ORAL LI

This is the first book to focus exclusively on an examination of early 21st-century adult reading aloud. The dominant contemporary image of reading in much of the world is that of a silent, solitary activity. This book challenges this dominant discourse, acknowledging the diversity of reading practices that adults perform or experience in different communities, languages, contexts and phases of our lives, outlining potential educational implications and next steps for literacy teaching and research.

By documenting and analysing the diversity of oral reading practices that adults take part in (on- and offline), this book explores contemporary reading aloud as hugely varied, often invisible and yet quietly ubiquitous. Duncan discusses questions such as: What, where, how and why do adults read aloud, or listen to others reading? How do couples, families and groups use oral reading as a way of being together? When and why do adults read aloud at work? And why do some people read aloud in languages they may not speak or understand?

This book is key reading for advanced students, researchers and scholars of literacy practices and literacy education within education, applied linguistics and related areas.

Sam Duncan is an adult literacy researcher and teacher educator at the UCL Institute of Education. She has a background in adult literacy and community education and teaches on a range of education, literacy and research-related modules. Sam is the author of *Reading Circles, Novels and Adult Reading Development* (Bloomsbury, 2012) and *Reading for Pleasure and Reading Circles for Adult Emergent Readers* (NIACE, 2014). She has just completed an Arts and Humanities Research Council (AHRC) Fellowship to research contemporary adult reading aloud practices across Britain.

LITERACIES
Series editors: Julia Gillen, Lancaster University, UK and
Uta Papen, Lancaster University, UK

This long-established series publishes innovative and high-quality research and scholarship in the field of literacy studies. *Literacies* provides a home for books on reading and writing which consider literacy as a social practice and which situate it within broader institutional contexts. The books develop and draw together work in the field; they are accessible, interdisciplinary and international in scope, and cover a wide range of social and institutional contexts.

LITERACY, LIVES AND LEARNING
David Barton, Roz Ivanič, Yvon Appleby, Rachel Hodge and Karin Tusting

GRASSROOTS LITERACIES
Writing, Identity and Voice in Central Africa
Jan Blommaert

DESIGN LITERACIES
Learning and Innovation in the Digital Age
Mary P. Sheridan and Jennifer Rowsell

LITERACY AND THE POLITICS OF REPRESENTATION
Mary Hamilton

DIGITAL LITERACIES
Julia Gillen

UNDOING THE DIGITAL
Sociomaterialism and Literacy Education
Cathy Burnett and Guy Merchant

ORAL LITERACIES
When Adults Read Aloud
Sam Duncan

For more information about this series, please visit: https://www.routledge.com/Literacies/book-series/LITERACIES

ORAL LITERACIES

When Adults Read Aloud

Sam Duncan

Routledge
Taylor & Francis Group

LONDON AND NEW YORK

First published 2021
by Routledge
2 Park Square, Milton Park, Abingdon, Oxon OX14 4RN

and by Routledge
52 Vanderbilt Avenue, New York, NY 10017

Routledge is an imprint of the Taylor & Francis Group, an informa business

© 2021 Sam Duncan

British Library Cataloguing in Publication Data
A catalogue record for this book is available from the British Library

Library of Congress Cataloging-in-Publication Data
Names: Duncan, Sam, author.
Title: Oral literacies : when adults read aloud / Sam Duncan.
Description: London ; New York : Routledge, 2020. | Series: Literacies | Includes bibliographical references and index.
Identifiers: LCCN 2020028598 | ISBN 9780367086626 (hardback) | ISBN 9780367086992 (paperback) | ISBN 9780367087005 (ebook)
Subjects: LCSH: Oral interpretation. | Reading. | Elocution. | Books and reading.
Classification: LCC PN4145 .D86 2020 | DDC 808.5/4–dc23
LC record available at https://lccn.loc.gov/2020028598

ISBN: 978-0-367-08662-6 (hbk)
ISBN: 978-0-367-08699-2 (pbk)
ISBN: 978-0-367-08700-5 (ebk)

Typeset in Sabon
by Taylor & Francis Books

FOR EVA AND MARCO; I LOVE YOU SO MUCH.

CONTENTS

ILLUSTRATIONS

Figures

Tables

PREFACE

I finished writing most of this book just before COVID-19 really 'hit' Britain. I had emailed a draft manuscript to the series editors and then, in the ten days that followed, life changed dramatically. I did not go back and make changes to the book in light of the experiences of these past months, and yet, it does not seem possible to simply ignore *it*. Many people died; many more were sick, and everyone has had to deal with new uncertainties, frustrations and fears. This study, which had preoccupied me for years, suddenly seemed so much less important. But at the same time, some of the ideas within the book became more obvious or acute in the new world of 'lockdown.' People reported on social media that they were finding it harder to read books but were listening more to audiobooks or books on the radio. Others were reading *and* listening more (while others read and listened less). More audiobooks became free, and recordings circulated. Reading groups had live online sessions. Religious groups posted, watched and listened to online services. Virtual choirs 'went viral.' Patrick Stewart read Shakespeare's sonnets aloud, posting videos online. The powers of the voice and ear seemed particularly important as ways to be together while not together. And yet we continued to miss each other. We missed *people* (we miss people), voices coming from bodies that we could see and smell and touch. If previously I had thought of this book as a celebration of oral reading and what it can mean, it now feels more like a celebration of people and what we can mean to each other, do for each other, and be for each other.

ACKNOWLEDGEMENTS

Thank you to the AHRC for funding the RABiT project and to all those who took part in the questionnaire, responded to the Mass Observation directive, talked to me in an interview or let me record you reading aloud. THANK YOU all so much for your time and ideas. Thank you to Steve Morrison for helping me put together the research bid. Thank you to the members of the wonderful RABiT Advisory Group: Jane Mace, Mike Baynham, Lesley Allen, Kirsty Pattrick, Ann Swinney, Farid Panjwani, Greg Brooks, Maxine Burton, Jonnie Robinson, Sarah Turvey and Debbie Hicks, and to project partners Alex Stevenson at the Learning and Work Institute; Carina Spaulding and Genevieve Clarke at the Reading Agency; and Jonnie Robinson and colleagues at the British Library. Thank you to Jessica Scantlebury, Joe Williams and Kirsty Pattrick at the Mass Observation Project and, again, to all the Observers. Thank you to Mark Freeman for being such a supportive mentor, to Greg Brooks for help with the history, and to Charlie Owen and JD Carpentieri for help with the questionnaire.

I am very grateful to Gordon Wells, Gillian Munroe, Caoimhin O'Donnaile and everyone at Sabhal Mòr Ostaig in Skye; Karen Fraser and colleagues at Shetland Library; Wendy Kirk, Donna Moore and everyone at the Glasgow Women's Library; and to Lilias Fraser and Samuel Tongue at the Scottish Poetry Library. Thank you to Vahni Capildeo for generous and insightful help throughout the project, and for making the Scottish Poetry Library event so wonderful. Thank you to the other hosts of the Regional Community Events: Carole Murcutt and the group the Pontypool Adult and Community Learning Centre, Sarah Turvey and my hosts at Prison Reading Groups, and Sheridan Browne and John Everson at the Nottingham Institute of Education. Thank you to Abayneh Haile and Tekle Belachew for help and expertise in Ethiopia, to Mary Blance in Shetland, to Nafisah Graham-Brown for a very special case study and to Kerry Scattergood for a great discussion.

Thank you to Louisa Semlyen and Eleni Steck at Routledge Literacies, to Julia Gillen and Uta Papen for being such supportive series editors and again to Uta Papen for invaluable feedback on a draft. Finally, thank you to Dorothy Sheridan and to the late Brian Street for generosity with time, encouragement and ideas at the very beginning of this project.

Three chapters of this book, Chapters 1, 3 and 4, draw on previously published work. Many thanks to the Taylor & Francis Group and to my co-author Mark Freeman for permission to reproduce much of the article Duncan, S., & Freeman, M. (2019). Adults reading aloud: A survey of contemporary practices in Britain. *British Journal of Educational Studies*, 68(1), 97–123, including tables and figures as three paragraphs of Chapter 1 and much of Chapter 3. This work is reprinted by permission of the publisher (Taylor & Francis Ltd, http://www. tandfonline.com). Thank you to editor John Yandell and once again to the Taylor & Francis Group for permission to reproduce most of the article, Duncan, S. (2018). Lend me your ears: Mass observing contemporary adult reading aloud practices, *Changing English*, 25(4) in Chapter 4. This work is reprinted with permission of Taylor & Francis Ltd, http://www.tandfonline. com, on behalf of the Editors of Changing English.

Mass Observation material reproduced with permission of Curtis Brown Group Ltd, London on behalf of the Trustees of the Mass Observation Archive. Copyright © The Trustees of the Mass Observation Archive.

1

INTRODUCTION

The narrator of Haruki Murakami's short story 'Sleep' (Murakami, 2003) finds herself not able to sleep and, more intriguingly, not needing to sleep. She starts to read at night. We know she reads alone, but we are not told whether she reads out loud or silently. People all over the world have read this story, in over forty languages. Someone is probably reading it right now. Many readers will wonder about the relationship between the narrator's drinking and her reading, or about how her choice of text relates to her marriage and experiences of motherhood. Most readers will wonder what exactly is going on at the end of this story and what will happen next. I would guess that few readers, however, will wonder whether she does her reading out loud, using her voice, or in complete silence. Most of us will simply assume that she reads novels however we read novels, whether this is aloud or silent.

Close your eyes and picture her reading. Or picture anyone reading. What do you see? Many would see someone sitting alone, reading silently. 'Reading' in this early twenty-first century world is often assumed to be silent and individual, particularly when we are thinking about adult reading. In some contexts – much of Europe and North America, for example – this assumption is particularly strong. Do adults read out loud today? Sometimes? Never? Perhaps for some sorts of reasons? With some sorts of texts? Stories or meeting minutes? Poems or prayers? Food packaging, *Anna Karenina* (like the narrator of 'Sleep') or graffiti?

Do adults read aloud today?

I really cannot fathom why anyone would want to or even enjoy reading out loud.

(Mass Observer M91)

30/8/17 Wednesday – Read a recipe aloud while baking with the girls at home in the kitchen. Read a couple of poems aloud to get the rhythm and flow of them and try to understand. I work at home, my desk is in the living room so I mainly work while everyone else is out.

Read out Google search results while discussing my son's homework at the kitchen table. He's 11.

(Mass Observer F43)

While anecdote or bus-stop chats can tell us that some people enjoy reading poetry from the top of their voice in the bath, that others read to their partners under the covers in bed and still others may read instructions in a whisper to get a grip on what has to be done and in what order, more traditional academic literature will tell us very little. A great deal has been written about reading aloud as a teaching and learning tool, an educational means-to-an-end (for example, Duncan & Paran, 2018, Pergams et al., 2018, Westbrook et al., 2018), as will be examined in Chapter 11. Oral reading also features in ethnographic studies – for example: Besnier's examination of Polynesian language use and its religious practices as 'between literacy and oracy' (1995, pp. 116–39); Heath's (1983) ethnography in the Piedmont Carolinas; Barton and Hamilton's (2012) study of everyday literacy in Lancaster; and Mace's earlier work on mothers and literacy (1998), and her later (2012) analysis of contemporary Quaker practices. This work provides us with important glimpses of contemporary oral reading but without a focus on examining the different forms of reading aloud going on in these contexts or on the particular purposes and powers of oral reading.

Quite a bit more popular and scholarly attention has focussed on parents and other carers reading out loud to children; for example, building on 2013 research, a 2018 survey by Nielson Book Research argues that there has been a decline in the proportion of parents reading to preschool children (Flood, 2018). The family literacy literature argues that reading to and with children is key to a child's literacy (and wider language) development (see, for example, Brooks et al., 2008; Carpentieri et al., 2011; Vandermaas-Peeler et al., 2009). This body of work does not, though, refer to other forms of reading aloud that adults may be taking part in and how these practices may relate to what parents do with children. Similarly, while studies of book groups, book clubs or reading circles provide examples of some groups that choose to read out loud together (see, for example, Duncan, 2012, 2014; Jones & Harvey, 2015, 2020), these studies do not address adults reading aloud outside of these specific contexts.

Over the past few years, there has been a resurgence of media and popular attention to oral reading: from poetry and prose collections advertised as to be read aloud, such as *A Little Aloud* (Macmillan, 2010), *Poetry by Heart* (Motion, 2014) or *Dancing by the Light of the Moon* (Brandreth, 2019), to Michael Rosen's popular *Guardian* article 'Why reading aloud is a vital bridge to literacy,' highlighting the benefits of continued reading aloud with children and teenagers (2019) and the development of the *Read with Audrey* initiative, an online community where users can read aloud to each other (Skarlatos, 2019). Two books published recently for popular audiences, Dimitri's *To Read Aloud* (2017) and Gurdon's *The Enchanted Hour* (2019), both encourage readers to take on the beneficial (they feel) habit of reading aloud to each other, though seemingly assuming that most readers will not already be doing this, while Williams' (2017) study of reading aloud in the eighteenth-century home brought renewed attention to how reading may have been something a little different in the past. Williams and Dimitri were interviewed together on BBC Radio 4's *Books and Authors* on the 26th of November 2017 (BBC Radio 4, 2017), further evidence, perhaps, of a reading aloud zeitgeist and providing a fascinating discussion. Yet it was a discussion about something done in the past and something that should (Dimitri argued) be done today. It was not a discussion of oral reading as a contemporary practice – something already done by many different people, in many different contexts, and for as many different reasons.

This means that though it may feel like more and more is being said about reading aloud in the media and popular discourse, it does not get us much further towards a sense of what adults today – in all different parts of the world – actually do and why. It does not add to wider conversations about what reading *is* or *involves* across adult life. I am arguing that the dominant conceptualisation of 'reading' in most of Europe, North America and much of the rest of the world is that of a silent, solitary activity. 'Reading' means silent reading; reading *aloud* is the form that needs specifying: the unusual, the exceptional, the weird even (Duncan, 2015; Radway, 1994). Historians of reading and the book tell us that this was not always so. Oral reading was once the unmarked form, with silent reading less common.

Vincent (2000) shows that mass literacy was only achieved during the nineteenth century, even in the industrial economies of North America and north-western Europe.[1] Thus, for most of human history since the invention of writing there have been more people who could not read than could, and therefore more need for those who could read to read aloud to those who could not. Before the invention of reading glasses around the turn of the fourteenth century, even those who had once been able to read needed others to read to them once they became too long-sighted to read for themselves. The enduring tradition of Cuban cigar factory 'lectors' reading to rows of employees busily rolling cigars is one of the best-known examples of people reading aloud to those who may (or may not) themselves be able to read but whose hands were/are simply busy doing other things (Manguel, 1996; Tinajero, 2010). There are many other examples, though, including domestic scenes of reading aloud to family members doing needlework or shelling peas and the seventeenth-century French *veilleé* or German *Spinnstube*: spinning circles of young women or girls reading aloud to each other as they spun or knitted (Houston, 2002, pp. 103–4). Moreover, historians of the book (see, for example, Cavallo & Chartier, 2003; Eliot & Rose, 2009; Vincent, 2000) note that even after the invention of the printing press and the expansion of the market for published texts books remained expensive and often difficult to get hold of, especially before the spread of the lending library from the eighteenth century (Raven, 1996) and the arrival of

3

cheap(er) paperbacks in the twentieth. Reading aloud, then, was also a way to allow many readers/listeners access to one book.

There are a great many references in classical and medieval sources to oral reading, so much so that some scholars (see, especially, Balogh, 1927; Hendrickson, 1929) have argued that silent reading was rare and that those who could read habitually did so aloud even when alone. This view has influenced and been repeated by many others. Manguel (1996, pp. 41–53), for example, asserts that reading aloud was the norm in the ancient world and that 'well into the Middle Ages' this affected the way in which texts were written and presented. However, other classical scholars, in particular Knox (1968) and Gavrilov (1997), not only rebut the interpretation of many of the key texts frequently cited in favour of the rarity of silent reading in the past – especially the famous passage in Augustine's *Confessions* in which he describes seeing Ambrose Bishop of Milan reading silently – but also show that there are about as many references to silent reading in classical and medieval sources as there are to oral reading. Gavrilov (1997, p. 59) reaches a balanced conclusion on the controversy: 'Reading to oneself was known to antiquity very early and was not felt to be something extraordinary. Nevertheless, because they loved the sonorities of language, people usually read aloud, especially with works of artistic literature.' A recent commentator (McCutcheon, 2015) appears to agree with this.

Conversely, others show reading aloud persisting into the early modern period: Fox (1996, p. 132), for example, shows that authors read their books publicly in the seventeenth century, as Dickens famously did in the nineteenth, and Raven (1996, pp. 176, 199) suggests that although there was certainly some silent reading in eighteenth-century England reading aloud remained important in a number of contexts, including both public and private libraries. Yet even after this, as the above-mentioned Williams (2017) explores in relation to the eighteenth-century British home, Reay (2004) discusses in a study of nineteenth-century rural England, and the Reading Experience Database Project (2019) demonstrates in its diverse examples from between 1450 and 1945 oral and silent reading co-existed within households and families. Just as some people read aloud today, so others in the past read silently as well as aloud. There has, however, been a shift in the dominant cultural understanding of what 'reading' signifies: as argued above, while 'reading' once most strongly suggested oral reading, today in much of the world, it predominantly indicates silent reading. There has also been a corresponding shift in the conceptualisation of what it means to be 'a good reader,' with theorists agreeing on a late nineteenth-century move from reading as 'articulation' to reading as comprehension (Graff, 1991; Monaghan & Barry, 1999; Venezky, 1986). Elster (2003, p. 685) argues that 'the dominant discourse of the modern era [foregrounds] a scientific and technological literacy'– that is, the encoding and decoding of factual information foregrounding a conception of adult reading as silent, individual and largely instrumental.

This book aims to challenge this dominant discourse of silent, individual adult reading and indeed to challenge the idea that oral reading is itself 'one thing' (that it is all about reading stories to children, for example) by examining as wide a range of forms of contemporary reading aloud as possible, thus acknowledging the diversity of reading (on and offline) that adults perform or experience in the different contexts, communities, languages and phases of their lives. This is part of a desire to better understand the role of reading in community life and the relationship between forms of reading and other cultural practices, such as speechmaking, storytelling or professions of faith. And it is certainly part of an endeavour to recognise and celebrate the diversity of what comes under (or we might choose to put under) the battered umbrella of 'reading,' which, for a start, includes both looking at a text message to identify the date of a hospital appointment and chanting a religious text in unison with hundreds of others.

As Chapter 2 details, over the years, as an adult literacy teacher and reading researcher, I found myself wanting to know more about whether, when, why, where and how adults might read out loud today, despite what I saw as a view of reading within educational and research discourses that seemed to be presenting adult reading as something silent and uniform (more or less the same thing, just done with different texts and in different contexts). When I tried to find records or accounts of adults talking about these practices, I struggled. This led me to a small pilot study in my home borough of London, Lewisham, and then funding from the (UK) Arts and Humanities Research Council (AHRC) for a two-year project working across Scotland, Wales and England: Reading Aloud in Britain Today (RABiT). This book builds on the data from this larger study, exploring it in relation to a wider, and more international, literature, to create a record and analysis of contemporary adult reading aloud practices – that is, when adults might read out loud or listen to others read.

But why do we need such a record?

There are at least two responses worth thinking about: the future and the present.

The future

Scholars of the future wishing to understand reading in the early twenty-first century would be able to find out quite a lot. They could find the books that sell well and those most often checked out of libraries, and they could find out a bit about who was doing the buying or borrowing. They could find out about newspaper and magazine subscription, paper and online, and about other online reading choices. They could find out about the posters put up on different transport systems around the world, about the flash fiction on social media most often 'liked,' and by whom, and about where there are shop or market signs that use words and where they use pictures. They could find governmental and workplace documents, economic agreements, political treaties, different sorts of holy texts and the reading lists for hundreds of thousands of courses or qualifications. They could find out things about parts of the world where most people learn to read in a language they do not speak at home and parts of the world where they do. They could also find out about how different people across the world were taught to read, at least a vision from curricula documents, lesson plans and materials. They would be able to find some accounts written by readers about favourite books or poems, how texts make us feel, about why one person loves being scared by horror fiction and someone else adores history. They could also find studies of the reading process and theories of how the most fluent readers read, and as many accounts of reading difficulties, disabilities, differences and support.

But they would not find much on whether that reading was silent or out loud: in our heads, with lips moving or not, whispered, spoken aloud, quietly or loudly, chanted, sung, shouted. They would find that often there is no mention at all of whether the voice is used, particularly when reading is done alone and/or behind the closed doors of the home. They may find examples where it says that someone was reading and someone else listening – a newsreader, in a Synagogue or to a child – but even in these cases, it is unlikely that they will find much of an analysis of what is going on with the voice and the ear. What difference does the voice make? When and why does one person listen? And when do many people listen? How does reading aloud join people together as a group, help one person feel less pain or another compose the perfect email?

This record is not only for future literacy or reading scholars, though, but also for social historians and anyone else interested in what we value and how we live, individually and in groups. The accounts I have tried to capture in this book were elicited to say something about oral reading, but they also tell us something about different adult lives: what one person finds meaningful, what another person struggles with, how different people choose to spend the minutes and hours of their lives, and about where people have had few choices. This book is a part of such a record for the future.

The present

I also feel that we need to know more about contemporary reading *now*, about the reading that happens across different people's lives, and in different contexts, traditions and parts of the world. There is quite a bit written about the reading taught and used in formal education, from early years to university, as well as within different forms of adult and community education, but less has been written about the reading of adults outside of these educational contexts. It is my belief (shared with many others) that what is taught as literacy needs to reflect the breadth of reading and writing in adult life. This concern with the relationship between the forms of literacy taught and valued 'in school' (or in formal education) and the literacy used within the home or various community contexts is closely aligned with that of the New Literacy Studies, or the ethnography of literacy more broadly, championed by the work of Heath (1983, 2012), Street (1984), Brandt (2001) and Barton and Hamilton (2012), among others. In this view, more recently termed as Literacy as Social Practice (LSP) (Street, 2016), literacy is recognised as a contextual, varied, ever-evolving set of social practices. Focussing on reading, Bloome and Kim put it like this: 'a reading practice is a particular way of using written language associated with a particular type of social situation' (Bloome & Kim, 2016). Central to this view of literacy as social practice is the recognition that what 'reading' and 'writing' mean is not self-evident, and we cannot assume that we understand the same things by these terms as others. Rather, we need continual examinations of the real-life usages of different communities, and continual discussions to inform our understandings. This is one of Brian Street's key messages for those wishing to understand literacy as social practice: challenge orthodoxies, challenge dominant views, ask questions and listen (Robinson-Pant, 2018).

Within teaching contexts, whether teaching children or adults, this nuanced and evolving understanding of diverse literacy practices is important not only to motivate or engage learners but, crucially, so that the conceptualisations of reading and writing that underpin curricula, assessments and research agenda continue to evolve. In other words, literacy as taught needs to have a relationship with literacy as lived, and literacy as lived is diverse and ever-changing. The teaching of reading, for example, cannot be based on a pretence that all adult reading is silent. The key point here is not that 'school' literacy (Street & Street, 1991) or literacy as taught in formal education necessarily needs to mirror all forms of 'home' or community literacy, but rather that it needs to be broad enough to acknowledge or include the diversity of out of school practices. Those teaching, assessing, advocating for or judging others' reading or writing in any way, therefore, need to be working from carefully observed and evolving ideas of reading and writing within and across different human lives and communities.

Literacy, oracy and the words we use

The title of this book is *Oral Literacies*. Though 'oral reading' is often used in place of 'reading aloud' (as I am doing in this book, partly to give us a break from 'reading aloud' or 'reading out loud'), when 'oral' is placed in front of 'literacies,' the effect is oxymoronic. The juxtaposition between 'oral' and 'literacies' jars or 'hangs' in the ear. It suggests a paradox – something being both about oracy and literacy in a world where these are too often seen as distinct and too little interrogated. How can reading or writing be oral? When is oracy a form of literacy? When is literacy oral or aural? What are the main differences and overlaps between literacy and oracy? My aim was for the title to suggest all these questions, as they are core to exploring reading aloud and will be picked up throughout the book in different ways.

The investigations in this book problematise the notion of an easy or fixed distinction between literacy and oracy by exploring their linkages and overlaps. For example, we may think of a written text as something where the words are in a fixed order, as opposed to the interactional nature of an oral/aural conversation. But how, then, can we understand the composition, 'storage' and performance of poetic or religious texts using only the voice, ear and memory (see, for example, Griffiths, 1999)? Or in considering the various ways that reading relates to both physical writing and composition, we could think about how the placing of words or characters on a page relates to how that text is meant to be read (aloud or silently), how texts were and are composed in particular ways to aid their memorisation and recitation, and how people may read aloud as part of writing processes (more of this in Chapters 7 and 9). We can think about where and when the written seems to hold more legal power than the oral, or vice versa, and when power seems to come from a combination of the two, as in many national legal systems where written statements must be read aloud. We can trace changes over time and between cultures. We can think through the different possible relationships between the languages we converse in and those we read, silently or aloud, including what reading 'aloud' could mean for those who use signed languages, such as British Sign Language (Aldersson, 2018).

Part of this unpacking of what is understood by literacy and oracy, and their multifarious relationships, involves thinking through some other terms. Reciting, proclaiming, performing, presenting, revising, chanting, singing, skimming, scanning, understanding, comprehending, decoding, deciphering, conjuring, spelling-making, learning by rote, learning by heart, embodiment, inculcation – how do each of these words relate to each other and to reading or reading aloud? Introducing a fascinating study of women readers in the middle ages, Green (2007, p. 6) writes that the French twelfth-century theologian Hugh of St Victor 'explicitly refers to three kinds of reading,' corresponding to the three roles of *'docentis, discentis, vel per se inspicientis'*: the teacher (or person reading aloud to someone else), the pupil or listener, and the individual reader/ student (reading to herself, whether aloud or silent). This is simply one way that the idea of the acts of reading and the roles involved were conceptualised in the European Middle Ages (and there are certainly many more across different time periods, places and languages). It is also part of Green's opening argument that present-day scholars (or readers or listeners) need to train themselves to see 'reading' more broadly; for example, to include the person listening to someone else reading aloud, and to recognise the difference between that act of service or communication between two people and the act of a person reading or studying alone.

The aims and scope of this book

This book aims to be a record and analysis of contemporary adult reading aloud for anyone interested, now or in the future, in painting a picture of what reading can be for adults today. It is a book that aims to answer some questions but asks a lot more, and it is certainly more a start of something than an ending. This is both an academic book and also not such an academic book. I hope it will be of some interest to those studying or researching literacy as well as others who might be interested in how other people read and feel about their reading. It aims to contribute to reading research and to the theorisation of literacy as social practice, but, more than this, to display the range of forms and purposes of oral reading that I have come across in my research, and the ways that individuals have understood or described them. For this reason, I am including as many of my research participants' own words as possible.

This is a form of both social history and applied linguistics (and at the same time, some would say, not quite either). It is a book written very much within adult literacy studies as an academic discipline and area of teaching and teacher education. Though this book is not primarily teaching-focussed, my aim is very much to feed into adult literacy teaching through contributing to under-standings of reading (which are themselves the basis of curricula and pedago-gies). The 11 remaining chapters will offer typologies of reading aloud, looking at practices and purposes across different lives and contexts. I am inviting readers to join me in thinking through ways to analyse data and reflect on possibilities, and for this reason, I will move between the pronouns *I* and *we*, with the *we* signifying my desire to imagine this book as a conversation, a communal reflection involving me, the writer, and you, the reader, walking alongside the RABiT participants, theorists and others whose ideas we will explore. In this way, we will examine how we can understand practices as more or less 'visible' or valued and what this means for a sense of a practice as common or 'everyday.' We will look at reading aloud and its varied roles across different domains of adult life, including family, romance, work, religion, lit-erature and education. We will look at themes emerging to do with spaces and places, the fixed and the varied, role-taking and the *wordhord*.

This examination is also a tentative contribution to the theorising of literacy as social practice (LSP) through the application of Shove et al.'s (2012) model of the dynamics of social practices (competences, meanings and materials) to lit-eracy in particular. I will argue that though others in literacy studies have noted how literacy practices involve skills and technologies, as well as meanings and values (see, for example, Papen, 2005), Shove et al.'s three-part model and emphasis on dynamism is a particularly useful tool for examining how different practices relate to (and differ from) each other and feature within the learning and experience of individual lives. What it means to consider literacy as social practice, and how we can understand forms of power, visibility and mediation, is threaded throughout the book.

Above all, though, this book is an invitation to listen to what the participants of the RABiT project say about reading aloud across their lives and in doing so to think a bit more about 'what we think about when we think about reading' (to borrow from Raymond Carver, 1981).

Here I am reminded to be explicit about the scope of this book and the slightly shifting dance it involves. This book comes out of a particular, and Britain-focussed, research project. At the same time, its investigation aims to be broader than this, more international where possible through the use of international examples. There is no doubt, though, that the rationale behind this study is born of my own personal and professional experiences in Britain and the United States (and some of the rest of Europe). This is where I have experienced a sense of adult reading assumed to be silent, with forms of reading aloud unnoticed or ignored. It is in this context, therefore, where I felt there is most need for a study like this, where so much is written about literacy but so little about the oral. This is not necessarily the case in other contexts, and again I invite others to reflect on potential differences (and how the ideas in this book relate to examples from their own differing national and cultural contexts). For these reasons, while in the explorations of this book I am aiming to move towards a more internationally focussed conversation where possible, this 'opening out' is tentative, and the core focus remains, necessarily, closer to home.

It is also important at this stage to say that much, if not most, of what this book is exploring is specific to those who can use their voices to read out loud and/or use their ears to listen to the reading of others. This includes different groups, languages, cultures, ethnicities, but it excludes those who cannot use their voices or who cannot hear, many of whom may be users of signed languages and have other ways of interacting with written text to be together, work, pray, produce or engage with literature, study or learn, alone or with others. In the analysis of this book, I am never suggesting these uses of voice and ear are the only ways to, for example, focus, meditate or share a story, only that they are a way valued by some. I look forward to reading a different study which looks at the uses of signed languages in relation to the themes of this book, or a study that offers a comparison.

Finally, a note on the naming of research participants. Within this book, I will refer to the words and ideas of four different groups of research participants, and how I refer to each is a product of the permissions process agreed in each case, as well as any other institutional conventions at play. Questionnaire participants, given the high numbers and anonymity of questionnaire participation, are simply identified as 'questionnaire' or 'questionnaire participant.' Mass Observers – that is, the panel of writers of the Mass Observation Project (see Chapter 4) – are referred to as Observers, and individual contributions are labelled by their gender and age (where and how given), as are the interview participants of the London-based pilot study; for example, F43, or M70s. Interview participants and those recorded reading aloud who have asked not to be named in project publications are referred to using pseudonymised initials (for example, RF), while those who have agreed to be named are referred to using their real initials alongside the British Library Sound and Moving Image Catalogue number of their recording where one exists (see Chapter 5); for example, MM, C7765/61, so that readers can follow up and listen to these recordings if they wish.

Structure

There are two parts to this book. The first, starting with Chapter 2, will introduce the rationale behind and activities of the Reading Aloud in Britain Today (RABiT) research project, as well as exploring its findings in three chapters based on the three main methods of data collection: the questionnaire (Chapter 3), Mass Observation (Chapter 4) and interviews/recordings (Chapter 5). The second part of this book then addresses these findings thematically, analysing them using a wider literature. Chapter 6 takes on reading aloud with family, friends and lovers; Chapter 7 looks at reading aloud in our working, public and political lives; Chapter 8 examines religious practices and Chapter 9 explores the literary. Chapter 10 is a reflection on reading aloud alone, and Chapter 11 asks how reading aloud intersects with education. The conclusion, Chapter 12, brings together key ideas and looks to the future.

Note

1 This and the following two paragraphs (the historical account) have been previously published as part of Duncan, S., & Freeman, M. (2019). Adults reading aloud: A survey of contemporary practices in Britain. *British Journal of Educational Studies, 68* (1), 97–123, reprinted by permission of the publisher (Taylor & Francis Ltd, http:// www.tandfonline.com). Many thanks to both Dr Mark Freeman and the Taylor & Francis Group for permission to reproduce this work here.

References

Aldersson, R. (2018, November 17). *Rethinking 'aloud' in the context of sign-language users*. RABiT Symposium: Everyday Reading: Explorations of Literacy and Oracy, UCL Institute of Education, London.

Balogh, J. (1927). *'Voces paginarum': Beiträge z. Gesch. D. Lauten Lesens u. Schreibens*. Dieterich.

Barton, D., & Hamilton, M. (2012). *Local Literacies: Reading and Writing in One Community*. (2nd edLinguistics Classics). Routledge.

BBC Radio 4. (2017, November 26). The Great American Novel and the merits of reading aloud. In *Books and Authors*. https://www.bbc.co.uk/sounds/play/p05p38cn.

Besnier, N. (1995). *Literacy, Emotion and Authority: Reading and Writing on a Polynesian Atoll*. Cambridge University Press.

Bloome, D., & Kim, M. (2016). Storytelling: Learning to read as social and cultural processes. *PROSPECTS, 46*(3), 391–405. https://doi.org/10.1007/s11125-017-9414-9.

Brandreth, G. (2019). *Dancing by the Light of the Moon*. Michael Joseph.

Brandt, D. (2001). *Literacy in American Lives*. Cambridge University Press.

Brooks, G., Pahl, K., Pollard, A., & Rees, F. (2008). *Effective and inclusive practices in family literacy, language and numeracy: A review of programmes and practice in the UK and internationally*. CfBT Education Trust.

Carpentieri, J. D., Fairfax-Cholmeley, K., Litster, J., & Vorhaus, J. (2011). *Family Literacy in Europe: Using Parental Support Initiatives to Enhance Early Literacy Development*. NRDC.

Carver, R. (1981). *What We Talk About When We Talk About Love*. Alfred A. Knopf.

Cavallo, G., & Chartier, R. (2003). *A History of Reading in the West*. Polity.

Dimitri, F. (2017). *To Read Aloud*. Head of Zeus Ltd.

Duncan, S. (2012). *Reading Circles, Novels and Adult Reading Development*. Bloomsbury.

Duncan, S. (2014). *Reading for Pleasure and Reading Circles for Adult Emergent Readers: Insights in Adult Learning*. National Institute of Adult Continuing Education.

Duncan, S. (2015). Reading aloud in Lewisham: An exploration of adult reading-aloud practices. *Literacy*, 49(2), 84–90. https://doi.org/10.1111/lit.12046.

Duncan, S., & Paran, A. (2018). Negotiating the challenges of reading literature: Teachers reporting on their practice. In J. Bland (Ed.), *Using Literature in English Language Education: Challenging Reading for 8–18 Year Olds*. Bloomsbury.

Eliot, S., & Rose, J. (Eds.). (2009). *A Companion to the History of the Book*. Wiley-Blackwell.

Elster, C. A. (2003). Authority, performance, and interpretation in religious reading: Critical issues of intercultural communication and multiple literacies. *Journal of Literacy Research*, 35(1), 663–692. https://doi.org/10.1207/s15548430jlr3501_5.

Flood, A. (2018, February 22). Big decline in number of parents reading daily to toddlers. *Guardian*, 14.

Fox, A. (1996). Popular verses and their readership in the early seventeenth century. In J. Raven (Ed.), *The Practice and Representation of Reading in England*, (pp. 125–137).

Gavrilov, A. K. (1997). Techniques of reading in classical antiquity. *The Classical Quarterly*, 47(1), 56–73.

Graff, H. J. (1991). *The Literacy Myth: Cultural Integration and Social Structure in the Nineteenth Century*. Transaction Publishers.

Green, D. H. (2007). *Women Readers in the Middle Ages*. Cambridge University Press.

Griffiths, P. J. (1999). *Religious Reading: The Place of Reading in the Practice of Religion*. Oxford University Press.

Gurdon, M. C. (2019). *The Enchanted Hour: The Miraculous Power of Reading Aloud in the Age of Distraction*. Hachette UK.

Heath, S. B. (1983). *Ways with Words: Language, Life and Work in Communities and Classrooms*. Cambridge University Press.

Heath, S. B. (2012). *Words at Work and Play: Three Decades in Family and Community Life*. Cambridge University Press.

Hendrickson, G. L. (1929). Ancient reading. *The Classical Journal*, 25(3), 182–196.

Houston, R. A. (2002). *Literacy in Early Modern Europe*. Longman/Pearson.

Jones, S., & Harvey, K. (2015). 'He should have put them in the freezer': Creating and connecting through shared reading. *Journal of Arts & Communities*, 7(3), 153–166.

Jones, S., & Harvey, K. (2020). Participation, perplexity and plurality: Exploring the shared reading of a 'difficult' poem. *Changing English*, 27(1), 34–49. https://doi.org/10.1080/1358684X.2019.1702455.

Knox, B. M. (1968). Silent reading in antiquity. *Greek, Roman, and Byzantine Studies*, 9(4), 421–435.

Mace, J. (1998). *Playing with Time: Mothers and the Meaning of Literacy*. UCL Press.

Mace, J. (2012). *God and Decision-Making: A Quaker Approach*. Quaker Books.

Macmillan, A. (2010). *A Little, Aloud*. Chatto & Windus.

Manguel, A. (1996). *A History of Reading*. Viking.

McCutcheon, R. W. (2015). Silent reading in antiquity and the future history of the book. *Book History*, 18(1), 1–32.

Monaghan, E. J., & Barry, A. L. (1999). *Writing the Past: Teaching Reading in Colonial America and the United States, 1640–1940. The Catalogue.*

Motion, A. (2014). *Poetry by Heart: 200 Poems for Learning and Reciting.* Viking.

Murakami, H. (2003). Sleep. In *The Elephant Vanishes*, Trans. A. Birnbaum (pp. 74–109). Vintage.

Papen, U. (2005). *Adult Literacy as Social Practice: More than Skills.* Routledge.

Pergams, O. R., Jake-Matthews, C. E., & Mohanty, L. M. (2018). A combined read-aloud think-aloud strategy improves student learning experiences in college-level biology courses. *Journal of College Science Teaching; Washington, 47*(5), 10–15.

Radway, J. (1994). Beyond Mary Bailey and old maid librarians: Reimagining readers and rethinking reading. *Journal of Education for Library and Information Science, 35* (4), 275–296. https://doi.org/10.2307/40323023.

Raven, J. (1996). From promotion to proscription: Arrangements for reading and eighteenth century libraries. In *The Practice and Representation of Reading in England.* Cambridge University Press.

Reading Experience Database Project. (2019). *The Reading Experience Database (RED).* http://www.open.ac.uk/Arts/RED/index.html.

Reay, B. (2004). *Rural Englands: Labouring Lives in the Nineteenth-Century.* Palgrave MacMillan.

Robinson-Pant, A. (2018, September 10). *Exploring Brian Street's understandings of literacy* (Presentation). Literacy as Social Practice CTLR and BALID, University of Sussex.

Rosen, M. (2019, March 9). Why reading aloud is a vital bridge to literacy. *The Guardian.* https://www.theguardian.com/books/2019/mar/09/why-reading-aloud-is-a-vital-bridge-to-literacy.

Shove, E., Pantzar, M., & Watson, M. (2012). *The Dynamics of Social Practice: Everyday Life and How it Changes.* Sage.

Skarlatos, T. (2019, August 4). Crossing divides: Why I read aloud to strangers. *BBC News.* https://www.bbc.co.uk/news/world-48725722.

Street, B. V. (1984). *Literacy in Theory and Practice.* Cambridge University Press.

Street, B. V. (2016). Learning to read from a social practice view: Ethnography, schooling and adult learning. *PROSPECTS, 46*(3), 335–344. https://doi.org/10.1007/s11125-017-9411-z.

Street, B. V., and Street, J. (1991). The schooling of literacy. In D. Barton and R. Ivanič (Eds.), *Writing in the Community* (pp. 143–166). Sage.

Tinajero, A. (2010). *El Lector: A History of the Cigar Factory Reader.* University of Texas Press.

Vandermaas-Peeler, M., Nelson, J., Bumpass, C., & Sassine, B. (2009). Social contexts of development: Parent-child interactions during reading and play. *Journal of Early Childhood Literacy, 9*(3), 295–317.

Venezky, R. L. (1986). Chapter 4: Steps toward a modern history of American reading instruction. *Review of Research in Education, 13*(1), 129–167.

Vincent, D. (2000). *The Rise of Mass Literacy: Reading and Writing in Modern Europe.* Wiley.

Westbrook, J., Sutherland, J., Oakhill, J., & Sullivan, S. (2018). 'Just reading': The impact of a faster pace of reading narratives on the comprehension of poorer adolescent readers in English classrooms. *Literacy, 0*(0). https://doi.org/10.1111/lit.12141.

Williams, A. (2017). *The Social Life of Books.* Yale University Press.

Part 1

2

THE READING ALOUD IN BRITAIN
TODAY (RABIT) PROJECT

Part 1 of this book will examine the Reading Aloud in Britain Today (RABiT) project in particular, while Part 2 will explore identified themes in relation to wider examples, including from an international literature. This chapter will address the RABiT project: its context, genesis, rationale, project activities and challenges. Here I will also briefly explore the ideas about literacy that underpin its methodology. The next three chapters will present the project's three main methods of data collection and their findings. Chapter 3 will explore the questionnaire, how it was created and what it tells us. Chapter 4 looks at the Mass Observation directive and the 160 pieces of writing sent in by the Observers, and Chapter 5 turns to the interviews and recordings of practices. Chapter 5, as the last chapter of Part 1, will also include a brief conclusion to this first section of the book.

RABiT: genesis, context, rationale

> Now I occasionally read aloud to my wife – often sitting on a bench in the open air. A few years ago, when she was ill with cancer and feeling weak and unwell, we both chose to start a habit of me reading aloud to her.
>
> (Mass Observer, M80)

The RABiT project was a two-year UK Arts and Humanities Research Council (AHRC) funded research project, and it was also a stage in a professional and personal journey. As an adult literacy teacher, teacher educator and researcher, and as someone with interests in literature and religious practice, I had long been fascinated by how, when and what we read and what our different reading experiences mean to us. This interest led to research into what are sometimes called reading circles, reading groups or book groups (Duncan, 2012, 2014) and how these seemed to fulfil a range of different individual and communal needs.

While recognising that reading circles vary hugely in a range of ways, I noted three shared characteristics. Firstly, as Elizabeth Long (2003) notes, when people gather to discuss a book they have all read, they are not (usually) presenting or exchanging fully formed interpretations or ideas about what they have read. Rather, they are usually developing their interpretations, refining their ideas or adapting their conclusions, in conversation with each other. In this way, the meaning-making, interpretive, inferential work of reading can be communal. I also came to see that though a reading circle is a shared activity, each member of the group is actually also (at the very same time) doing something slightly different from the other members of the group. Each member comes to the group sessions with a particular motivation or combination of motivations: one person might want to widen her reading choices, someone else wants to meet new friends, another person wants to improve his discussion skills, another to get out of the house, and so on. These motivations or pre-occupations change, if slightly, the focus and therefore experience of each person within the group situation. This means that a reading circle is both a shared activity and many different individual activities, all happening at the same time. This reminded me of the oscillations between individual and shared experiences that characterise our lives. It also provides a striking example of how reading encompasses many different activities, some shared, some individual, some solitary, some communal, some 'private' and some 'public.'

Finally, I found that some reading circles involve members reading their book, or parts of it, together, out loud, while others do not. What difference, then, does the aloud-ness bring? Why do some groups do this while others do not? Here I recalled debates about the uses of reading aloud in adult literacy and language provision, as well as in other forms of teaching. I remembered a US online forum exchange about uses of reading aloud in the adult literacy and language classroom, where someone posted, 'unless a learner wants to be a newsreader, reading aloud will be of no use to them' (National Institute for Literacy, 2009). I was struck by this comment and its place in the surrounding discussion for two reasons. It was part of an exchange that was conflating a discussion of reading aloud as a teaching tool (to what extent it is effective or not and why) with a (potential) discussion of reading aloud as a 'real-life' literacy practice (something adult learners might want to be able to do in specific life contexts). This comment also suggests a narrow view of oral reading in adult life: that it is only something done by newsreaders. I am giving the writer of this comment an undeserved hard time, but this is because this comment so succinctly captures the way the topic of reading aloud was often handed within adult literacy education in Britain, in my own experience as a teacher and teacher educator between 1999 and 2017, where discussions were most often about reading aloud as a teaching technique – a means to an end (that end being fluent, silent, 'adult' reading), rather than an end in itself, with little, or nothing, said about forms of oral reading across different areas of adult life.

It is certainly the case that reading aloud has been controversial as a teaching tool (as Chapter 11 will discuss), and my experience as an adult literacy teacher in Scotland and England between 1999 and 2010 was of reading aloud either not mentioned at all or cautioned against. Many adult learners, though, told me they wanted to read aloud, both in and out of the classroom. Again, (at least) two things are at play and need teasing out. On one hand, we have important questions about the effectiveness or not of oral reading as a teaching tool to develop aspects of literacy, mainly centred on how it is handled: is reading aloud enforced, voluntary? Is it 'round the room'? Individual or in unison? Are learners given the chance to prepare first? What are other learners meant to be doing while one learner (or the teacher) is reading? Does the teacher know why they are asking for it to be done? And do the learners? On the other hand, there is the possibility of learners wanting to prepare themselves for forms of oral reading in parts of their lives outside of the classroom; for example, reading to children, as part of religious worship or to read aloud menu items.

There is a literature on the former – and the consensus seems to be that it can certainly be useful for language, literacy and other purposes *if* carefully thought through (see Chapter 11). But there was not, I came to realise, a literature on the latter, on the different roles that oral reading may play in adult life today. This is what I decided to investigate.

Pilot study

To get started, I undertook a small pilot study between January and June 2014, interviewing adults in one London borough (Duncan, 2015). I spoke to people in parks, community centres, libraries and through personal contacts and was lucky enough to gain the voluntary participation of seventeen people. The youngest was 24 and the eldest 82. They did different sorts of work and came from different educational, ethnic, faith and linguistic backgrounds, capturing some of the diversity of the borough. The interviews lasted between 25 and 40 minutes and were loosely structured; I asked participants whether they currently read aloud or listen to others reading and whether they did in the past, prompting for more detail and their thoughts about purposes and meanings. With permission, I audio recorded and transcribed each interview.

These seventeen people described reading aloud recipes and poems, speeches and legal documents, museum signs and fairy tales, lists of rules, from YouTube, Holy books, schedules for electrical testing and more. They read aloud as part of their spiritual or religious lives, for work, for study purposes and as part of family life, and they read to study or learn things, to communicate, to entertain, for enjoyment, to be with others, to understand something, for worship and to write or compose. They described reading aloud completely alone as well as with and to others; they read aloud in pairs and groups, singing, chanting and shouting, and in workplaces, courtrooms, places of worship, care homes, cars, cafes, kitchens, living rooms, bedrooms, bathrooms, schools and libraries.

They shared memories and experiences, explanations and explorations.

> I think it's an emotional thing you get from it, it's spiritual as well [...] it's like shouting at the wind, you know if you are at the top of a mountain and you shout, it's a feeling of power and it's expressing

myself, and if I could never read aloud again I'd feel a bit lost [...] words are flat on a page, when it's read, it has a profile, it has an intensity [...] there are words on the page and they have a meaning in themselves, but when they are delivered and delivered with passion, if you like, they become alive, those words live, you know, 'once more on to the breach, dear friends!' [...] it's a spiritual, emotional experience.

(M60s)

If it's really dense language, it kind of helps to say it out loud [...] when the voice in your head can't seem to quite – the words are knocking together without making any sense, and sometimes you just need to hear it [...] where it's just a bit jarred or jammed, the language.

(M20s)

Sometimes I do if I need to refocus; sometimes when I'm reading quietly, I, my mind goes somewhere else, and I find that if I read out loud for a moment or two it brings me back.

(M70s)

Whenever I read the Quran, I read out loud [...] I know how to read Arabic, but I don't know the meaning [...] In an overall spiritual sense, you know why you are reading that but not the words, so when you read aloud you memorize [...] every morning before leaving for work I read [...] I read aloud to make my memory fresh.

(M40s)

Occasionally, I go to a mass and there will be Latin, and it's more about the ritual rather than the language. It sort of flows over you and takes over, and you've got some [...] but you don't know word for what what's being said [...] it sort of flows over you and sweeps you up, doesn't it? [...] if you listen to opera, I defy anyone to understand the words but you know what the storyline is, and it sweeps you along and you can, you can be involved, can't you, be part of it.

(M60s)

If I've got a visitor, and if I've read something that I think oh you know you might find this – it could be a newspaper article, it could be something I've found off the internet or in a magazine, and it will just pop into my head to share it with them, and I'll either read it out to them or give it to them to read and then we'll have a good chin wag about it and put the world to rights as it were.

(F50s)

When you are looking at the newspaper, I read it silently, you know, and at a certain point I find myself actually reading it aloud – it depends on the impact I get from reading that article; you know, I sometimes find myself automatically, I find myself reading it aloud [...] it's like I'm in that position, I'm in that state, or if it's a story about a young person's death, then I'm relating to the mother already, I'm feeling into the situation, I'm saying her words, I'm actually getting that feeling.

(F70s)

It feels like you are being given a bit of a gift, I think, when somebody perhaps reads to you. They are giving you time, they're acknowledging you, and giving you something quite special really.

(F50s)

Chanting with a whole room of people, reading the same text, the power can surprise you, surprise me even after all this time [...] It's a shared event. It is different. You are getting different tones of voice and echoes of the same word, and it focusses the mind on what you are actually reading, not on if you are reading it right or if anyone is listening. You are in a sea of it, and you focus inwards on the words.

(F60s)

There's so much meaning that can be conveyed in the voice as well, that maybe can't through text, if that makes sense.

(F20s)

Here we have ideas about power, expression, 'proclamation' and spirituality, of reading aloud to understand 'jammed' language or refocus attention, of reading aloud in different languages with different meanings, of reading aloud to memorise and to make 'memory fresh' and being 'swept along' in a religious 'storyline.' They reflect on reading aloud to share and discuss news with others and on forms of identification or intersubjectivity, of gifts of time, 'inward focus' and what the voice can convey.

These interviews raise key questions about the nature and power of the human voice as a 'mode' of multimodal communication and its relationship to notions of identity; about reading aloud and acts of intersubjectivity (if we 'become' someone else when reading certain texts, do we 'become' them 'more' or differently when we literally lend them our voices as we say their words?), about oral reading and processes of understanding, focus and memorisation and about the relationship between group and individual practices (when we read aloud our work as a lone writer, are we mimicking communal interaction, becoming both reader and listener, or is something else going on?). These questions, along with the striking diversity of practices within this small number of interviews, provided the impetus to try for a larger piece of research.

The RABiT research design

But larger how? More interviews? The pilot study interviews allowed people to talk about their experiences of, and ideas about, reading aloud and offer their own analyses. These interviews also elicited an initial response to the effect of 'I don't know why you want to interview me, I don't really read aloud,' and then, in conversation, remember or notice instances they hadn't previously (for example, the electrician who felt he doesn't really read, let alone read aloud, but found he reads aloud emails from a tablet as he reports to different jobs to do PAT testing). *More* interviews, therefore, seemed like a good idea: aiming for between thirty and fifty and expanding the geographical boundary from one London borough to the whole of Britain.

Several colleagues suggested a questionnaire, a research tool that can allow the gathering of data from larger numbers of people and across larger physical spaces, as questionnaires can be posted or conducted online. How could a (non-facilitated) questionnaire, though, allow me to ask about practices of which participants may be less aware of carrying out? And how could I distribute a questionnaire to reach at least something of a cross-section of the adults currently living in Britain, people with all different interests and backgrounds? How could I avoid a sample of only reading-aloud fanatics or only those who feel themselves to be quite 'bookish' and therefore more inclined to answer a questionnaire about reading? These were considerable challenges. Potential benefits, though, could (and did) include the chance to access not tens but hundreds of different people and the possibility of gathering the experiences and ideas of those who might not have the time or inclination to sit and talk to someone face-to-face but may be willing to give a questionnaire a go (after all, you can abandon a questionnaire at any time). Chapter 3 provides a more detailed look at the questionnaire design and sampling issues, as well as offering an analysis of the responses.

Someone else suggested the Mass Observation Project as another way to 'go larger,' and Mass Observation became not only another data collection strand but a key theoretical underpinning of the entire research design (and a great joy). Once referred to as 'scientifically, about as valuable as a chimpanzee's tea party at the zoo' (as discussed in Pollen, 2013), one story is that the original Mass Observation was born of the British Abdication Crisis of the 1930s and the desire to find out whether 'the masses' really think what the newspapers think they think. Paid Observers took notes on clipboards, professional photographers took pictures, and unpaid armies of diary writers all contributed, in their different ways, to a gathering of reports about the everyday life and views of 'ordinary people.' Closed in the 1950s then restarted in the 1980s and housed at the University of Sussex, the (renewed) Mass Observation Project sends 'directives' three times a year to around 500 'Observers': people of different ages and backgrounds living in different parts of the UK. These directives ask for observations, experiences and opinions about a particular event, issue or phenomenon (Christmas cards, the Gulf crisis, having an affair, menstruation, serial killers ...) and Observers respond with sentences, paragraphs and often many pages.

I worked with the Mass Observation archivists to write a directive on Reading Aloud (*Directive 109, Summer 2017: Reading Aloud*). It allowed us to ask hundreds of Observers to write about their experiences (including keeping a diary of their reading aloud). As explored in Chapter 4, Mass Observation offered two distinctive advantages to the RABiT project. It provided access to a team of committed Observers, who could choose to respond as much or as little as they liked, over period of several weeks or even months, allowing time for reading, rereading, reflection and writing in the privacy of their own homes. Crucially, also, Mass Observation directives arrive in through Observers' post-boxes or email accounts three times a year, regardless of previous interest or not in the topic (reading aloud or any other Directive focus), making it possible to capture diverse reactions including surprise, delight or horror at the Directive topic itself.

Importantly, Mass Observation is not only or even mainly a data collection endeavour. It is also a social history, collaborative writing and life-writing project; an archive which allows the words of its participants to speak for themselves, to be read directly as written, outside of any researcher's frames of analysis or preoccupations. Reflecting on the value of such an archive, currently at around a total of 69,000[1] responses (received since 1981) either handwritten or typed, on white, cream, yellow and blue paper of different sizes, and posted in as well as emailed, led me to approach the British Library to work with me in producing another type of archive, this time a sound archive of adults talking about their practices (the interviews), alongside audio recordings of examples of adults reading out loud (see Chapter 5).

In this way, the RABiT research design was finalised: three methods of data collection – a questionnaire, Mass Observation and interviews/recordings to be analysed separately and together – as well as two archives providing anyone interested with direct access to the written words of the Mass Observers, the spoken words of the interviewees and audio-recorded examples of adults read-ing out loud. This became the first year of a two-year project, funded by the AHRC, with the second year devoted to exploring the implications of this data. A one-day symposium at UCL on 'Everyday reading: explorations of literacy and oracy' generated discussions between researchers, academics and students, and five 'regional community events' gathered the ideas of different groups with an interest in adult reading: one with adult learners and educators in Wales; one with members of the *Story Café* at the Glasgow Women's Library; one with poet Vahni Capildeo at the Scottish Poetry Library for poets and poetry fans; one with student teachers and teacher educators at the Nottingham Trent Institute of Education; and one with a reading group in a male prison. The academic symposium led to a Special Issue of the journal *Changing English* in early 2020 gathering and celebrating research around forms of 'everyday' reading and relationships between oracy and literacy (Duncan, 2020). The discussions at the community events led to downloadable 'resources for discussion, reflection and next steps' (available on https://www.ucl.ac.uk/ioe/research/projects/reading-aloud-britain-today). Here are some examples from across the resources:

> We have memories of reading out loud: sisters, friends, fathers, mothers, partners, spouses. These are memories of the texts, and of the voices, and of the time spent together.
>
> How we feel about reading aloud (and being read to) is very individual. Some like audiobooks and some don't. Some prefer listening to 'live' people reading rather than audiobooks or recordings. Some can concentrate better listening than when reading ourselves (aloud or silent). Others feel exactly the opposite and prefer to read things ourselves.
>
> If reading aloud is slower in our heads, does that allow for greater resonance and better depth of meaning?
>
> To what extent does how we read aloud to learners impact on their understanding of characters and text more broadly?
>
> When we read aloud are we giving our voice to someone or something else, or taking on the voice of someone else? Is there a third thing, a 'voice of the poem or text'?

These ideas, and more, from each of these events feed into the analysis throughout this book.

Theoretical underpinnings

The aims, research design and other activities of this project were born of a certain view of literacy, just as every form of literacy research reflects particular definitions, assumptions or priorities. As noted in Chapter 1, this work is aligned to a view of literacy or literacies (the plural form often used to emphasise multiplicity) as social practice (LSP): socially and historically situated, embedded in cultural and institutional relationships, contextual, ideological, performed or experienced for different purposes and carrying different meanings or values (see, for example, Barton & Hamilton, 2012; Bloome & Kim, 2016; Street, 1984, 2016). The idea of literacy as social practice gives us a way to talk about the different ways people and communities use, understand and value literacy – literacy *practices* – and to refer to specific events, occasions or happenings that involve versions of these literacy practices – literacy *events* (Heath, 1983). More than this, though, core to a view of literacy as social practice is the idea that literacy is more than, or something other than, a set of individual skills (see, for example, Papen, 2005). That skills are somewhere within literacy practices has never been disputed, despite a 'skills approach' frequently being seen as in opposition to a social practices approach within adult literacy studies (see, for example, discussions in Green & Howard (2007) and Gates et al. (2009)). However, I am arguing that Shove et al.'s (2012) model of social practices as made up of three interrelating elements – *meanings, materials* and *competences* – could be a particularly valuable tool for thinking through how competences ('skill, know-how and technique') relate to materials ('including things, technologies, tangible physical entities and the stuff of which objects are made') and meanings ('in which we include symbolic meanings, ideas and aspirations' (p. 14)) across different literacy practices, and I will be playing around with this model in this book. Shove et al. emphasise the importance of theorising social practice as 'dynamic' and 'part of an examina-tion of social reproduction and social change' (p. 13), asking 'how are elements, practices and links between them generated, renewed and reproduced?' (p. 14). This is a useful perspective for looking at how individuals both develop specific 'competences' related to the 'meanings' and 'materials' of particular literacy practices and, potentially, adapt their experience of one literacy practice to engage in new practices, as 'elements of know-how are typically modified, reconfigured and adapted as they move from one situation or person to another and as they circulate between practices' (p. 52).

Shove et al.'s model also provides a fresh reminder of the centrality of meanings to the idea of literacy as social practice and the relationship between how we understand literacy and how we choose to research it. This idea is core to the New Literacy Studies or LSP literature, but expressed particularly powerfully by both Mace and Baynham, if in quite different ways. In the introduction to her book *Literacy, Mothers and Time*, which draws on both interviews and a 1995 Mass Observation directive 'Mothers and Literacy,' Mace writes:

> I want to persist with the notion that literacy engages our imagina-tions, intellects, emotions and memories: and as such, is a matter of enormous mystery, beyond simple measurement. In this book I hope to show that any researcher who accepts this and who seeks to find out what literacy may mean to an individual or a group, has to go beyond mere observation [...] for while such observation can tell us some things, there is much it cannot. If, for example, I watch someone else reading a newspaper on a train, I can notice which page they turn to, or how long they take to read an article; but I cannot tell what mental images or lines of thought their reading sets up. If I see someone writing a postcard in a café, I may notice they are left-handed, using a felt-tip pen, and pausing over every other word; I may even – when they go up to the counter to buy another cup of tea – catch sight of a word or two of what has been written [...] But I have no idea of the unwritten words that they have decided not to write.
>
> (Mace, 1998, p. 15)

Writing of 'narrative as evidence in literacy research' (as part of research, which, like Mace's and mine, includes both interviews and Mass Observation), Baynham argues

> Narratives provide a way into the subjectivity of literacy practices, into understanding how participants construct what they do according to which ideologies and values, which historical trajectories, as well as what kind of self-preservation or identity work they are currently engaged in.
>
> (Baynham, 2000, p. 100)

Mace and Baynham are both making the same argument: we cannot access the meanings of literacy practices without some form of first-person account. In this way, observation is not enough to research literacy as social practice; we need to gain a reader's perspective to fully understand reading, whether oral or silent. Street's consistent argument was that an 'ethnographic perspective,' a mixture of observation and conversation, 'can be helpful in addressing the local uses and meanings of literacy – that is, in discovering what people are doing with reading and/or writing in specific social contexts' (2016). This raises two points. The first is that the RABiT project is certainly not fully ethnographic in this view, as it includes observation only in the (indirect) way that the Mass Observation Project does – that is, through the perspectives of participants. The second is that Street's use of 'local' here (and elsewhere) is not a physical place or a source of influence that should be contrasted with 'the global' (see debate in Brandt & Clinton, 2002; Street, 2003a), but rather what anthropologists call the 'emic' view: an on-the-ground perspective, a way of expressing a focus on literacy as lived by individuals and communities, an interest in what reading is for the reader or readers. This is a reader's-eye-view, an interest in how things work, what they mean, how they are experienced, enjoyed, rejected, struggled with, adapted, developed, learnt, loved and shared in the lives of individuals.

Street's 'ethnographic perspective' is very much in keeping with the original Mass Observation's desire to capture both 'what people do and what they think about what they do' (Johnes, 2017), just as the revived Mass Observation Project's way of accessing 'what people do' by asking them to write about it is in keeping with RABiT's approach of asking people – in different ways – about what they do (and what they think about it) rather than aiming for researcher observation. And just as a Literacy as Social Practice approach (LSP), as articulated by Street (Street, 1984, 2003b, 2016), aims for literacy research to challenge orthodoxies in order to see what is unexpected, forgotten or invisible (Robinson-Pant, 2018), Mass Observation, Dorothy Sheridan argues, aims to use the richness of 'idiosyncratic' Observer accounts to challenge accepted truths (Sheridan, 2017). This is part of what I will describe in Chapter 4 as the 'Mass Observation ethos,' fundamental to both the RABiT project and this book. I am not aiming to say that all people do this or that, or even most people do this or that. Rather, I wished to gather ideas of what some people do and others just might do. I aimed to find out more, and in more detail, about the different ways that adults read aloud, listen to others read and think about these practices – a search for specificities, reflections and feelings rather than generalisations or trends. This is about exploring what is possible,[2] and therefore what should not be discounted, ignored or forgotten.

The research questions and aims that guide this book are the same as those underpinning the RABiT research project.

> What, when, where, how and why do adults today read aloud or listen
> to others reading aloud?
> What roles does reading aloud play in adult lives?

The aim of this book, like the wider RABiT project, is to document and analyse contemporary adult reading aloud practices in order to:

- Identify whether, what, when, where, how and why adults today read aloud;
- Better understand reading aloud as a contemporary practice;
- Better understand the role of reading aloud in adult lives across different regional, linguistic and faith communities, including, but not exclusively, the domains of family, faith, work, leisure and the arts;
- Examine the wider significance of contemporary adult oral reading practices in relation to current conceptions/discourses of reading – that is, to expand notions of what 'reading' is, means or involves to better include the diversity of contemporary practices.

Conclusion

In around 2008, I started from a place where, as an adult literacy teacher, teacher educator and new researcher, I wanted to find out more about whether, what, why, when and how adults might read out loud instead of in silence. The RABiT project is an attempt to create the record that then I wanted to read but was unable to find. It builds on a pilot project to find out more, from more people, in more places around Britain. It is based on a view of literacy as socially situated, contextual, varied and where materials and competences are bound up with meanings that we cannot understand without gaining first-person accounts of different sorts: questionnaire responses, Mass Observation writing and interviews. And while these accounts will not give us a full or complete picture of reading aloud, they are an important part of the picture, to be read and listened to alongside other forms of research. I hope they provide what both Street and Sheridan stress we need: challenges to orthodoxies, provocation for reflection, a questioning of the dominant.

Notes

1 Many thanks to Jessica Scantlebury of the Mass Observation Archive for this figure.
2 Towards the end of April 2020, the first full month of 'lockdown' in Britain, Katherine Rundell and Bloomsbury Publishing released a free online edited book hosted by the National Literacy Trust: *The Book of Hopes* (Rundell, 2020). Rundell explains in her introduction, 'Real, true hope isn't the promise that everything will be all right – but it's a belief that the world has so many strangenesses and possibilities that giving up would be a mistake; that we live in a universe shot through with the unexpected' (p. xiii). And that, I realised, is what I was trying to do in this book, to search out strangenesses, possibilities and the unexpected.

Rundell, K. (Ed.). (2020). *The Book of Hopes*. Bloomsbury. https://literacytrust.org.uk/family-zone/9-12/book-hopes/.

References

Barton, D., & Hamilton, M. (2012). *Local Literacies: Reading and Writing in One Community*. (2nd edLinguistics Classics). Routledge.

Baynham, M. (2000). Narrative as evidence in literacy research. *Linguistics and Education*, 11(2), 99–117.

Bloome, D., & Kim, M. (2016). Storytelling: Learning to read as social and cultural processes. *PROSPECTS*, 46(3), 391–405. https://doi.org/10.1007/s11125-017-9414-9.

Brandt, D., & Clinton, K. (2002). Limits of the local: Expanding perspectives on literacy as a social practice. *Journal of Literacy Research*, 34(3), 337–356. https://doi.org/10.1207/s15548430jlr3403_4.

Duncan, S. (2012). *Reading Circles, Novels and Adult Reading Development*. Bloomsbury.

Duncan, S. (2014). *Reading for Pleasure and Reading Circles for Adult Emergent Readers: Insights in Adult Learning*. National Institute of Adult Continuing Education.

Duncan, S. (2015). Reading aloud in Lewisham: An exploration of adult reading-aloud practices. *Literacy*, 49(2), 84–90. https://doi.org/10.1111/lit.12046.

Duncan, S. (2020). Editorial. *Changing English*, 27(1), 1–4. https://doi.org/10.1080/1358684X.2020.1718333.

Gates, V. P., Jacobson, E., Degener, S., & Purcell-Gates, V. (2009). *Print Literacy Development: Uniting Cognitive and Social Practice Theories*. Harvard University Press.

Green, A., & Howard, U. (2007). *Skills and Social Practices: Making Common Cause: An NRDC Policy Paper*. NRDC.

Heath, S. B. (1983). *Ways with Words: Language, Life and Work in Communities and Classrooms*. Cambridge University Press.

Johnes, M. (2017, July 11). *Christmas and the Mass Observers*. Mass Observation 80th Anniversary Conference, University of Sussex.

Long, E. (2003). *Book Clubs: Women and the Uses of Reading in Everyday Life*. University of Chicago Press.

Mace, J. (1998). *Playing with Time: Mothers and the Meaning of Literacy*. UCL Press.

National Institute for Literacy. (2009, May 27). Basic skills reading discussion list. http://library/nald/ca/learning.

Papen, U. (2005). *Adult Literacy as Social Practice: More Than Skills*. Routledge.

Pollen, A. (2013). Research methodology in Mass Observation past and present: 'Scientifically, about as valuable as a chimpanzee's tea party at the zoo'? *History Workshop Journal*, 75(1), 213–235. https://doi.org/10.1093/hwj/dbs040.

Robinson-Pant, A. (2018, September 10). *Exploring Brian Street's understandings of literacy*. Literacy as Social Practice CTLR and BALID, University of Sussex.

Sheridan, D. (2017, July 11). *Closing panel keynote talk*. Mass Observation 80th Anniversary Conference, University of Sussex.

Shove, E., Pantzar, M., & Watson, M. (2012). *The Dynamics of Social Practice: Everyday Life and How it Changes*. https://doi.org/10.4135/9781446250655.

Street, B. V. (1984). *Literacy in Theory and Practice*. Cambridge University Press.

Street, B. V. (2003a). The limits of the local-'autonomous' or 'disembedding'? *International Journal of Learning*, 10, 7.

Street, B. V. (2003b). What's new in New Literacy Studies? *Current Issues in Comparative Education*, 5(2), 1–14.

Street, B. V. (2016). Learning to read from a social practice view: Ethnography, schooling and adult learning. *PROSPECTS*, 46(3), 335–344. https://doi.org/10.1007/s11125-017-9411-z.

3

THE QUESTIONNAIRE

Surveying contemporary reading aloud

My husband once read Lord of the Rings to me when we were camping.

(questionnaire)

I wish I read books aloud to myself more often, as although it slows my reading down, sometimes this is good as I take in things more. I don't like people overhearing me though. I feel embarrassed and don't know why.

(questionnaire)

What have other questionnaires told us?

There are questionnaires about adult reading habits and preferences. Sharon (1973), Kling (1982), Scales and Rhee (2001) and Liu (2005) all created questionnaires to survey adults' reading habits and preferences, looking at what, why, when and even where adults might read and how adults feel about their reading habits, skills and materials, but they did not examine what is read aloud as opposed to silently. Ivey and Broaddus (2001) and Hughes-Hassell and Rodge (2007) created questionnaires to survey the reading habits of teenagers, in and out of the classroom, but, again, did not touch on oral versus silent reading. There are questionnaires examining how often adults read to children (Scholastic, 2018; YouGov, 2018); for example, the aforementioned survey by Nielsen Book Research showing a decline in the proportion of preschool children who were read to on a daily basis by their parents (Flood, 2018). Most of this questionnaire research on adults reading to children is what could be described as works of advocacy, part of a drive to encourage more adults to read to their children, and, some would argue, to place more responsibility for children's literacy on parents. None that I found were concerned with other forms of reading aloud going on in families. This seeming lack of previous surveys into adult oral reading made the creation of such a questionnaire more appealing and yet also more daunting – where to begin?

Creating and distributing a RABiT questionnaire: aims and challenges

As noted in Chapter 2, the aim of the questionnaire was to get *more* data: to reach more people, in more parts of the country, to gather more ideas and experiences, in response to more questions. These aims carried considerable challenges. How would it be possible to design a questionnaire that could be completed unaided, that would encourage people to think of reading as something broader than reading books, that would allow participants to remember the forms of reading aloud that they may not think about as 'reading' or even notice, without leading people into thinking that certain answers were expected or desirable? This first challenge is quite specific to this project. The second challenge is common to many different research projects, but no easier for it. How do you distribute a questionnaire to reach as wide a range as possible of the population of Britain, reaching adults living in different places, with different educational backgrounds, interests, attitudes and preferences around reading, from different linguistic, cultural, ethnic and religious backgrounds, of different genders and ages? We could see the first challenge as a question of design and the second as a question of distribution and participation.

Challenge A: design

In both the pilot study and when discussing reading aloud at presentations, participants would usually start off by saying 'I don't really read aloud' and then discover many more instances than they had realised. How does one design a questionnaire tool that encourages participants to reflect in this way, without leading them to a set list of practices? And how to allow room to probe for frequency and types of texts and purposes without creating an overly complex or long format? Other questionnaires on adult reading habits and reading to children provided ideas for how questions could be structured, and these combined with advice from questionnaire experts led to the decision to develop an online survey, with a paper-based option for those who would prefer it. This was for ease of distribution and from a view that many participants prefer the experience of completing a questionnaire online (as it can be done on a phone, tablet or computer; no need to find a pen or remember to post back somewhere), the lesser of evils. Nevertheless, I noted the impact this may have on the sampling (see below).

I decided to begin (as many questionnaires do) with brief introductory text and used this text to be explicit: 'We would like you to think about reading as broadly as possible. For example, reading can mean reading road signs or food boxes, not just books or newspapers.' The introductory text ends with: 'We are interested in everything and anything you read, at any time and in any language' (see https://www.ucl.ac.uk/ioe/research/projects/reading-aloud-brita in-today for the full questionnaire). I also developed structured grid questions, probing, for example, frequency of reading aloud different text types.

31

I modelled a breadth of texts while deliberately not including all text types (I left out poems, for example) and added 'other' text boxes to encourage participants to add in additional texts types. This became a general pattern: closed questions (with a set of possible responses), followed by open text boxes for further examples and ideas.

Once a draft was completed, I began two phases of piloting. The first was a 'think-aloud' process with eight adults of varied educational and language backgrounds. I sat with each person and asked them to complete the survey online while talking me through the questions and their thoughts as they went. This was invaluable for insights into which questions were confusing or misleading, where more or fewer open questions were needed and which demographic questions irritated participants. It also provided a better sense of how many questions was simply too many. After making changes based on this first phases of piloting, the second phase of piloting involved emailing out a new draft to a slightly larger number of adults (37) to complete the questionnaire on their own, including an additional question at the end about their experience completing it and any recommended changes. Once again, this led to considerable changes – new questions added, others removed, changes of wording, order and guidance.

The final questionnaire had twenty-nine questions in eight sections: 1) *reading and your life*; 2) *reading aloud: what?*; 3) *reading aloud: alone or with others?*; 4) *reading aloud: why?*; 5) *computer, table or phone screens*; 6) *languages*; 7) *thoughts, feelings, practices*; and 8) *about you*. Throughout, it addressed both reading aloud and listening to others reading. It was distributed electronically (with the option of a hard copy) in both English and Welsh.

Challenge B: distribution and participation

But how to get a range of people to fill it out – people living in different parts of Scotland, Wales and England, urban and rural, people of different cultural, linguistic and educational backgrounds and in different economic situations? How to reach people who don't like reading, as well as those who do, and people who never or rarely read aloud, as well as those who do it a lot? The aim was not to appeal primarily to those with particular interests in oral reading, and with this in mind, I titled the questionnaire 'everyday reading' and started with initial questions about reading more generally before moving into an explicit focus on oral reading in the second section. It was also not the aim to appeal primarily to people who see themselves as 'bookish' or 'into' reading, but this was harder to achieve, and it did not seem possible or ethical to pretend that the questionnaire was not about reading. It remained an aim, though, to distribute it through organisations with no connections to reading or libraries as well as those that did. The questionnaire was distributed via smaller community centres and groups working with older people, the Research and Practice in Adult Literacies (RaPAL) Regional Advocates network, and two of the RABiT project partners, The Reading Agency (UK) and the Learning and Work Institute (England and Wales), with combined national networks including Unionlearn and UNISON. The questionnaire was also distributed through the project website, social media and online professional networks, including networks of ESOL and adult literacy teachers, who passed it on to their adult learners.

In this way, in the autumn of 2017, over 600 adults anonymously completed most of the questionnaire, including 47 paper responses. As we will see later, those who completed the questionnaire cannot be seen as representative of the wider British population in a number of ways, and yet I was surprised and delighted at both the number of people who filled it in and the detail of the responses.

Who filled it in?

The following analysis of those who completed the questionnaire, and the analysis of the questionnaire results to follow, was carried out in partnership with Dr Mark Freeman. Mark and I are the 'we' of much of the rest of this chapter, as the majority is from an article we wrote together.[1]

Around 600 people filled in all or most of the questionnaire. For the purposes of the analysis in this chapter, we are using the data from the 529 respondents who also completed the demographic questions about their ages and genders. Of these 529 respondents, 414 (78.2%) are female and 112 (21.2%) male, with a small proportion neither or not responding; around 6.5% live in Wales, 12.2% in Scotland, and 40.8% in London and the south-east of England. Around half live in a city, just under a third in a town and just below a fifth in rural areas: this is approximately representative of Britain as a whole. In terms of age, 15.5% are 18 to 30, 33.7% from 31 to 45, 38.9% from 46 to 66, and 11.7% are 67 and over. Just under a half report no religion; around 44% associate themselves with a form of Christianity, 3% with Islam and the rest a mixture of other religions. Nearly a third consider themselves bi- or multilingual, with 59 languages other than English mentioned. Of the 271 who completed an open question asking about their ethnicity or cultural heritage ('if you would like to indicate your ethnicity or cultural heritage, please do so in the terms you prefer'), 162 describe themselves as some form of 'white,' 12 use the word 'Black/black' and 42 use other terms suggesting Black or minority ethnic identification (Pakistani, African, Ethiopian, Latino, Turkish and Cantonese are examples). More than 95% of the whole sample describe finding reading 'easy' or 'usually easy,' as opposed to 'difficult' or 'usually difficult.' Around three-quarters indicate having attended university; only two report that they have had no compulsory schooling.

The sample, then, is unrepresentative, most obviously in two respects: a heavy preponderance of female and university-educated respondents. Moreover, as noted above, only a few respondents report that they find reading difficult. Those who completed the questionnaire were almost certainly aware that it was about reading (though not necessarily, initially, of the focus on oral reading), and this, combined with uses of technology to distribute project information and the questionnaire, very likely created a self-selecting sample of those reasonably confident in their own reading and use of technology. It is therefore important to note that our sample cannot be taken as representative of the wider British adult population. It does, however, capture aspects of the diversity of contemporary British society, providing an insight into the oral reading practices of a range of adults living across England, Wales and Scotland today, and suggesting trends for examination in future studies. And it tells us a lot, through the fullness of the responses, about the reading aloud practices of this particular group of adults, which includes those who, in response to a demographic question about religion, write 'while raised in a non-practicing Protestant family, and if pressed I would call myself agnostic, when completing Equal Opportunity forms I always tick "none," though I did list myself as a Jedi on the 2001 census,' 'Jewish and Buddhist,' 'I follow the Indian Master Avatar Meher Baba (1894–1969). Ironically he was silent!,' 'Hindi, Catholic upbringing, Jewish ex,' 'none. I consider myself a rationale human being,' and 'not sure but I do believe in God and I do say my prayers.' It also includes those describing their ethnicity or cultural heritage as 'Pale Sarcastic British European,' 'I am Black British,' 'I was born in South America from a Spanish father, Indigenous South American mother, raised in the United States by a Jewish family, married an English man,' 'Mixed German/Cantonese,' 'I'm a European born and bred in south east England, with grandparents of Irish and Welsh ancestry,' and 'My parents are born in Somalia but we are originated from Yemen. We are known as Barawanis. I speak Chimini, which is a dialect of Swahili.'

What do the questionnaire responses tell us?

A key finding of the survey is that, simply but importantly, adult reading aloud is widespread in our sample: almost nobody *never* reads aloud, although the frequency and purposes of doing so vary significantly. Figure 3.1 shows the self-reported frequency of reading particular texts aloud. ['Occasionally' includes those reading the text type aloud less often than once a year or only once or twice a year, while 'often' includes those reading the text type aloud at least once a week or once a month.] With the exception of religious texts, a considerable majority of respondents report reading all the named texts aloud sometimes, even if only occasionally. Almost all report at least some occasions of reading instructions or recipes aloud, and a similarly high proportion for shop signs and newspapers/magazines. In terms of very frequent reading, the most common type of text read aloud – with 22.1% and 38.4% of respondents reporting daily and frequent reading aloud – is social media posts, with newspapers/magazines, shop signs and instructions/recipes close behind. Emails and letters are read aloud daily by 19.5% of respondents, and often by 35.4%. Children's books are the most commonly read texts on a daily basis, with

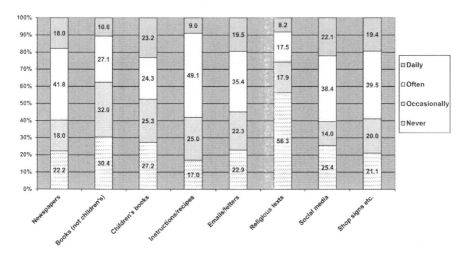

Figure 3.1 Frequency of reading common text types aloud (% of total sample)

23.2% reporting this. The frequency of some practices may reflect life circumstances and the life course, with parents and grandparents predominating in the reading aloud of children's books. This is supported by the responses to an open question asking about whether participants' reading aloud practices have changed: of the 199 who replied to this, 87 wrote about changes to reading aloud practices due to becoming grandparents or their children growing up.

A more surprising (perhaps) finding is in the proportions reading aloud books other than children's books, with 10.6% doing this daily and 27.1% frequently. This may lead us to wonder about the particular pleasures and purposes of reading aloud and the perceived benefits of shared literacy as opposed to – or as well as – other practices such as watching television as a couple or in a family group.

Participants were invited to comment on other texts they read aloud, and 134 people provided information about text types (for example, poems or menus) that are not explicitly included in the questionnaire. Here some of the less frequently noted activities give us a sense of the variety of things that are read aloud. For example, the (one) person who notes reading aloud amusing graffiti from toilet doors and walls, the (again just one) person who reads bus numbers and car number plates aloud, the person who reads out plant labels, the three who read from museum or gallery placards, the four who read from food packaging, or six from menus. Meanwhile, the prevalence of some practices is also notable: there were also 20 mentions of reading plays or scripts and 38 of poems. When asked, in a different open question, about the text type they read aloud *most often*, the findings echo those in Figure 3.1: as many as 140 respondents read to children, 88 mention social media and/or text messages, 79 write about 'news' and 55 about recipes/instructions.

These findings are striking, and they are strengthened by examining some of the practices in relation to each other. Almost all of our respondents read *something* aloud daily or frequently: 482 (90.9% of the total) read something aloud at least monthly, and 275 (51.9%) report reading at least one type of document or text aloud daily. Conversely, only 32 respondents (6.0% of the total) report never or only occasionally reading anything aloud, and just 17 of these (2.6%) answer 'never' to all the questions. These figures may be partly an artefact of the sample, but they highlight adult engagement in a wide range of reading aloud practices and suggest that oral reading is certainly more widespread and diverse than is often acknowledged.

There are some differences between men and women, although the overall patterns are not dissimilar. In the case of every text type, men are less likely to read aloud daily or frequently and more likely to answer 'never.' Table 3.1 makes these differences clear: almost two-thirds (66.1%) of men in the sample never read religious texts aloud, while only 1.9% read instructions or recipes aloud on a daily basis. These proportions may reflect higher levels of religious observance, and greater participation in cooking, among women. Of the 32 respondents who read aloud only occasionally or never, exactly half are male, representing 14.3% of the sample of men, and the other 16 female, or 3.9% of the women who responded to the survey; and of the 14 who claim never to read aloud at all, 11 are male, or 9.8% of the men in the sample. Yet a clear majority of men in the sample read at least *something* aloud monthly or more often – 91 or 81.3% – and nearly half (45 or 40.2%) do so every day.

There are some differences between the age groups covered by the survey, although some practices seem quite similar in extent between the different cohorts. Table 3.2 shows little variation in the proportions reading newspapers or magazines aloud, for example, or emails and letters, although those in the oldest age group are more likely to report *never* reading newspapers/magazines, letters and emails, shop signs, instructions/recipes and social media posts aloud. On the other hand, they were slightly *more* likely to read religious texts. The frequency of reading children's books aloud is likely to reflect the life course, with those aged 31 to 45 most likely to read these on a daily basis, and those in the older age groups more likely to read them often, but *not* daily. Many of those in the 31 to 45 age group may well be parents of young children, while non-co-resident grandparents will be in the older age groups. Those aged 30 and below are least likely to read children's books aloud. Conversely, they are the most likely to read social media posts aloud on a daily basis; however, the proportion reading these aloud often *or* daily is actually slightly higher among the 46 to 66 age group. Among those aged 67 and over, reading social media posts aloud is relatively uncommon, with nearly half reporting that they never do this, and a further 9.1% doing so only occasionally. The age spread of those who read aloud only occasionally is roughly in line with that of the sample as a whole, as is that of the small group who never read aloud at all.

Table 3.1 Frequency of reading common text types aloud (% of total), by gender

	Never		Occasionally		Often		Daily	
	Women	Men	Women	Men	Women	Men	Women	Men
Newspapers	19.3	33.0	18.5	15.6	44.0	33.9	18.3	17.4
Books (not children's)	29.1	35.2	32.1	31.5	27.8	25.0	11.0	8.3
Children's books	23.0	44.3	25.7	23.6	26.2	17.0	25.2	15.1
Instructions/recipes	13.1	32.1	23.5	31.1	52.7	34.9	10.6	1.9
Emails/letters	20.6	31.5	22.1	21.3	36.3	32.4	20.9	14.8
Religious texts	53.9	66.1	18.7	13.8	18.5	14.7	9.0	5.5
Social media	21.7	39.3	14.3	13.1	39.3	34.6	24.7	13.1
Shop signs etc.	16.6	37.6	21.0	15.6	40.8	34.9	21.5	11.9

Table 3.2 Frequency of reading common text types aloud (% of total), by age group

	Never				Occasionally			
	30 and below	31–45	46–66	67 and above	30 and below	31–45	46–66	67 and above
Newspapers	20.7	24.4	19.8	26.3	24.4	18.2	16.8	12.3
Books (not children's)	26.8	35.0	28.9	25.9	40.2	26.6	32.0	37.0
Children's books	43.2	17.9	27.8	32.1	29.6	17.9	31.3	21.4
Instructions/ recipes	16.0	13.6	16.9	29.1	24.7	20.5	29.9	21.8
Emails/letters	18.8	24.1	22.5	25.9	25.0	17.2	26.0	20.7
Religious texts	67.9	52.5	57.3	48.2	14.8	17.5	21.1	12.5
Social media	19.5	25.0	21.8	49.1	18.3	13.6	13.9	9.1
Shop signs etc.	14.8	21.9	20.7	28.8	22.2	12.4	27.1	15.3

	Often				Daily			
	30 and below	31–45	46–66	67 and above	30 and below	31–45	46–66	67 and above
Newspapers	41.5	39.2	46.0	35.1	13.4	18.2	17.3	26.3
Books (not children's)	28.0	23.7	29.9	25.9	4.9	14.7	9.1	11.1
Children's books	18.5	17.3	27.3	44.6	8.6	46.9	13.6	1.8
Instructions/ recipes	53.1	55.1	44.3	41.8	6.2	10.8	9.0	7.3
Emails/letters	32.5	35.1	36.5	36.2	23.8	23.6	15.0	17.2
Religious texts	13.6	16.9	16.1	30.4	3.7	13.0	5.5	8.9
Social media	30.5	36.9	46.5	25.5	31.7	24.4	17.8	16.4
Shop signs etc.	39.5	41.6	38.9	35.6	23.5	24.2	13.3	20.3

The questionnaire also asked *why* people read aloud, offering 11 options (see Table 3.3) and inviting free-text responses. The tabulated results show that, across the sample as a whole, among both women and men and all age groups, the most popular answer is 'to share what I have read with someone,' which is perhaps not surprising, although a majority in all groups also use reading aloud to memorise and learn. Indeed, more than half in most age groups – and more than half of women and 44.6% of men – report reading aloud to learn or read another language. This could range from sustained study to casual reading of signs while travelling abroad: one respondent noted that she reads aloud '[o]n holiday, reading signs like "EXIT" etc., or a menu.' Women and those in the youngest age groups are most likely to read aloud to help or serve another person: such help or service can range from reading to a partially sighted relative to reading something for someone who has forgotten their glasses. As is the case elsewhere, responses under this heading may reflect the life course and the distribution of caring responsibilities. Reading aloud for religious purposes becomes a little more common with age. In terms of gender, all of these reasons for reading aloud are given more often by women than men, but the rank order is much the same for both. Strikingly, Table 3.3 shows that 58.5% of women in the sample, and 46.4% of men, comprising 56.0% of the total, read aloud 'because I enjoy it'.

Before being faced with these 11 options, participants were asked to write down, in an open question, *why* they read aloud. This invitation was taken up by 397 participants, with the most popular response being a version of 'to better understand a text' (84 mentions), with 'sharing information' mentioned 80 times. These initial responses are notable for the sheer range of purposes expressed: some describe the pleasures of simply hearing voices (including their own), while others use reading aloud when alone to memorise information or compose text. Some read aloud to learn, practise and enjoy different languages, and others to settle, teach, motivate and interact with their children. Some delight in the sounds of words and phrases as they say and hear them, and others find it a good way to be with other people, whether in different sorts of groups or in the intimacy of a couple. These responses are notable not only for their range but also for the nuance they present. For example, many free-text responses concern 'sharing' texts with others but with quite different conceptualisations of the value or need for sharing. 'Wanting someone to hear' the logistical information contained in a letter or email seems quite different from explanations such as 'you can share something you love with other people' or 'to pass on information and start a conversation.' Or, to take another example: 'when reading a funny or interesting line in an article or book I can emphasise certain words or phrases for effect and share the humour (or horror!) that I find in it.' Similarly, participants explained the practice of reading aloud to children in quite different terms, ranging from 'reading aloud to my grandchildren because they are too young to identify and read the words yet,' to 'with my child, there's a connection when we read together,' to 'it feels fabulous,

Table 3.3 Reasons for reading aloud: % answering 'yes' to question 'Do you ever read aloud for these reasons?'

	All	By gender		By age group			
		Female	Male	30 and below	31 to 45	46 to 66	67 and above
To share what I have read with someone	88.5	90.8	80.4	92.7	86.6	91.7	77.4
To a child	72.0	74.9	60.7	61.0	79.9	70.4	69.4
To memorise or learn something	70.7	74.2	58.0	75.6	68.7	73.8	59.7
To understand difficult text	67.5	71.0	55.4	76.8	64.2	68.9	59.7
To entertain others	66.5	68.6	58.9	64.6	63.7	71.8	59.7
To help someone	62.8	67.1	46.4	70.7	59.8	66.5	48.4
To help me write something	59.9	62.6	50.0	62.2	55.3	62.6	61.3
Because I enjoy it	56.0	58.5	46.4	53.7	52.0	60.7	54.8
To help read/learn another language	55.0	58.0	44.6	59.8	55.3	54.4	50.0
Part of communal religious worship	31.8	33.1	26.8	23.2	34.6	30.6	38.7
Individual worship/spiritual purposes	26.3	27.8	20.5	23.2	28.5	24.8	29.0

Note: Figures given in descending order of % age of whole sample answering 'yes'.

40

enhances the meaning, brings the text to life and is an intimate activity.' Many participants emphasise the intimacy of the voice and physical closeness central to reading aloud with a child or another adult, while just as many others (and some of the same) stress the educational benefits of enhancing vocabulary, acquiring new pieces of information and developing literacy.

Diversity of purpose is related to the different formations in which adults read aloud. Table 3.3 suggests that reading aloud is both a shared and a solitary practice, and this is borne out by the responses to a question which asked directly about this aspect of oral reading. Figure 3.2 shows that more people read out loud to only one other person than in any other formation, with reading to a group next and reading aloud alone a little less common, though still done daily or frequently by almost half the sample. Only 9.8% say that they never read aloud to one other person, again emphasising the ubiquity of reading aloud in these personal and social lives. Reading to a group may be done in families and is also common in workplace situations. Religious practices – and perhaps other occasions involving group or individual singing, recitation or chanting – may account for the relatively high proportions who read aloud in unison in groups, with 17 individuals reporting doing this every day, and almost a quarter of the total doing it daily or often.

The 358 free-text comments on this question reveal further information about the contexts in which reading aloud occurs. Two-hundred and thirty-five participants write of reading aloud in home or family settings, including to partners and children, and even in some cases to cats and dogs. There are 151 examples of reading aloud in workplaces, 48 with friends, 44 in performance or artistic settings and 21 in religious contexts. Typical comments on this topic include: 'I am a librarian so sometimes read aloud to a group; emails etc[.] to relay information to staff'; 'I read aloud children's books to my daughter and

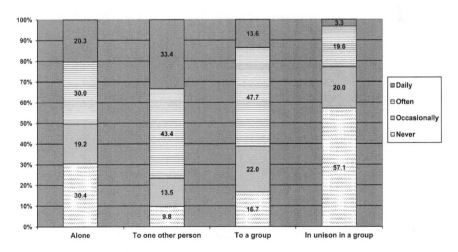

Figure 3.2 Frequency and formations of reading aloud (% of total sample)

41

textbooks to my class. I used to volunteer and read letters and information to a blind couple'; 'I read aloud from religious texts to my church group. I read online articles aloud to my friend. I read books or instructions to myself to help me understand things better'; '[w]e read aloud from the Bible in church – one reads and everyone follows'; 'I am a member of a book club and we often read relevant passages out to the group. When attending marriage ceremonies I read from a script and sometimes guests read out poems'; and '[I r]ead particular excerpts of books or newspaper articles to my boyfriend if I find them particularly interesting or think that he might enjoy them too.' Younger people often report reading emails and news items to partners, friends or work colleagues: one woman in her 30s notes that 'obviously if I see something amusing online ([US President Donald] Trump has proved fruitful news fodder for sharing with partner, in office, etc).' Of the 82 respondents in the '30 and below' age group, 64 wrote a comment here, and of these 29 explicitly mention reading aloud to their partner or spouse.

It is almost axiomatic that new media influence literacy practices, especially among younger people, and there is a large literature on the nature and impact of 'digital literacies' (see, for example, Burnett et al., 2014; Gillen, 2014). We asked our respondents whether they read aloud from screens, and 412 (77.9%) replied that they do, with only 109 (20.6%) saying that they did not. The results of this question are broken down in Table 3.4. Members of the oldest age group are less likely to read aloud from screens than the youngest, but a majority do so in all age groups, and among both women and men, though with an even greater preponderance among women. Of the 412 respondents who wrote that they do read from screens, 371 gave additional comments, revealing a mixture of texts (social media, emails, poems), reasons (understanding, sharing) and devices (phones, Kindles, computers); some suggested that they do most of their reading aloud (and reading more generally) from screens, including religious texts and their own writing, while others read aloud from screens only those texts that appear *solely* on screens (emails, social media posts, text messages). These additional comments also show that, in the case of the latter types of text, most are read from phones, whereas texts that appear in various formats are more often read from computer screens.

Table 3.4 Reading aloud from computer, tablet and phone screens (% of sample, and by gender and age group)

		By gender		By age group			
	All	Female	Male	30 and below	31–45	46–66	67 and above
Yes	77.9	81.2	65.2	89.0	76.5	81.1	56.5
No	20.6	17.1	33.9	11.0	22.3	17.0	40.3

We also asked whether participants read aloud in more than one language: just under half – 232 or 43.9% of the total number of respondents – said that they do, compared with just under a third of the sample describing themselves as bi- or multilingual. A number of respondents, as noted above and in Table 3.3, use reading aloud to help them learn or practise another language. It is clear, then, that reading aloud is common in both English and other languages spoken in Britain, and also for language-learning purposes. Participants read the news, social media posts, books and sometimes instructions and recipes in a range of languages: either because these are the languages they are most comfortable reading or the texts they have easiest access to, or in some cases in order to maintain individual or familial engagement with a heritage language. In total, 46 languages are explicitly mentioned in this context, including some 'dead' languages such as Old Norse and Middle English, which are read aloud for both pleasure and education; and some such as Quranic Arabic and Hebrew for religious purposes. This can involve reading aloud a language the reader does not use in daily spoken interaction (see, for example, Baker, 1993; Herbert & Robinson, 2001).

Another series of questions asked about listening to others reading aloud. Table 3.5 breaks down the frequency of hearing particular text types read aloud by gender: these are the same text types as in Table 3.1 but with the addition of audiobooks and books read on the radio. In general, there seems to be a slightly lower incidence of hearing things read than of reading them aloud oneself, and this is true among both men and women, for whom the proportion answering 'never' is higher for all but one of the categories – i.e. religious texts, in Table 3.5 than in Table 3.1. The same pattern emerges if the categories 'never' and 'occasionally' are added together. These proportions in part may reflect the fact that a considerable proportion of reading aloud is done alone, as shown in Figure 3.2. It is also possible that respondents are less likely to notice the various kinds of reading aloud that they hear on a frequent basis, although only nine respondents – three women and six men – report that they never hear *any* of the text types read aloud. For each text type, the proportion of men who never hear others reading aloud is higher than the proportion of women.

Listening to others read aloud can also be a solitary activity, with a number of respondents mentioning that they listen to reading on the radio or to podcasts, either alone or in company. (Some of these broadcasts may not, strictly speaking, involve reading aloud, but many do.) Table 3.5 shows that rather more women in the sample listen to audiobooks or books read on the radio daily (16.4%) or often (27.9%) than men (12.3% and 21.7% respectively). Indeed, female respondents are more likely to hear audiobooks or books on the radio daily than any other text type – although, conversely, a third of women and more than 40% of men report never hearing them. Interestingly, listening to audiobooks or books on the radio is somewhat more widespread among the 23 to 30 age group, of whom nearly a half (47.9%) in our sample report doing this daily or often, compared with 40.2% of those aged 31 to 45 and 43.7% in

Table 3.5 Frequency of hearing common text types read aloud (% of total), by gender

	Never		Occasionally		Often		Daily	
	Women	Men	Women	Men	Women	Men	Women	Men
Newspapers	32.3	42.1	24.6	17.8	32.8	26.2	10.4	14.0
Books (not children's)	47.7	57.5	29.1	25.5	19.4	14.2	3.8	2.8
Children's books	41.4	57.1	19.2	16.2	25.7	18.1	13.7	8.6
Instructions/recipes	32.2	47.2	27.8	25.5	35.8	24.5	4.1	2.8
Emails/letters	35.4	43.1	21.7	17.4	33.6	32.1	9.3	7.3
Religious texts	49.9	62.0	20.9	16.7	23.9	15.7	5.2	5.6
Social media	30.4	43.1	12.6	11.0	44.0	33.0	13.1	12.8
Shop signs etc.	29.4	48.1	23.4	22.6	36.9	24.5	10.2	4.7
Audiobooks or books on radio	33.8	41.5	21.9	24.5	27.9	21.7	16.4	12.3

the 46 to 66 group, and just over a third of those aged 67 and over. It is worth noting that a majority of those who listen to recorded readings-aloud often or daily do so only alone (140 out of 261 in the sample), but 101 do so both alone and in the company of someone else, and the other 20 *only* with someone else. When asked whether they read aloud more than they listen to others reading aloud, 33.3% of our sample said that they do, whereas 36.5% said the opposite, that they listen to others more than they read aloud themselves. In many settings, it can be hard to separate reading aloud and listening: they often occur together. As one participant commented, 'reading and listening are integral to each other, though to listen well in some circumstances is more difficult than reading aloud.'

The common and the visible

The findings of this analysis identify a number of features of adult reading aloud practices. They suggest that reading aloud happens in a number of different ways and for different purposes, across contexts and life domains. This is not to suggest that reading aloud is *more* widespread than reading silently: indeed, only 10 respondents agree with the statement 'I read aloud more than I read silently.' However, very few adults in our sample do not read aloud at all; most read more aloud than they initially realised, many read aloud a great deal, and some – in fact more than half of our sample – read aloud because they enjoy doing it. These findings suggest that more notice should be taken in literacy research of adult reading aloud practices, including areas that are largely overlooked, such as the quotidian activities of reading text messages and social media posts, the use of reading aloud when completely alone, or adults reading books to each other, all of which our survey highlights as 'common' practices in the lives of the participants.

A social practice often is described as being common or 'everyday,' and this can mean different things. Some texts are read often or daily by a majority of respondents, including newspapers and magazines, social media posts and shop signs, road signs and posters (see Figure 3.1). For some individuals, daily reading aloud is part of their work: teachers, poets, actors, ministers of religion and others identified themselves in the survey. Some other professions involve structured reading aloud: for example, one respondent noted, 'in my work as a psychotherapist I read prepared scripts to my clients all the time.' A similar point can be made about a significant minority who read aloud as part of their leisure or cultural lives: our sample included a number of individuals who regularly read poetry to larger or smaller audiences as well as those who read their writing to creative writing groups.

Another aspect of 'commonness' concerns practices that most individuals may do at some point in their lives but not regularly or frequently, but rather as part of rituals that are socially widespread: for example, three respondents mentioned reading aloud at funeral services and another three at weddings. These are not done often by any one individual (except by professionals such as ministers and registrars), but they are socially widespread, and they can involve a large number of hearers. Finally, there are practices that become common to people at certain points in the lifecourse, the most obvious being reading to children. The commonness of a practice, then, can be understood in terms of social pervasiveness – funerals and weddings take place daily, but most of us attend them relatively infrequently – or in terms of frequency within individual lives, as well as patterns across the lifecourse.

Another way we can understand the 'commonness' – or not – of a literacy practice is to explore notions of visibility – that is, how much practices are noticed or talked about within a wider culture or context, including by the readers themselves. An Internet search for 'reading aloud' will generate a great deal on the importance of reading to children. By contrast, the practices of adults reading to friends or family from newspapers or social media, or reading aloud alone as part of a writing or study process, are far less 'visible' – less often mentioned, written about less, and perhaps even sometimes not noticed by those who do it, as one respondent notes, 'I did not realize how much we read aloud. I probably have not included all the examples of when I read aloud, as we do this without thinking most of the time.'

Several aspects of visibility are highlighted by the questionnaire data. The first is that visibility is related to what we might – no doubt problematically – call the public and private spheres. Practices that occur in the public sphere, such as poetry performances, are likely to be more visible culturally than those occurring in the home. Such public occurrences of reading aloud are more easily noticed, even by non-participants, than partners reading to each other, the solitary reader helping himself get through a difficult text, or the volunteer reading to her blind neighbour. Reading aloud that happens in the home, per-haps especially in bed, as some respondents note, is particularly hidden from public view and usually involves only one or two people. In our survey (see Table 3.1), a third of male respondents and almost 40% of women report fre-quent or daily reading aloud of books other than children's books, not to mention other practices that are even more common in private family settings, such as reading newspaper and magazine articles, emails and social media posts. One respondent claimed that reading aloud is 'best done in the bath': though whether she does this alone or with an audience is not clear. Another explained that 'I live alone – maybe the sound of my own voice breaks the silence. I read to my imaginary friends.' The home, then, is a place of private and generally less visible reading aloud, with one notable exception: parents' reading to children enters the public sphere, probably because it is explicitly encouraged by the educational professions and, as noted above, in the popular media. Family literacy research (Carpentieri et al., 2011) repeatedly emphasises the importance of this practice within the home as well as in schools and libraries, and as such a domestic activity becomes a feature of widespread public discussion (this is picked up again in Chapter 6). For a range of reasons, then, some practices are more 'visible' than others.

It is also important to see these ideas of the visibility/invisibility of certain oral reading practices in the context of earlier discussions in the New Literacy Studies literature about visibility, dominance and power. Much has been written about the dominant literacies of powerful institutions or groups, as opposed to the 'vernacular' or 'ordinary' literacies of those with less power (see, for example, Crowther et al., 2001; Papen, 2005). Sheridan et al. write about the 'invisibility of literacy practices of ordinary people' (2000, pp. 5–7), particularly around who is and is not allowed to consider themselves a 'writer.' Tusting et al. (2000) conclude the influential *Situated Literacies* volume with an analysis of key themes, including those of power and visibility, looking at ideas from both Hamilton's (2000) chapter on what is and is not visible in a (photographable) literacy event and Wilson's (2000) chapter on 'permitted' and 'hidden' literacies, what is seen or noticed and how this relates to what is valued in prison contexts. Wilson's work highlights the contextual nature of dominance, just as Elster (2003) argues that certain Orthodox Jewish literacies, visible and powerful in a specific religious context, are made invisible in other (secular, educational) contexts. The questionnaire data supports this idea that the visibility (and therefore power) of a practice can be highly contextual: what is visible (or audible, or noticed) in one life domain or setting may be invisible in others. For example, the reading aloud practices of healthcare professionals may be widely noticed within their own settings but not elsewhere: many people would be unaware that therapy scripts and medical notes are routinely read aloud. From the point of view of literacy education, perhaps the most striking aspect of the relative cultural visibility of literacy practices is the invisibility of forms of adult reading aloud within many educational conceptualisations of reading. This point will be developed in Chapters 11 and 12.

Conclusion 1: what are the key messages from the questionnaire data?

Across the questionnaire responses, reading aloud practices are ubiquitous and remarkably varied; they are sometimes visible, and sometimes invisible, and often seem important to personal or cultural identities. While much of the literature proposes a historic shift from reading as oral and communal to reading as silent and individual, our questionnaire findings show that reading is (for at least some people) all of these things. Our analysis suggests ways that we can understand or unpack the 'commonness' and visibility of an 'everyday' literacy practice, exploring notions of frequency within individual lives, changes over the lifecourse, social pervasiveness and contextual visibility. Our analysis also suggests the need for closer examination of the forms of reading aloud performed, used and enjoyed by adults of different backgrounds, in different countries and contexts, for different purposes and with different meanings, in different languages and with different uses of technology. These are all areas that will be developed elsewhere in this book.

Conclusion 2: what else does the questionnaire tell us?

Though the questionnaire is quite long and demanding in terms of number and nature of questions, the majority of participants filled in these free-text boxes with an extraordinary amount of insight, candour and generosity with their time – and a sense of really having something they wanted to say, to make public in some sense. The sort of analysis presented above runs the risk of obscuring the more human 'I want to say this'-ness of it all: the voices, lives or experiences behind each response. Here is a taste.

Doing this survey has made me realise how much I read aloud/talk to myself mainly when on my own. I have reached an age when I don't think this is 'the first sign of madness.'

I have gone through stages of reading self-help mantras aloud to help with mental health issues.

I learn and relearn poems and short pieces of prose to keep reading for – very occasional – auditions and as an attempt to keep ga ga dom at bay.

Texts containing information, to help my partner. Choral music for singing. Is singing reading aloud?

Quran and when I pray. I prefer reading aloud otherwise sometimes I feel I am just reciting it subconsciously and my mind drifts, rather than a conscious engagement.

On three occasions I have been part of an Al-Anon group where each member reads aloud from the guidelines at the start of the meeting.

I think it is something we do more than we think we do. Especially if we're prone to talking to ourselves. I think it can be an act of great benefit because it 'lifts the words off the page' and can give them extra meaning. It can also bond people as in an act of common worship or common interest. But it can also exclude if people aren't familiar with a particular language or ritual.

My sister and I read aloud whole books to each other when we were growing up. I always read my mum's letters aloud to her. My elderly mother often reads poetry when I visit her.

It feels fabulous, enhances the meaning, brings the text to life and is an intimate activity. I read to my son when he was a child and now, he's an adult, occasionally we share a bottle of red and he reads to me, usually Sherlock Homes.

For instructions/recipes, it makes them clearer and easier to follow step by step. If I am reading a book for pleasure when tired, I will read the first few words of it out loud to ease into the story.

It makes me scared.

Note

1 Most of the rest of this chapter (pp. 33–47), including the tables and figures, was previously published as part of Duncan, S., & Freeman, M. (2019). Adults reading aloud: A survey of contemporary practices in Britain. *British Journal of Educational Studies*, 68(1), 97–123, reprinted by permission of the publisher (Taylor & Francis Ltd, http://www.tandfonline.com). Many thanks to both Dr Mark Freeman and the Taylor & Francis Group for permission to reproduce this work here.

References

Baker, J. M. (1993). The presence of a name: Reading scripture in an Indonesian village. In *The Ethnography of Reading* (pp. 98–138). University of California Press.

Burnett, C., Davies, J., Merchant, G., & Rowsell, J. (Eds.). (2014). *New Literacies around the Globe: Policy and Pedagogy*. Routledge.

Carpentieri, J. D., Fairfax-Cholmeley, K., Litster, J., & Vorhaus, J. (2011). *Family Literacy in Europe: Using Parental Support Initiatives to Enhance Early Literacy Development*. NRDC.

Crowther, J., Hamilton, M., & Tett, L. (2001). Powerful literacies: An introduction. In J. Crowther, M. Hamilton & L. Tett (Eds.), *Powerful Literacies* (pp. 1–4). National Institute of Adult Continuing Education.

Elster, C. A. (2003). Authority, performance, and interpretation in religious reading: Critical issues of intercultural communication and multiple literacies. *Journal of Literacy Research*, 35(1), 663–692. https://doi.org/10.1207/s15548430jlr3501_5.

Flood, A. (2018, February 22). Big decline in number of parents reading daily to toddlers. *Guardian*, 14.

Gillen, J. (2014). *Digital Literacies*. Routledge.

Hamilton, M. (2000). Expanding the new literacy studies: Using photographs to explore literacy as social practice. In D. Barton, M. Hamilton & R. Ivanič (Eds.), *Situated Literacies: Reading and Writing in Context* (pp.16–34). Routledge.

Herbert, P., & Robinson, C. (2001). Another language, another literacy. In B. V. Street (Ed.), *Literacy and Development: Ethnographic Perspectives* (pp. 121–136). Routledge.

Hughes-Hassell, S., & Rodge, P. (2007). The leisure reading habits of urban adolescents. *Journal of Adolescent & Adult Literacy*, 51(1), 22–33. https://doi.org/10.1598/JAAL.51.1.3.

Ivey, G., & Broaddus, K. (2001). "Just plain reading": A survey of what makes students want to read in middle school classrooms. *Reading Research Quarterly*, 36(4), 350–377. https://doi.org/10.1598/RRQ.36.4.2.

Kling, M. (1982). Adult reading habits. *Reading Psychology*, 3(1), 59–70. https://doi.org/10.1080/0270271820030109.

Papen, U. (2005). *Adult Literacy as Social Practice: More Than Skills*. Routledge.

Scales, A. M., & Rhee, O. (2001). Adult reading habits and patterns. *Reading Psychology*, 22, 175–203.

Scholastic. (2018). Reading aloud at home. https://www.scholastic.co.uk/readingreport/reading-aloud-at-home.

Sharon, A. T. (1973). What do adults read? *Reading Research Quarterly*, 9(2), 148–149.

Sheridan, D., Street, B. V., & Bloome, D. (2000). *Writing Ourselves: Mass-Observation and Literacy Practices*. Hampton Press.

Tusting, K., Ivanič, R., & Wilson, A. (2000). New literacy studies at the interchange. In D. Barton, M. Hamilton & R. Ivanič (Eds.), *Situated Literacies: Reading and Writing in Context* (pp. 225–234). Routledge.

Wilson, A. (2000). There is no escape from third-space theory. In D. Barton, M. Hamilton & R. Ivanič (Eds.), *Situated Literacies: Reading and Writing in Context* (pp. 54–69). Routledge.

YouGov. (2018). *Read aloud 15 minutes survey report: How America reads aloud to its children.* http://www.readaloud.org/documents/ReadAloudSurveyReport.pdf.

Liu, Z. (2005). Reading behavior in the digital environment: Changes in reading behavior over the past ten years. *Journal of Documentation*, 61(6), 700–712. https://doi.org/10.1108/00220410510632040.

4

MASS OBSERVATION

The original Mass Observation[1] was a reaction, at least in part, to a sense – during the British Abdication crisis of 1936–1937 – that the press did not really have any idea what 'the masses' really thought (or did), and so Tom Harrison (anthropologist), Humphrey Jennings (documentary filmmaker and artist) and Charles Madge (reporter, communist and poet) joined forces to develop Mass Observation. Both this original Mass Observation (1937 to the early 1950s) and the present-day revived Mass Observation Project (ongoing from 1981; hereafter MOP) can be seen in terms of multiple layers of duality: being both social science research and a political movement; both data collection and collaborative writing; and examining (as noted in Chapter 2) both 'what people do and what they think about what they do' (Johnes, 2017). The 'twin pillars' of the original Mass Observation – volunteers who wrote about what they did and paid observers who took notes of what others did (Summerfield, 1985, pp. 440–441) – are echoed by the present-day MOP's 'dual vision' (Kramer, 2014). MOP's 500-odd volunteer writers, or 'Observers,' are invited to respond in writing to 'directives' sent to them three times a year. Kramer argues that this writing is characterised by 'a dual vision': part autobiography and part 'amateur sociology,' ideal, as Sheridan, Street and Bloome (2000) have argued, for understanding the role of literacy in people's lives.

   The MOP had previously run directives on literacy such as *Viewing and Reading* (1983), *Uses of Reading and Writing & Literacy Diaries* (1991), *Reading* (1993), *Mothers and Literacy* (1995), *Childhood Reading* (2003) and *Books and You* (2009), providing rich accounts of the role of reading in people's lives. They tell us comparatively little, however, about what was read aloud as opposed to silently and why. These responses to these directives also tell us less about practices which people may not always associate with the word 'reading;' for example the types of reading one might do in a café, at work, in an art gallery or as worship, though some information on these practices can be found in the responses to other directives, e.g. *Going to a Funeral* (2009). I worked with the MOP archivists to create a directive (please see Figure 4.1 at the end of this chapter) asking the Observers about their experiences, memories and feelings about reading aloud and listening to others read, and to keep a reading aloud diary. This was sent out to 507 Observers in the summer of 2017.

One-hundred and sixty responses were returned by the end of January 2018, 96 by email and the rest posted in. This is slightly below the MOP target of 175 per directive but still considered by the MOP to be a healthy response. About half of these are between 1 and 3 pages in length, about a quarter between 4 and 7 pages, just under a quarter under 1 page, and the rest 8 or more pages.[2]

Much is written about MOP as a research enterprise or methodology, including observations that the Observers cannot be considered representative of the UK population as a whole (being too female, too old, too southern and too middle class), and their writing lacking in objectivity (Pollen, 2013). MOP writing was of course never intended to be representative or objective but rather to provide the 'illumination' and 'surprise' that an individual life and perspective can offer, potentially 'disrupting' established narratives (Sheridan, 2017). Further, Moor and Uprichard (2014) write of the 'unwieldy materiality' of MOP data, referring to both the physical excess of the hundreds of pieces of paper (of different colours, shapes and smells, many written in different styles of handwriting and colours of ink), as well as to the methodological challenge presented by hundreds of separate pieces of writing, each providing an individual offering of personal narrative and analysis. In this way, the Observers are less subjects of research, or even participants in research, and more writers and researchers themselves. To analyse, present or condense the 160 responses, I draw on these ideas about the nature and affordances of MOP writing. Below, Section 1 explores the 'atypical typicality' of the Observers and what we can learn from their reactions to the topic as well as from the practices they report. Section 2 examines the writing of the Observers as researchers, and Section 3 looks at the work of the Observers as writers or storytellers.

Atypical typical

As noted above, methodological writing on the MOP rightly stresses that the MOP Observers cannot be considered typical or representative of the UK population. However, this 'atypical' group may actually be well-placed to offer a kind of 'typicality' in relation to the focus of this (or any) directive. They are not self-selecting in terms of previous interest in or engagement with reading aloud; this directive dropped through their letter boxes or into their email accounts because of their relationship to the MOP, not because of any previous relationship to the topic. Crucially, the MOP Observers can and do take their time to respond (MOP colleagues tell me that most responses are returned within between two weeks and three months of a directive being sent out). Several Observers indicate that they started the directive and then left it, returning, after further reflection, some hours, days or even weeks later. Changes to ink colour also suggest that others may have done the same, without mentioning it. The MOP offers a ready and waiting group of adults committed to providing their views on the directives sent to them three times a year. Observers are not necessarily predisposed to or rehearsed in the topics concerned, but they are willing to think through them carefully and write candidly because of their commitment to the MOP endeavour. I am arguing that this means that the MOP Observers do offer a rare form of typicality, or varied reactions to diverse topics, and therefore the endeavour presents a unique opportunity to capture initial and reflective responses to the topic of adults reading aloud as well as examples of reading aloud practices themselves.

a) Reactions

The overwhelming reaction is that of surprise: surprise at the topic and surprise at their own practices. Observers express their surprise at adult reading aloud being the subject of a MOP directive. For some, this is simply a reaction to an unusual topic. F38 (as noted in Chapter 1, throughout this book I will refer to the Observers by their age and gender as given) considers it 'one of the strangest directives.' Others specify that their surprise is based on the feeling that reading aloud is usually associated with children, as F72 notes: 'adults and reading aloud don't go together,' while for others their surprise is linked to a strong dislike of reading aloud or a sense of its irrelevance, as M82 writes: 'I see no point.'

The second element of surprise may be more interesting. Twenty Observers write of their surprise at coming to *realise* (this word features heavily across the responses; for this reason I have italicised it in this section), through the directive prompts, that they read aloud more than they had previously thought. Many start their writing noting that they read aloud little and yet eventually end up writing about a great many more oral reading practices (including those who kept a reading aloud diary and discovered in this way that they read aloud more than they had realised), suggesting that they too read aloud more than first thought. M28 captures a common refrain:

> I imagine like other people, I had thought very little about reading aloud [...] It was something I immediately associated with childhood. However, the more I've thought about it, I've *realised* that I read aloud or am read aloud to in a variety of ways.

Similarly from M58, 'My first thought [...] Reading aloud – me, never [...] reflection shows that is clearly not true,' F61, 'my first reaction – I don't do it. But the more I thought about it, the more I *realised* that I do actually read aloud, more than I thought I did,' and F44:

> Initially I would say I rarely read aloud; however thinking and observing myself reading aloud over the course of a week it appears that I may read aloud more than I had thought. I think this is because I read very small amounts of text aloud – maybe a tweet, or a sentence or a few words at once. Most of this would take place at work.

M96 explains that despite memories of oral reading in the past, he doesn't think he reads aloud in his present life, and yet, 'having written that, I suddenly *realise* I am saying these words aloud as I tap them out on the word processor. Something I must be doing continuously without *realising* it.' Likewise, M44 writes that he needed help from his spouse to record when he reads aloud because he simply doesn't notice most of the reading aloud he does; it happens without him '*realising*.'

None of the 160 Observers write that they have never read aloud, though three declare that they do not read aloud in their present lives. F23 remembers both reading aloud and being read to as a child and hopes that she will be able to read to children of her own one day. M88 explains that while he read to his children when they were small, he does not read aloud at all now. However, he goes on to explain that he does understand that other adults may take part in reading aloud practices that have nothing to do with children. M71 provides the shortest directive response of them all, consisting only of these words:

> I own 8000 books, never read aloud, have never read aloud. Never since Primary school, in the 1950s, had books read aloud.
> I have never married and have no children. The Directive is an irrelevance.

The above is only a snapshot of the range of reactions to adult reading aloud present across all 160 responses, from those surprised by the amount of reading aloud in their lives (however small or big), to those who had already been aware of it (whether they love it or hate it) but were nevertheless surprised to see a directive on the topic; from those who read aloud a lot to those who do it very little; and from those who associate reading aloud with childhood and children to those who see it as a core part of their (adult) work, creative, romantic or religious lives.

b) Practices

The lack of a necessary predisposition towards the topic of adult reading aloud also makes the MOP writing of value in terms of the range of oral reading activities mentioned and the prevalence of certain practices. After reading through the 160 responses several times, I read through twice again, noting down all the different instances of reading aloud mentioned and how many Observers write of each, before grouping them into 20 categories (in bold below).

Eighty-eight mention **memories from childhood and youth**, including memories of reading aloud and being read to at school and home or of seeing one parent reading to another. Fifty-eight write of reading aloud as part of work roles, both more **generic work practices** – such as reading aloud from information boards, reading aloud in collaborative writing tasks and reading aloud or listening to minutes read at meetings – as well as more **specific work activities**, such as reading relaxation scripts as part of mental health work, reading aloud as a magistrate in court, as a receptionist confirming an appointment or a nurse reading notes to a patient. Reading aloud for **study purposes** features 48 times, including reading aloud for language learning (Basque, German or French, for example), reading aloud to memorise and reading aloud to better understand difficult text. Thirty-four write of reading aloud as part of **individual or communal writing processes** to hone writing or get help from others to 'proof-hear,' and 47 write of reading aloud as part of **dealing with correspondence**, reading emails, letters, cards or invitations to others in person (because they may be interested, cannot read, cannot see or have their hands full) or sharing them over the telephone.

Sixty-four write of reading aloud, alone or with others, **to follow instructions (including listening to a GPS), timetables or recipes or to choose food products while shopping.** Sixty mention reading aloud as part of **preparing for or giving speeches,** talks or lectures, including eulogies, wedding speeches, and at important events, such as an AIDS/HIV benefit or at protest marches, and 20 note reading aloud to play **board games, bingo, or do crosswords or quizzes.** Eighteen read aloud or listen to others reading as part of **book group or writing group activity,** 11 as part of **play-reading groups, drama groups or amateur dramatics,** and 38 read aloud **poetry,** including at gatherings, as part of performance poetry, and simply to one other person or to themselves. Nine write about reading aloud when **singing,** including as a choir, chanting or singing hymns. Fifty mention reading aloud or listening to others reading as individual or communal **religious worship.** Fourteen read aloud to **help** those who cannot see, cannot read or are unwell, including reading aloud to record a talking newspaper and a woman who remembers reading aloud to her mother who had never learnt to read.

Thirty-eight say they read aloud bits of **books or stories to other adults** – partners, friends or family, while 53 listen to **audiobooks, 'book at bedtime' or plays on the radio.** Eighty-one wrote of reading aloud **with children**: not only stories and books but also mathematics problems and other bits of homework. The most prevalent group of practices, though, at 116 mentions, is not reading with children but oral reading as part of **engagement with the news or social media,** such as reading tweets or other social media posts to others or reading 'snippets' from the newspaper across the breakfast table. At the other end of the spectrum, there are four mentions of **miscellaneous solitary practices**: reading aloud from a knitting pattern, doing throat exercises prescribed by a doctor, and two accounts of reading aloud when completely alone in order to hear a voice.

Beyond this picture of commonality and difference, six headline points are worth highlighting. First, despite its strong cultural association with the idea of reading aloud, reading with children is not the most commonly mentioned practice by the MOP Observers (thought it did get 81 mentions). The most prevalent practice reported by the Observers is reading aloud to share news from papers or social media with others: a communal engagement with, or mediation of, the outside world (see Chapter 6 for a discussion of this). Second, not all reading aloud of books or stories is done with children, much is done with other adults. Third, not all reading aloud is done with other people at all; a great deal is done when completely alone (and while one person notes that he rarely reads aloud because he lives alone, two others explain that they read out loud precisely because they live alone). While some practices are clearly to serve others (for example, to console, entertain or inform), others are to serve the reader; for example, to understand, memorise or write.

Fourth, reading aloud appears to be ubiquitous in the workplace for both more generic work purposes (for example, the reading of extracts of minutes at meetings) and for highly specialised activities: from offices to shops, legal to medical, teaching to the creative industries. Fifth, forms of reading aloud are a key part of the religious worship of many Observers (though the MOP responses appear to include only Christian examples), whether read, heard, sung, chanted and/or recited. This suggests that these practices are a significant part of the lives of those who engage in regular religious practice (but may be invisible to those who do not). Finally, the responses demonstrate considerable engagement in forms of creative writing, poetry and drama, indicating that as much as telling us something about reading aloud in Britain today this directive (as several Observers noted) may tell us something about contemporary adult life; specifically, that it involves more than work or family.

Observers as researchers

Shirley Brice Heath, in her Foreword to Sheridan et al. (2000), notes the Observers' striking sense of writing 'as individuals within a larger collection of people' (2000, p. xiii). Within the original MO idea of a 'science of ourselves' through the efforts of 'men and women of goodwill' (Summerfield, 1985, p. 443), and the theorising of the present day MOP's 'dual-vision' (Kramer, 2014), rests the idea that the Observers are not subjects being researched but rather researchers themselves, individually writing up their own findings or analyses in response to each directive. While providing 'raw' data for research-ers to analyse, Mass Observers also provide their own analyses of both their practices and the practices of others which they observe (Kramer, 2014; Sher-idan et al., 2000). This means that for this directive there are actually 160 sets of findings. This is reminiscent of Kristin Thomson's influential concept of 'cinematic excess' in film studies, where an excess of 'materiality' (which may be about costume, props, plot or acting) threatens or rather resists the illusion of the cinematic whole (Thompson, 1986). Similarly, the 'unwieldy materiality' (Moor and Uprichard, 2014) of the MOP responses resist the potential (and tempting) research illusion that 'data' can be smoothly compacted into a sleek set of findings. The MOP Observers as researchers write about themselves, others and their communities, each creating individual analyses that resist, to a certain extent, organisation and simplification.

Clearly, these 160 pieces cannot all be presented here (though I would urge any reader to visit the archive and read them all), and so in an attempt to nevertheless recognise Observers as researchers, here I am reporting on two notable shared analytical acts: the classification of practices, and explorations of the relationship between the artistry and purposes of reading aloud.

a) Classifying practices

The directive did not ask respondents to classify their own or others' practices, but this is exactly what many have done, at least implicitly, writing about their practices in particular groupings (alone, at work, with children, for example). This is one of the ways that the responses are most clearly analyses rather than simply description. Fifteen Observers, though, are explicit in offering a classification or typography. Nine offer classifications by situation or context; for example, F79 offers a four-way split: Quaker activity, throat exercises prescribed by the doctor, within her French classes, and reading newspapers aloud in French. F53 provides nine situations where she reads aloud, including sharing items from the BBC news feeds on her phone with her partner and reading aloud with a cat in bed on a Saturday morning. M74 offers a four-way classification of practices, not his own, but rather of situations where he believes reading aloud happens today: reading to children at bedtime, teachers reading to pupils or students, reading papers at meetings and reading at church.

Four Observers classify by purpose. F29 identifies three purposes of reading aloud: redrafting text, to regain focus when reading for pleasure and to bring people together socially. F47 also produces a classification of purposes but with a two-way division of purposes: practical – for example, reading instructions and to better understand information – vs life-enhancing: to be funny, for entertainment or to develop a relationship. One person (M52) offers a classification through the text types themselves (including jokes, recipes and TV listings) and another, M74, offers a binary classification based on the degree of deliberation or planning involved. He contrasts the deliberate, planned instances of reading aloud he does as a film editor, writer or parent (for example, read-throughs of scripts or reading a book to a child) with the 'countless everyday occasions when we indulge in wholly forgettable instances [...] the 'listen to this' at the breakfast table.

Here, we can see the Observers writing as researchers, not only noticing their and others' practices but working to characterise and categorise them in some way, thus analysing the role of reading aloud in adult life.

b) Artistry and purpose

The directive invites Observers to think about whether there is a relationship between *why* they read out loud and *how*. The 160 responses present a clear consensus that this is the case. F29 explains that she aims to be loud and clear when reading for a lecture audience but whispers if reading aloud to herself as part of her writing process or to focus on what she is reading. Many echo this general idea: if reading for others you need to be loud and clear, while if for yourself, you can read however you like, whether whispering or booming.

However, some Observers provide more complex analyses, exploring how they may be using their voices and bodies in different ways depending on the purpose of the reading. M79 explains his nerves at being a new magistrate, having to read aloud in court and learning the importance of eye-contact for highlighting the significance of what he was reading: 'If I did not make eye contact with the person being read to, it negated the importance of what was being read.' Similarly, exploring professional reading aloud, F71 writes about conducting marriage ceremonies, noting several different factors at play: the need to comply with the law means that the text has to be read aloud exactly as written; the need for everyone in the room to be able to hear means the text has to be read at an appropriate volume and pace; and the (highly challenging) need to represent both the gravity and the joy of the ceremony for those getting married means 'it was important [...] to strike the right manner; too much informality was inappropriate, but a certain warmth and sincerity had to come through in the voice.' In both these examples, we see choices made and skills exercised in order to convey more than the message contained in the words of the written text: to convey the significance of the occasion, to ritualise a stage in a legal process and, potentially, a stage in a lifecourse (we will return to these 'professional' examples in Chapter 7).

F26 offers a different example, writing that she attends a local Catholic church once a week, enjoying the familiarity and how 'your voice gets lost in a mass of other people [...] It makes me feel like I belong.' Here, like the marriage example above, the purpose of the reading is not primarily about conveying a new message contained within a written text. In both cases, the readers and listeners are likely to already possess a good sense of the meanings of the texts and have read or heard them before, in some cases many times. Rather, something else happens when the voice ignites those words, unifying two people or a congregation.

These analyses tell us that *how* one reads aloud is linked to *why* one reads aloud (and not only to the presence or absence of an audience); that the purposes of reading are diverse, as Griffiths (1999), Elster (2003) and Yandell (2012) have argued, and not always about decoding or communicating a previously unknown meaning. What we could call the artistry of reading aloud (and reading more broadly) therefore varies from practice to practice but could include decisions about volume, pitch, pace, stress on certain words and phrases, use of eye contact, facial expressions and body language, and more, to convey something *through* the written text, rather than simply *from* it. In each of these examples, we can see evidence of the relationship between the meanings (including purposes and values) of a literacy practice and the skills/knowledge/competences used.

58

The nature of the skills and knowledge needed to perform a certain literacy practice 'well' is determined by the meanings (including purposes and values) at play.

Observers as writers or storytellers

Another 'way in' to this data is to remember that whatever else they are doing
the Observers are writers in a collaborative writing project (Sheridan, 2017),
selecting and sharing the stories of their lives. Responding to questions about
reading aloud, the Observers tell stories, things that have happened to them and
to others. There are too many stories to recount them all here, but I will
examine examples of stories on two recurring themes: a) loss and pain, and b)
youth and encounter.

a) Stories of loss and pain

Many Observers tell stories of reading aloud at funerals, and/or reading aloud
to those ill, in pain or dying. F72 writes of reading at her mother's funeral. She
found a poem by a writer she knew her mother loved and read and reread it out
loud, over and over, in advance to learn it by heart in order to have a chance of
getting through it on the day. She remembers that during the funeral she found
the last verse so hard that the chaplain reached out to touch her and encouraged
her to take it slowly. She reiterates, 'it was hard, but I knew she [her mother]
would have loved the poem.'

As personal as this story is, it also shares a number of features with other
funeral stories. It highlights the significance of taking on the role of reading
at the funeral of a loved one; the importance of choosing words that they loved;
the need put on a decent performance in order to serve the both loved one and
the community; and the near-crushing difficulty of all of this. The identity
expressed is that of someone who loved and was loved, one side of a unique,
personal relationship with the deceased, whether as sister, daughter or lover.
Yet in stepping into the funeral reading/eulogy tradition another identity is
expressed as well: an identity as part of a cultural group, whether religious or
secular. The story told seems to be one of how these two identities co-exist: the
particular, individual or personal, and the communal or cultural. With the
union of these two identities comes both the importance and difficulty of doing
the reading and doing it well.

The stories of reading aloud to those ill, in pain and/or dying are more varied.
M82 writes that when his wife became weak with cancer, he began to read aloud
to her, usually outside on a bench in the fresh air. He notes that this habit has
continued, though, he seems to be suggesting, she is now stronger. F66 remembers reading aloud to her own father after her mother died and his dementia
deteriorated and also volunteering to read aloud in a hospice, and recently finishing (aloud, alone) a book in honour of the woman she had been reading it to,
who had passed away before the end of the book. F26 writes about reading to

My dying friend, bed-ridden and no longer able to go outside, particularly enjoyed listening to poems about nature and the seaside. It made her feel nostalgic and she imagined herself walking along a beach with sand between her toes.

These accounts are all different, yet they share the characterisation of reading aloud as an act of giving or sharing solace. Reader and listener share a distraction, an escape, a story and, once again, the meeting of the particular, personal or individual (time, place, love and voice) with the wider culture: the book or poem they are reading.

b) Stories of youth and encounter

There is an even more common story, an archetype or perhaps stereotype, running through the majority of the responses, linking experiences in childhood or youth with later adult practices; from stories of being read to as a child, creating a love of listening and reading, to memories of bullying or boring teachers putting them off for life. These are stories that locate present attitudes or practices in past experience. Yet, there are others, also about youth, which are a little different.

M60 recounts a memory:

> One incident sticks in my mind from schooldays. I'd never until now thought of it in the context of reading aloud; for decades I regarded it as a spontaneous expression of, I don't know, primitive Communism of some such thing. When I was about twelve or thirteen someone in my class at school managed to get their hands on a copy of the then-scandalous pulp novel Skinhead, and the problem arose that there were thirty or so of us desperate to read it all but only one copy [...] and instead of fighting over the book we all made our way to an empty laboratory (this must have been at lunchtime) and one of us – I seem to recall it was a girl called Alice – sat at the teacher's demonstration table at the front of the room and read the most choice passages out to the class. Even at the time I marvelled at the contrast between her delivery – which was that of a dutiful daughter reading out to her mother from the back of a packet of flour the recipe for making Victoria sponge – and the salacious, and, to us, inflammatory material on the page.

(Note the implied usualness of reading to your mother from the back of a flour packet.) He remembers this strange, electric, rebellious happening vividly almost 50 years later (*Skinhead* was published in 1970).

M93 tells another.

> I chanced one evening to accidentally receive Radio Cairo which was broadcasting, in Arabic I suppose, an extremely long reading [...] by a

man whose voice and style were so intense and passionate, that I was mesmerised by it all, and was compelled to listen. I didn't understand any of it, but recognised that some sentences were from time to time repeated as in an heroic poem. The passion and intensity of the reading increased to an extreme degree as the reading continued until, abruptly it ended – very precipitately as if the reader had been shot dead. I sat stunned: its emotional effect was enormous although I understood not a word. I remember it even now, more than half a century later, and can still hear that reader's passionate voice – it still has an effect upon me.

What do these two stories tell us? They both present a paradox in that they are quite specifically 'about' reading aloud. In the first, the contrast between the delivery and the content is striking, and in the second a lone reading voice reaches a listener over hundreds of miles and across languages. Yet they are also *not* about reading at all but rather about chance encounters. In the first, the teenage boy has an encounter with a countercultural (and highly controversial) text, a wider cultural movement, and the chance of being able to access it, in a group of other youngsters, an empty room and a few minutes of freedom before discovery and a return to lessons. In the second, a young man has an encounter with someone from across the world, a chance meeting with a voice reading a poem in an alien language and yet a somewhat familiar tradition. Just as in the stories of pain and loss, the reading voice forms a link, a line, an oscillation between the individual, particular or personal, and the larger, communal or cultural, creating – potentially – a recognition of simultaneous difference and kinship, the familiar and the new. Reading aloud is not incidental to these stories but central.

Discussion and conclusion

The MOP responses – longer, shorter, handwritten, typed, word-processed, angry, indifferent, glowing, unsure, comic, confused, didactic – make up a unique, long-term resource which allows us to better understand the role of reading aloud in contemporary adult life. MOP writing, as argued above, is part sociological data and part autobiographical writing, part analysis and part storytelling. It is also more. Observers also include in their responses poems they have written, accounts of conversations they have had and lists of books they have read, when and to whom. MOP Observers' contributions are notoriously complex to 'capture'; there are ideas and accounts enough for several volumes. To say that MOP writing presents analytical challenges (and the challenges are considerable, not least that one can never be sure one is reading the handwriting correctly and therefore any 'count ups' are approximate) is to miss a more interesting point: not only does MOP writing *resist* being tamed, it can take the reader to a place where a neat analysis no longer seems desirable, and to the realisation that the actual power of the MOP can only be experienced sitting in a corner of the archive building itself, touching, smelling, reading and rereading as many of the individual pieces of paper as possible. The effort it takes to get to the archive is more than repaid by the volume, range, candour and passion of the responses, each a glimpse into a life as well as a contribution to the understanding of reading aloud today.

Yet there are things an analysis such as this chapter can provide. These 160 pieces take us further in understanding contemporary adult reading aloud. Here we have voices of surprise at the idea of adults reading aloud apart from to children, surprise at the extent of some of our individual (and previously unnoticed) reading aloud practices, and surprise, for some, at the chance to talk about this aspect of their reading. These 'surprises' are all different but together tell us that adult reading aloud practices are indeed largely invisible, echoing the questionnaire responses. These surprises also provide a useful reminder of just how different one's own literacy practices may be from one's neighbour and, therefore, of the challenge of fully understanding the role that literacy plays in someone else's life. The list of practices performed by this group of adults includes the more often cited practices (such as reading with children, in worship or performing poetry) while also, illustrating Sheridan's (2017) point about MOP writing being able to disrupt dominant discourses, presenting a picture of reading aloud as far more varied and quietly ubiquitous across various life domains: work, leisure, learning, romance and creative life as well as family and faith. Observers write of adults reading to each other as well as to children, of reading out when completely alone as well as with larger and smaller groups, and to understand, memorise, write and *feel* as well as to communicate, share or inspire. Another group of 160 adults would certainly reveal some different practices and attitudes (and may not include a man, as this group does, who reads aloud to alleviate his wife's constipation) but is also likely to reveal some of the same. The consensus within these MOP responses suggests patterns that may well be replicated in the wider population and indeed match patterns within the RABiT questionnaire and interview data.

As researchers, the MOP Observers classify their practices and explore their artistry, sharing findings about the diversity of purposes and their relationship to how we may read aloud. As storytellers, they tell tales of pain, loss and forms of 'being there' for others, and of youth encountering worlds of difference, working between individual human connections and larger, communal traditions. They say something about the thundering significance of forms of reading which may, at times, be neither particularly frequent within any one individual life nor widely visible culturally (as noted in Chapter 3) but still *matter*. In this way, the MOP writing for this directive also reinforces a message about reading more broadly: that reading is not one act for one purpose, requiring a predetermined and finite set of skills, but rather a bigger umbrella under which sit a diversity of practices, involving different bundles of skills, acts of judgement, challenges and pleasures. Reading is engagement with text but not always to find out what is written, as the rest of this book will explore.

MASS OBSERVATION
Recording everyday life in Britain

The Mass Observation Project
Summer 2017 Directive

Part 2: 'Lend me your ears: when adults read aloud rather than in silence'

This Directive is about how and why adults read *aloud* in their everyday lives. We want you to write about all of the instances where you experience reading aloud, either as speaker/reader or listener, however long or short these moments might be. This may be alone or in a shared experience with others, at home, work, or within your community or communities.

> Please start each part of your Directive reply on a new sheet of paper with your MO number, sex, age, marital status, the town or village where you live and your occupation or former occupation.
>
> Remember *not to identify yourself or other people* inadvertently within your reply. It is best to use initials instead of real names.

We would like you to reflect on all the occasions when you read aloud, even if only a few words. For example, an article in the newspaper, a TV guide, a book, menu, bingo numbers, religious text or a letter. Reading aloud is often thought of as reading to children. If this is something you do, we would be delighted to hear about it, but we are also particularly interested in other adult reading aloud practices, including those performed alone or shared with other adults.

How you read

We are keen to hear whether you read aloud in a very quiet voice, murmuring or whispering, or you may shout it out, chant or sing. You may read aloud in different ways with different texts or for different purposes. We are interested in all of these.

If you read aloud, or listen to others reading aloud, in a different language from the language or languages you may usually use for communication, we would love to hear about this.

You may have experience of reading aloud as something planned (perhaps even rehearsed) or you may have experience of reading aloud that was spontaneous and/or unexpected.

You could write about why you do it, how it feels, how you developed this practice and why you think it is important to be reading aloud rather than reading in silence. What does reading aloud give you? What does the voice bring?

Do you find that others read aloud in similar ways or differently? Why do think this is?

What proportion of your reading is aloud rather than silent?

Technology

We are also interested to hear about your experiences and thoughts on the role technology plays. Do you, for example, read aloud from digital devices or listen to audio books? Do you listen to 'Book at Bedtime' on the radio or something similar?

Figure 4.1 Mass Observation directive

Task: Reading aloud diary Please complete a week's diary briefly listing instances of reading aloud, or being read aloud to:

- *Where* are you when you are reading aloud or being read to? For example, is it at work or at home, in your leisure time, in community life or another domain?
- *What* kind of text is it? For example, a recipe, a poem, a newspaper article or something else?
- *Who* are you with when you are reading aloud, or being read to? If you are reading aloud with others, why is this important?

Finally, if anything comes to mind that you usually do, but didn't do this week, please note this down too.

Reflecting on the past and the future

What have been the situations in which you read aloud, were read aloud to, or took part in shared reading aloud, in the past? Please tell us more about when and why this happened.

Were you ever taught how to read *aloud* in particular? Or did you find a way to learn certain techniques?

Is your experience of reading aloud today similar or different to your past? Why do you think this is? Does it *feel* different today?

Looking to the future do you think your experience of reading aloud, to yourself or others, might change? Why do you think this is?

Feelings and Challenges

What memories and emotions do you attach to the practice of reading aloud? This could be in the present day, or reflecting on your past.

Are there times when you find reading aloud particularly challenging, or particularly enjoyable or fulfilling?

This study/project

Finally, in reflecting on these questions, do you believe that it is beneficial to create a record of adult reading aloud practices across Britain? Why do you feel this way?

Please post your response to: **Freepost: RTGU-AYJE-YSSC, The Mass Observation Archive, The Keep, Woollards Way, Brighton, BN1 9BP or by email to: moa@sussex.ac.uk**
KP/JW Summer Directive No. 109

Figure 4.1 (continued)

Notes

1 Most of this chapter was previously published as 11 pages of the 12-page article: Duncan, S. (2018). Lend me your ears: Mass observing contemporary adult reading aloud practices, *Changing English*, 25(4), copyright © the Editors of Changing English reprinted with permission of Taylor & Francis Ltd, http://www.tandfonline.com, on

behalf of the Editors of Changing English. Thank you to the editor of Changing English, John Yandell, and to the Taylor & Francis Group for permission to reproduce this work here.

2   Thank you very much to Jessica Scantlebury, Kirsty Pattrick and Joe Williams at the Mass Observation Project, and, of course, to all of the Mass Observers. Mass Observation material reproduced with permission of Curtis Brown Group Ltd, London on behalf of the Trustees of the Mass Observation Archive. Copyright © The Trustees of the Mass Observation Archive.

References

Elster, C. A. (2003). Authority, performance, and interpretation in religious reading: Critical issues of intercultural communication and multiple literacies. *Journal of Literacy Research*, 35(1), 663–692. https://doi.org/10.1207/s15548430jlr3501_5.

Griffiths, P. J. (1999). *Religious Reading: The Place of Reading in the Practice of Religion*. Oxford University Press.

Heath, S. B. (2000). Foreword. In D. Sheridan, B. V. Street & D. Bloome (Eds.), *Writing Ourselves: Mass-Observation and Literacy Practices* (pp. ix–xiv). Hampton Press.

Johnes, M. (2017, July 11). *Christmas and the Mass Observers*. Mass Observation 80th Anniversary Conference, University of Sussex.

Kramer, A.-M. (2014). The observers and the observed: The 'dual vision' of the Mass Observation Project. *Sociological Research Online*, 19(3), 7.

Moor, L., & Uprichard, E. (2014). The materiality of method: The case of the Mass Observation archive. *Sociological Research Online*, 19(3), 10.

Pollen, A. (2013). Research methodology in Mass Observation past and present: 'Scientifically, about as valuable as a chimpanzee's tea party at the zoo'? *History Workshop Journal*, 75(1), 213–235. https://doi.org/10.1093/hwj/dbs040.

Sheridan, D. (2017, July 11). *Closing panel keynote talk*. Mass Observation 80th Anniversary Conference, University of Sussex.

Sheridan, D., Street, B. V., & Bloome, D. (2000). *Writing Ourselves: Mass-Observation and Literacy Practices*. Hampton Press.

Summerfield, P. (1985). Mass-observation: Social research or social movement? *Journal of Contemporary History*, 20(3), 439–452. https://doi.org/10.1177/002200948502000306.

Thompson, K. (1986). The concept of cinematic excess. In P. Rosen (Ed.), *Narrative, Apparatus, Ideology* (pp. 130–142). Columbia University Press.

Yandell, J. (2012). Different ways of reading, or just making the right noises? *Changing English*, 19(3), 283–294. https://doi.org/10.1080/1358684X.2012.704579.

5

THE INTERVIEWS AND RECORDINGS

I used to work at [...] an Alzheimer's home, I worked in nursing, and I used to read, particularly things about the past, to my elderly people that I were caring for, and that used to actually take their imagination because they could remember that actually happened you know, because as you know they go back in time [...] I think reading to somebody is taking world into them as well. It's inviting world into them, instead of them being ostracised because they can't get out. I mean that's just my idea.

(MH, British Library C1765/15)

In keeping with the 'dual vision' of the Mass Observation Project (Kramer, 2014), the interviews and other audio recordings have a dual purpose within the research design. They are research data gathered for analysis along with the questionnaire and Mass Observation data to build an analytical account of reading aloud in Britain today. But they are also, crucially, a different form of record: 91 audio recordings held within the British Library Sound Archive, available for listening by anyone today and (the hope is) in the future. These audio recordings include both examples of practices and the majority of the interviews and were recorded in thirty-eight different locations across Scotland, England and Wales (including on a boat in the ocean off Shetland). They involve a total of 125 participants aged between early 20s and 103, who each gave permission for their recordings to be held in the British Library Sound Archive and for their real names to appear in the Sound & Moving Image (SAMI) catalogue. These recordings each have a catalogue number (British Library, C1765/1–91), and where I refer to these archived recordings in this book (and appropriate permissions have been given), I provide the catalogue number so that readers can follow up the recordings if they wish. The British Library SAMI catalogue can be viewed online and provides an overview of all 91 RABiT recordings (C1765/1–91).

The interviews

I interviewed adults of different ages, educational, cultural and linguistic back-grounds, of different ethnicities and religions, with different levels of confidence and interest in reading, living in different parts of Britain, and including those who had already thought a lot about reading aloud and those who had not. Some participants came forward themselves as a result of a note at the end of the RABiT questionnaire or because they had heard of the project through social media or project partners. These make up a minority of the participants. I gained the voluntary participation of the majority through contacting local and national organisations and networks, travelling to different parts of the country and working through word-of-mouth – talking to as many people as possible. For example, I travelled to Shetland after first putting a notice out through Shetland Library. Three people contacted me on reading this notice, and we arranged the interviews before I arrived. I met two others while in Shetland. In this way, between October 2017 and July 2018, I conducted forty-nine interviews, five with pairs of interviewees, one with a group of three and the rest one-to-one. Forty-eight of these interviews were audio recorded and (with the kind permission of the interviewees) are now in the British Library Sound Archive. Where interviewees have given permission to be named in pro-ject outputs, I refer to them in this book using their (real) initials. Where interviewees have asked for their real names not to be used, I refer to them using pseudonymised initials (and do not include their Sound Archive catalogue number, where one exists).

These interviews took place in homes, community centres, places of worship, colleges and workplaces, in and around London, Pontypool, Glasgow, Hud-dersfield, Leicester, Portsmouth, Hull, Rotherham, Gloucestershire, Somerset, Skye and Shetland, and one was done online with a woman based in Anglesey, Wales. At the time of the interviews, the interviewees (35 women and 20 men) were aged from their 20s to 80s and all resident in Scotland, England or Wales. Nine were born outside of Britain, eleven had grown up speaking a language other than English and nine are speakers of what we could call minority British languages (Scottish Gaelic, Welsh and Shetland dialect). Some interviewees are atheists and others practise Islam, Judaism, Baha'i and various forms of Chris-tianity. Ten interviewees identify as belonging to a minority ethnic group.

Each interview was semi-structured, and I started by asking interviewees whether they ever read aloud and allowed the conversation to develop from there, prompting for more detail – for example, interviewees' ideas about pur-poses and contexts and languages used –and I asked about listening as well as reading. For example, 'Do you ever read aloud? Or did you in the past? Do you ever listen to others reading? Can you tell me when? Why do you do that? And is that alone or with others?' etc. Most interviews lasted between 20 and 40 minutes. I also asked each interviewee if they wanted to be recorded doing some of the reading aloud they had discussed (some did and some did not).

Recordings of practices

I had originally planned for this third strand of the RABiT research design to include interviews only, but the more I thought about the lack of writing about, or records of, contemporary oral reading, the more I thought about making another kind of audio recording: examples of oral reading. These could be examples of the kinds of practices people were discussing in their interviews, as well as examples that perhaps had not featured. How to approach making these recordings, though, was complex and bound up with the purpose of creating such an archive. If one wished to strive for authenticity – that is, to influence what was being recorded as little as possible – one would have to devise some sort of system where a mic could be attached to someone and left there for weeks – one would then sift through the material afterwards to capture instances of oral reading or perhaps to record practices first and ask for permission afterwards (problematic ethically, and practically). Other research teams may have made a success of these or similar approaches, but this did not seem right for this project.

My purpose in making these recordings was to provide some examples of contemporary reading aloud as an addition to the archive, for interesting parties to listen to and gain an idea of the different things reading can be – as a start to the endeavour of shedding light on contemporary reading aloud. I was less interested in ensuring I captured practices happening exactly as they would 'naturally happen' and more interested in gaining a range of different examples that would demonstrate some of the diversity of what goes on across the country. Additionally, in keeping with the Mass Observation ethos and duality (see discussion in Chapter 4) – where participants are acting as researchers as well as participants – I was happy to be led by the participants to see what they thought would be useful or desirable to record. In some cases, this meant being invited along to audio record an event that was already happening; for example, a Middle Welsh class at the Gaelic-medium Sabhal Mór Ostaig, Skye, which involved different people reading aloud and discussing Middle Welsh poetry (British Library C1765/58) or the Drama Queens play reading group at the Glasgow Women's Library (C1765/18). At other times, this meant participants demonstrating or re-creating (illustrating or curating even) practices that would usually happen in private, or at least in another time and place; for example, MB reading a poem in Shetland dialect as she frequently does alone (C1765/84) or CC reading aloud a Gospel passage in Tamil as he explained he frequently does at home, reading to his wife (C1765/79).

In this way, I made forty four audio recordings of adults reading out loud, in groups and individually, some with interviewees and some with people who were not interviewed (including one recording which is both an interview and example of reading aloud). These recordings include different varieties of English and Scots (including Shetland dialect) as well as Arabic, Urdu, Scottish Gaelic, Hebrew, Ecuadorian Spanish, Welsh, Middle Welsh and Tamil. This

RABiT collection will, I hope, give listeners a sense of some of the diversity of contemporary oral reading practices, but there is certainly a place for someone else to create a far larger, and possibly quite differently approached, collection of sound recordings.

What do the interviews and recordings tell us?

My approach, as with all the RABiT data, was to try to find ways to present and analyse this data that are somehow in keeping with its nature, that shows what is particular or potentially especially valuable about this strand of data. The interviews and recordings present us with a striking diversity of different forms of reading aloud in varied locations and formations and for different purposes, bound up with identity, pleasures and preferences and involving intersecting arrangements of competences, materials and meanings (remembering Shove et al., 2012). For this reason, I will first provide an overview of the range, with thought to domains (Barton & Hamilton, 2012), purposes and 'types' of oral reading. Then, I aim to present two ways that the interviews in particular can provide a 'deeper' examination of oral reading: through examples of the roles of reading aloud *across four individual lives*, and through examples of *three conversations* getting to grips with understanding oral reading.

Overview of practices, domains and purposes: types *of oral reading*

There are fourteen examples to do with **helping or caring for others**; for example, reading to a grandparent, sick mother or partner; a husband reading aloud with his wife as she learns to read again following a stroke; a woman reading to her partner when he forgets his glasses; and reading aloud in old people's homes and hospices. Fifteen examples are part of individual or collaborative **writing processes**, whether to write fiction or poetry, help a friend write his autobiography or edit teaching materials. Thirteen examples are of oral reading as part of **work roles**, including in broadcasting (for example, reading listeners' letters on air), reading aloud in therapy work, and presenting health and safety information to others as a cleaning services manager. There are seven descriptions of reading aloud **out and about**: road signs, shopping lists, ingredient lists on food packets and menus, and placards at museums. And forty-nine examples are related to **education and learning**, including learning languages and developing literacy in and out of formal education, and as part of teaching a range of subjects, from biology to information technology, Gaelic poetry to Middle Welsh.

There are fifty mentions of reading aloud **in childhood or to children**, including memories of being read to as a child, reading with children at a local primary school, reading aloud as a Brownie Leader, and listening to oral reading at children's storytelling events. Thirty-seven mentions are of reading aloud or listening to others reading aloud for **religious reasons**, at a church, mosque, synagogue, Baha'i temple, Quaker meeting house, and at home, alone and in groups, and in various languages. There are fifteen examples of **singing**, including reciting song lyrics from memory, singing from word and music sheets in choirs and Taizé chanting from multilingual booklets, and twenty-five of reading out loud **as a way to be with others**, whether reading aloud when cooking with a daughter, reading out at family Christmas gatherings, at weddings and funerals and a husband reading a certain cartoon to his wife every single day of their married lives. Eighty-four examples are of forms of reading and listening to **literature, drama, poetry** etc., including to audiobooks, and there are eight 'other alone' practices, such as a woman reading novels to herself or a man reading aloud to hear a voice. There would have been other ways to cut these classifications, but an exercise like this provides a sense of prevalence (what is more and less common) as well as range and variety; just as the Mass Observation and questionnaire data suggests (see Chapters 3 and 4) not all reading aloud is done with children, not all with other people of any age, and certainly not all with narrative texts. This itself is worth emphasising, given the ways that reading aloud is most often talked about in much of Europe and the Anglophone worlds.

Looking at the above overview, several other ways to sort or present come to mind. A domain-based analysis is considered by Wallace (2013) to be core to a social practice approach to literacy, and Barton and Hamilton (2000, 2012) have been influential in both their definition of domains (as 'structured, patterned contexts within which literacy is used and learned') and for their emphasis on the 'permeability of boundaries,' 'movement' and 'overlap' between domains (Barton & Hamilton, 2000, p. 11). This idea of understanding literacy use and learning within distinct and yet overlapping domains underpins the structure of Part 2 of this book, and the idea of an individual at the centre of the multiple domains of their life taking part in the different literacy practices core to each domain is one which we will return to. For now, here we could look at the different life domains where, for these interview participants, reading aloud happens and where it seems to be particularly important; for example, as part of religious and spiritual life, education or learning, family and home life, the workplace and as part of both the creation and enjoyment of the arts, literature, drama or poetry. Within and across these domains we can also see purposes: reading aloud to memorise or write something, for example, falls across uses around the arts, for study and for religious purposes, as does reading aloud to aid understanding, 'unpick' dense text or allow meanings to be processed or savoured – and this is done alone and with others. Oral reading as a way to be with others is evident in family, religious and even workplace practices. Importantly, looking at both domains and purposes, we can see that reading aloud cannot be seen as one practice (or process) that simply happens in different places, situations or with different texts but that 'reading aloud' is itself a broad umbrella that covers extremely diverse activities.

We could also play with the idea of there being three main 'types' or categories of oral reading within the interviews and other recordings. The first is when the reading is to serve another person or group of people. This sort of reading aloud is done for the benefit of the listener(s), whether to impart information (for example, from a letter, menu or text message) to someone who cannot read, does not have their glasses or is too far from the text to read it themselves; to entertain or amuse (for example, a funny poem to an adult or a storybook to a child); or facilitate worship (as in the cases of the 'reader' in some religious traditions, where one person reads a passage to an assembled group, whose listening is their worship). This category could also include a teacher or manager reading precise instructions to a group. In each of these cases, what makes the reading aloud 'good' or successful is the degree to which it has achieved its aim with the listener or audience. Has it imparted the desired information? Entertained? Soothed? Facilitated worship?

The second category is when the reading out loud (whether alone or with others) is to meet a particular cognitive, creative or practical goal; for example, to remember something, to learn something, to write something or to understand something, whether this means working out clausal structure in dense philosophical text or reading out instructions for building a new bedside table in order to figure out what to do. Here reading aloud is a means to an end, for the reader or readers (for example, interviewee HM reading out recipes line-by-line to herself as she cooks, to ensure she is following the recipe correctly). This oral reading is to achieve a particular purpose using the voice and ear (as will be discussed further in Chapter 10).

A third category could be 'reading aloud for its own sake': for the experience of saying or hearing the words, as an aesthetic, meditative, religious or spiritual experience. In this category, the reading is not to serve another person or people, and it is not to achieve a specific, earthly or easy to define purpose. When discussing this idea with interviewee NS, a literature professor and Anglican priest, I referred to it as 'reading aloud as an end in itself.' NS suggested that it may sometimes be more of 'a *beginning* in itself,' referring to religious and literary practices where the oral reading may be seen as a way in to something much larger, as Chapters 8 and 9 examine.

The interviews and recordings also demonstrate that these three categories clearly overlap. An adult reading aloud a story to a child can be both a service to the child and an experience for and in itself of enjoying language and each other's company. The reading of a Baha'i prayer while watching others around the world do the same over YouTube, as described by interviewee MA, is both an experience in itself and also a tool to achieve a certain purpose, whether togetherness with a geographically scattered community or personal calm. We could also think about a fourth category: reading aloud as way of being together, as a community, a family, a couple (as explored in Chapter 6). This sort of categorisation is imperfect but is still, I would argue, useful in encouraging us to think about the extent of the differences between these diverse forms of oral reading.

Going deeper 1: the lives we live

The interviews also allow us to see what individuals say about the roles of oral reading across their lives. Below are extracts edited from longer interviews.

1) JR: a man in his early 70s: everyday life, teaching and acting C1765/ 04–06

Well, I've categorised it. Everyday reading and listening would be one. I got married quite late [...] and I do a lot of shopping, so shopping involves her reading me lists and me talking about them, so negotiating shopping, everyday stuff. We talk a lot and we listen to the radio, you know online stuff that we share, newspaper items we get [...] And then, because I've got a family and [she]'s got a family, we arrange a lot of meetings, so we read from emails, you know 'can you do Wednesday week?' 'No, my sisters coming.' 'Oh blast, blah blah blah,' and we'll look at something else and then we'll read again, so everyday stuff is one thing.

 [...] I trained as a secondary teacher in English, so in my everyday work I would from time to time read poems, stories, listening to students reading [...] I'd also read the admin stuff that teachers have to do, you know, 'on Thursday week we'll be going on a trip' or whatever, that sort of stuff. And increasingly, and oppressively, I'd have to read stuff that was online, that [was] sent to me as administration, which seemed to go berserk, you know, so I'd be, I'd read that aloud, once I'd digested it, to the kids, or the FE students [...] In FE, I taught theatre [...] where you had set texts for performance at A Level so I would have go through from the page to the stage; [the] rehearsal process which involved, roughly speaking, a first reading by students and then me reading bits, helping, you know, generally helping them through it, then, 'standing the text up on the book,' so, I would do some reading and would listen to them reading, so we were standing up 'on the book' so you would be doing moves but you're not off the book yet, and, then, we'd work again reading aloud on character work, again on the book [...] you know, how do you, if you don't like someone but you can't show it, how might you read, inflection, intonation, stress, juncture, how might you get that across, without actually smacking someone on the nose, that sort of stuff.

 [...] Professional actor stuff [...] learning audition pieces, ok, you'd go back to the text, you know, a sonnet, say, you go back to the text, you read it, you read it out loud, you get somebody to listen to it, you learn – if you'd got an audition coming up, you read it so you have to really be connected with it [...] *When my love swears that she is made of truth, I do believe her, though I know she lies, That she might think me some untutored youth* – that's the sonnet that got me into the RSC, but I remember sitting in the loo of the Barbican machine-gun reading before I went in [...] So that you are connected to it. So that it's part of you. You know. So that it becomes, you know, habitualised. Like making a cup of coffee properly, you know making a cup of coffee, like, the way you like it, without thinking too much, you know, because then you don't get nervous if it's really, you know, if it's kind of part of you.

2) SB: A woman in her 40s: children, faith and a love of listening
   C1765/07–08

I think at the moment I read out loud to my daughter mainly because I want her to get into reading and she's just turned ten and she's not much of a reader like my other kids have been, for various reasons, so I, to encourage her, I've sort of been reading to her, not bedtime reading but just anytime reading [...] I think the first book that we read together like that was *Harry Potter*. And she got quite into it. She likes me to do voices, which I'm not that good at doing voices, because my husband, I've heard him do it and he can do really good voices. So, compared to him, I'm really not very good. But I still have to do them because she really likes it [...] I personally think that it's been having that time with me as well, not just the actual story, I think for her definitely. I don't know about my son. For her it's both, it's having that time with me, and actually then she can get into the actual story as well [...]

So anyway, at the moment I'm reading to her and the other time I read aloud is when I read the Quran. Yeah, I think, the reason why I read out loud is because I think it's supposed to be read out loud. So I think Quran is something that – because the first word that was sort of revealed in the Quran is the Arabic word 'Iqra,' which means to actually read out loud as opposed to read in your heart. So I think it's because of that I always read it aloud, and also I can't imagine because some of the letters of the Arabic are very throaty and in different parts of your mouth so I can't imagine reading it silently [...] When I was in Damascus I learnt it – it's the science of reading the Quran. It's called Tajweed [...] you learn each sound and where it comes from in your mouth, so I did learn it quite well [...] That was the reason why I sort of started reading out loud, to hear my own mistakes, and, and I think it's an act of worship, you're supposed to be reading it out loud, on your lips.

[...] I think for a listener it's nice to hear voices. Because when I'm listening to an audio[book], I think it's nice 'cause they always change a little bit don't they, voices, it's not one tone. [...] I hate doing housework, so if I'm in the kitchen I always put something on [...] When I had the flu for a few days, I told my daughter to read, because I really – when I'm ill I really like, I hate watching things, and sometimes you know when you can't read because you have a headache, so I like, I really like listening to things [...] When I was pregnant with my daughter, my older daughter – there's 8 years difference – when I was feeling ill she literally read to me, and it was really silly because I don't know if you know *Milly Molly Mandy* books [...] I really love them, I don't know why, and I listened as she read them all to me, and I really enjoyed listening to them, as an adult. And I always say to my kids, I think when I'm older, I think I'd like, like in *Little Women*, they used to go and read to the old granny. I'd like to be one of those. I'll pay someone to come and read to me. I think it's really nice.

3) PO: A man in his 60s: family, work and a men's club C1765/67

I often read a paper aloud if I'm with my wife. If I'm reading it, I'll suddenly start reading aloud to her, that's quite common. Bits of it that she might be interested in – once you get to sport I don't talk more about it [...]

With the granddaughter, I read to her because I like her to learn things [...] With the wife, I'm only reading it because it sounds interesting and she might be interested in it, so it's [a] different sort of context isn't it? [...]

Other times reading aloud? Well, sometimes when, because I'm a supervisor, I've got, say, ten cleaners in, I might start reading aloud so they all get to hear about something rather than issue it out individually, that kind of thing [...] Any health and safety, any up to date information, any news, anything they need to know or anything that's of interest, that sort of thing, to make sure they all hear it at the same time. A lot of them don't use computers, so it helps that way [...] I do the training here for the cleaners, so on their induction, so I read aloud in front of all of them, because English is very often not their first language or they might not be able to read themselves or whatever but I always read to ensure that they do understand [...] It's absolutely essential, I mean from a health and safety point of view, it's very important that we get that message over [...]

Sometimes there's little things, like for example, I go down to the Working Men's Club on a Saturday, and I've often been sat in there and someone's reading out about what acts are going to be on; they tend to sit and read out and tell everybody, 'you know them people so and so' – 'oh yeah I've seen them before,' you know [...]

About 7 years ago, 8 years ago, my wife had a stroke, and she couldn't read then – the words kind of didn't make any sense, but after a bit of trying, we got to the point when she was starting to read again, and since then, we've always read every night because once we started, she started to read again, we carried on, to make sure we carried on reading, so now we read every night.

4) GK, A woman in her 60s: poetry, song and Welsh C1765/89–91

Mostly I read out loud poetry. I can't actually read poetry unless I read it out loud, so I always read poetry out loud if, I mean if I can – unless there's company and I'll shut up at that point, but [...] it's usually when I'm on my own, and I suppose reading out loud with small children, I mean my granddaughter and other people, with small children – and my own children obviously, before, but that was a long time ago [...]

I think poetry to me – it's about the sound of the poetry as much as the meaning of the poetry, and I think possibly in Welsh in particular there's a lot of poetry that is, there's lots of very kind of strict rules and forms and all that, it's called Cynghanedd in Welsh, and it's basically quite complex rules of alliteration, and it enhances it to read it out loud, so I always have had that approach to read poetry I guess, from it being in my first language [...].

I sing a lot so actually I like expressing myself vocally; I think I'm a frustrated performer [...] there would be, it was a very kind of collective approach the [singing] group that I was in, and there's about 12 of us, and we would rehearse it sometimes by ear, more often with the music, and then we would rehearse. First of all, you had to get to grips with any complexities in the music, then you had to memorise the words, and that's quite interesting because there was this one song once that I'd known for years, 'The World Turned Upside Down,' and I know the song so well, and we would sing it collectively, and I went to a folk club kind of thing, and I got up you know from the floor or something like that to sing this song, and on my own I couldn't remember it, it was very interesting, kind of like 'oh god I can't remember what comes next,' so there's something about singing collectively that you have this kind of collective memory that helps you to remember the words as you go along [...].

I think maybe singing a song is, is slightly different [...] how can I put it? Poetry, when I read poetry out loud, it's more about feeling like I'm expressing something that I feel, although it's not my words, and that is true to a certain extent with singing as well but less so, possibly, whereas when it's poetry that I like, it's – I kind of own it [...].

I think, now, reading Welsh poetry is one of the ways I get to hear my own language, and because I don't speak it, I mean I always used to speak to my mother in Welsh, but she died, how many years ago? Ten years ago, twelve, something like that. She lived in Wales, so we used to phone up and talk at least once a week, but since she died that doesn't happen, and I very occasionally get opportunities to speak Welsh, and I always get terribly excited, you know, because it is still my first language [...].

My mother loved poetry, both Welsh and English, and I remember as a child I learnt chunks of poetry that – like from Shakespeare, and so I could even now. I was 11, I could read, I could recite Wolsey's farewell speech from Henry the 8th because my mother used to recite it, so, I think I've driven my kids mad over the years.

I have included these in some length to provide a sense of how participants express the roles of oral reading within and across their lives. We will return to the ideas expressed in Part 2 of this book.

Going deeper 2: conversations

These three conversations, edited down from longer paired interviews, illustrate how participants offer their own analyses of the roles of oral reading in adult life.

1) 'The ownership of the word widens completely' (a discussion between two members of a female Roman Catholic Religious Community)

ST: I would read out loud in our chapel because we have our own worship, so there will be readings out loud in chapel, we will have quite a bit with, whether it's Intercessory Prayer, so out loud is quite an important thing for the rest of the community and the public to hear. In my work as a spiritual director, doing spiritual accompaniment, I will be encouraging my 'retreat into my person' actually to read biblical material out loud. There's one kind of particular way of praying called *Lectio Divina*, which is divine reading, where it is important to hear the text out loud, and I would also do that for myself. In my own prayer life, too, I will frequently read aloud poetry, for example, because I like to hear the resonance of sound and expression, and it becomes much more alive for me [...].

CO: Like [ST] says, it's something about just hearing this text that already gives something to the context of the group, to the prayer life. It might also be in terms of worship, I mean, [ST] talked about reading the Psalms, but we also sing the Psalms more often and that, in that we have the text in front of us too, so it's a form of, of reading and of vocalising it in a very different way than reading it, because you have the music that you have to take into consideration there too, when, when you're making your voice work [...]

The fact that the words on the page are being verbalised, it gives them a different, a different resonance; it gives them a different meaning, it sometimes, I, you know when I'm in class and I'm reading the, you know, the phrase that I really wanted to, it's like 'oh ok I really understand that differently now,' or with the children reading, even for myself, reading out the newspaper aloud, it's like 'whoa ok, there's something else,' there's a different resonance, there's a different feeling to it, there's a different, it's almost like a play, it's like 'ok I can accent this word this way,' I can put this emotion on this word, I can feel text in a different way than if I was just skimming through it and reading it for myself on my own.

ST: There's a double dimension, isn't there? I would agree with you what you are saying. It's something to do with your body, something to do with your voice, the ownership of the word widens completely, and I think there's something quite mysterious actually [...].

2) 'A reinforcement that I'm doing it right' (a discussion between two adult learners)

AL: Sometimes signs if I'm walking on the road or if you're driving, can't pronounce something, I'll say it aloud.

HM: You do it subconsciously sometimes –

AL: Yeah.

HM: Recipes, if you read them or if there's something on the telly and those things come up at the bottom and I might read them off so it reinforces the information, but I do it quite often, actually, but I think I do it subconsciously because I don't think about it. [...] Yes for learning, for me to learn, it's better when I read it myself than if I sit in silence and I don't take it in, I find as well.

AL: If I'm on my own and I'm revising, I'll read it aloud; if I'm on my own though [...] I think it reinforces it reading it back to yourself, and I'm a writer, so when it comes to the final process of a short story, it's vital to read it all out to hear how it sounds back to you.

HM: So I think that just reinforces, and like you said, the sound of it, hearing it, you know if you've punctuated it properly or you're pausing in the, in the right places or those type[s] of things [...]

AL: [and] I read on the phone, I do read aloud on the phone, or I'm reading it back to my partner [...].

HM: Yes, sharing information, we do that, when we sit down, 'oh look, so and so, oh that,' 'that's happening and that's happening.' And social media, the girls are like, 'oh Mam, look at this is so and so and so and so's thing, this is what they said,' and they'll read it off to me or to friends, you know, they invest a lot in that, don't they?

AL: Or if my partner's driving and he has messages, I'll read them back to him [...] or emails, usually I, I'll get them mixed up [...] And in supermarkets I tend to read aloud. Yeah, reading ingredients and stuff –

HM: Like your gluten-free stuff.

AL: I've gone gluten-free, and I just pick something up and read – I probably look like a crazy person just standing there reading to myself, but you see a lot of people doing it [...]

HM: I do it for clarification that there's no wheat in it; it sounds silly, but in my head it makes sense, and if I read it aloud, and I've read every word, and I've spoke every word, then it means that's not in it, if I haven't seen wheat in it or gluten in it, then that's not in it.

AL: I think it's back to, same as revision, reading aloud enforces it for me –

HM: Enforces it. And recipes I find if I do a recipe on my phone or on my tablet, I find myself talking to my tablet, relaying the information, 'right, now I'll do that now, I'll do that now' – and I'm relaying the information; it's a reinforcement that I'm doing it right and putting the right things in the right time and the right amount, I don't know.

3) Crossword Sundays, 'crazy' poems, 'comfort' and 'the edge of your seat' (a discussion between two colleagues) C1765/68

AR: I have to say, I've only just started learning to read, so I'm a bit slower, and if there is a word I don't understand, then I will say it out loud [...] Breaking it down [...].

JP: [...] I read out loud when my granddaughter's here; we go to the library – as she's choosing a book, she'll look at the pictures, but she doesn't know the words, so I'll read perhaps the first two or three pages of it, and then she'll decide whether or not she likes that book, so I read out loud like that [...] but I also read out loud because me and my daughter, we do crosswords, and she'll read something, and I'll have a go and I'll read something – sort of across from each other on crosswords [...] I think we started doing that about three or four years ago. We meet every Sunday, and we go into town, and we'll just sit somewhere quietly, and we'll do crosswords and things, so, yes, we're always reading out loud [...] My daughter writes poems, and she'll read her poems to me every week.

AR: Now that's nice.

JP: They are really crazy and silly poems – not romantic things – they are really crazy, about the pets she owns and all this, yes, she's very good at anything like that [...] and now and again I'll write her a poem, and I'll read that to her as well and then we'll swap poems, and I'll take hers and I'll take it home and read it to the rest of the family, yeah, we do crazy things.

AR: That's nice being creative, isn't it? Does that take you back to your childhood?

JP: It does, it's comforting.

AR: You're changing the roles aren't you? From you being a mum who's reading to a child. That's really nice that [...] I've got a lot of audiobooks [...] I like to listen to them in bed; I fall asleep half way through, but I like it

[...] I just like to be read to, I never had that as a child, I just, I just I don't know about anybody else, I just find it so soothing because the reader is, she's got a really nice, nice, soothing, melodious – I don't know if that's the right word – melodious voice. And she's very, it's very nice to just lay there and have somebody tell you a story and you can picture what's happening. I can picture everything [...]

JP: You can travel in your mind, can't you? [...]

AR: And I love listening to someone else reading [...] For me it's the telling. I can't remember his name, but there was a crime writer that came here not so long ago –

JP: Oh, the Liverpool guy? Gosh, I can't remember his name.

AR: [...] it was the telling of the stories [...] and it was all, the descriptions, and I thought, wow, you actually –

JP: You can see it, can't you? As he's describing it, picture in your mind exactly what he's talking about, can't you? [...] He was very good at reading, yes.

AR: That's what I'm saying – he drew you with his voice, he drew you with his –

JP: The dramatic pause, he made his voice more dramatic and then it was more gentle [...]

AR: He had you sitting on the edge of your seat, well it did me.

Once again, we will think through the ideas expressed in the analysis of the second part of this book, but the hope is that these edited conversations provide a taste of the exploratory, reflective nature of the interviews.

Conclusion

The overall picture of the range and purposes of practices emerging from the interviews and recordings is very similar to those coming from the survey and the Mass Observation. The interviews also allowed participants to discuss their practices across different stages and domains of their lives, and their conversational nature allowed probing and exploration of key ideas: how reading aloud relates to making words or text 'part of you'; the multiple meanings or purposes of reading with children; oral reading as safety at work and support in a marriage; linguistic and family identity; the 'mysteries' of the 'widened ownership' of the vocalised word; clarification and reinforcement; and the different ways that reading aloud can be part of interpersonal relationships, with comfort, 'craziness' and drama. These point at themes or issues which will be tackled, and with reference to other literature, in the rest of the book.

This is also the end of the first part of this book, the account of the RABiT project, its rationale, challenges and a flavour of its findings. The data from this project will continue to run throughout Part 2 as we look at family, friends and lovers; working and public life; religion; the literary life; aloud alone; and education. It feels fitting, though, to end this part with a final urge to, if at all possible, visit the Mass Observation and British Library archives. The recorded interviews and examples, like the overflowing boxes of Observers' writing, are research outputs in themselves, to be read and listened to, as participants themselves provide their accounts, explanations and examples of the roles of reading aloud in adult life.

References

Barton, D., & Hamilton, M. (2000). Literacy practices. In D. Barton, M. Hamilton & R. Ivanič (Eds.), *Situated Literacies: Reading and Writing in Context* (pp. 7–15). Routledge.

Barton, D., & Hamilton, M. (2012). *Local Literacies: Reading and Writing in One Community*. (Linguistics Classics2nd ed). Routledge.

Kramer, A.-M. (2014). The observers and the observed: The 'dual vision' of the Mass Observation project. *Sociological Research Online*, 19(3), 7.

Shove, E., Pantzar, M., & Watson, M. (2012). *The Dynamics of Social Practice: Everyday Life and How it Changes*. Sage.

Wallace, C. (2013). *Literacy and the Bilingual Learner: Texts and Practices in London Schools*. Springer.

Part 2

6

FAMILY, FRIENDS AND LOVERS
Community, domesticity, intimacy and mediation

In her Reading Aloud Diary, one Mass Observer, F45, records:

> Sunday: Mum is reading yesterday's colour supplement from *The Times*. Mum likes to read bits out to other people a lot, and she is very expressive, sometimes to the point of me cringing. I think I cringe because I am her daughter and she is embarrassing me. [...]
>
> When I've done my hair, Mum reads out bits from a beauty feature in the same magazine. She is incredulous because the items are stupidly expensive [...] This then leads the two of us on to what we each consider to be essential beauty items, and it's a darn sight less stuff, and far cheaper. [...]
>
> Dad comes in and Mum reads the article out loud to him – edited highlights only – and he also scoffs [...]
>
> Dad has moved on to something on Facebook, a brochure for the TVs and radios made at the factory where my grandfathers worked. He reads aloud some stuff about the specifications of a record player, but I am too busy reading the paper and don't pay more than a cursory bit of attention [...].
>
> Monday: In the evening my daughter (aged 16) who is out with friends sends me an amusing whatsapp message and I reply. We have a couple of exchanges about what I'm watching on TV at the moment. I read the exchange aloud to my son (aged 14) and he laughs.

This chapter examines reading aloud as a way of being with others, as members of smaller and larger groups or communities, as friends, lovers, partners, spouses and family members. It will look at the ways that we read aloud as part of creating, expressing, sustaining or developing these relationships, exploring oral reading in and as domesticity, intimacy and mediation: between inner and outer worlds, personal and political worlds, familial and global worlds.

In A. S. Byatt's 1978 novel *The Virgin in the Garden*

[...] on the new bedsprings, which twanged, Daniel consummated his marriage. There was a moment during this time, when his face was on hers, cheek on cheek, brown on brow, heavy skull on heavy skull, through soft skin and flesh. He thought: skulls separate people. In this one sense, I could say, they would say, I lose myself in her. But in that bone box, she thinks and thinks, as I think in mine, things the other won't hear, can't hear, though we go on like this for sixty years. What does she think I *am*? He had no idea what she was.

(Byatt, 1978, p. 278–9)

It is hard to read this without reflecting on how our physical bodies both unite and separate us, and the ways that our thinking both is and is not accessible to others. Our 'bone boxes' are built to protect and enclose but also to open up and make sounds that others can hear. Reading aloud, this chapter will argue, is one way that we join ourselves with others, whether taking on particular roles in relation to others (grandmother, Rabbi or partner), becoming 'one with others' as one merged voice or entity (one choir, one family, one congregation), or perhaps both.

Community

This afternoon I attended a session of the university Baking Society, and I found myself reading aloud the recipe and commenting on it to the people around me. In that regard, reading aloud can be seen as a social activity; as a way to stimulate conversation between people who would otherwise be strangers.

(MO M23)

Oral reading can certainly be a way that people join with others socially, whether in the case of the young man above, who feels reading aloud brings a form of closeness or camaraderie to a group of Baking Society members who would otherwise be 'strangers,' or the cases of the many crossword societies, board-game clubs, writing or poetry groups and reading circles where reading aloud provides a way 'in' to more friendly or personal conversation (this is something that happens in many different countries around the word; see discussions in Duncan (2012, pp. 90–92) on Japanese, Canadian and American reading circles, as well as Long (2003) on Texan groups and Nafisi's account of *Reading Lolita in Tehran* (2004)).

We can also see oral reading as part of forms of community or belonging around religion, language, social class and ethnicity. Examples of reading aloud as a way to be together in the context of religion are plentiful, and Chapter 8 provides a more detailed examination of this area. I want to touch on this briefly here too, though, as this is one of the most striking ways that reading aloud is used as a way of joining ourselves with others, whether in person or remotely. From Chapter 4, we might remember Observer F26, who noted that her participation in a weekly Catholic mass means her 'voice gets lost in a mass of other people [...] It makes me feel like I belong to something.' Interviewee MA describes something similar but virtual, as she watches, listens to and joins in with filmed online Baha'i worship from her home in Glasgow: 'there is energy, and when we [listen and take part] we enjoy to hear other people [...] not only ourselves' (British Library, C1765/23). Another interviewee, SM, describes her family's practice of reading aloud, singing and chanting Islamic prayers every week at home and how important this is 'to connect' as a family:

> we involve them [the children] and encourage them and get them to, to live and experience what we are living and experiencing because I think we, we passed a time when we weren't doing that, and we found our children were quite disconnected, and we didn't know how to connect them, so for us this is a really good opportunity to connect spiritually together.
>
> (C1765/49)

In 2019, in Addis Ababa, I observed adults and children taking part in an Ethiopian Orthodox 'Reading School' (see Kalewold, 1970; Woldeyes, 2017 for discussions of this tradition) in the greenery outside a church, reading Psalms and Gospel passages in small groups. Some groups were reading out loud in unison and others reading the same text but starting from different places and reading aloud at different paces. Standing among them, I heard about twenty different voices reading a dozen different texts and in both Amharic and Ge'ez (the language of the Ethiopian Orthodox Church). The year before, in Skye, I observed a Church of Scotland service in Gaelic where a Psalm presenter sang a line (from a written text) in a particular rhythm and the congregation sang a response, in that same rhythm and in one voice. In each of these cases, I observed something incredibly beautiful and sacred, something that happened regularly, and something involving people using their voices and bodies (sitting, standing and moving between the two) to do and be something together.

Overlapping at times with religious practice, the languages we read aloud in (and listen to others reading in) also bind us to others, into bigger and smaller groups and identities, and bind us to the languages themselves no less. Interviewee VC expresses the 'emotional life' of her family's multilingualism:

> I grew up in Trinidad, which is an island just north of the equator, close to Venezuela, and I remember hearing about reading aloud as important. My mother went to the Sisters of St Joseph of Cluny Convent School – nuns required a student to read aloud in French every lunchtime to them, and this is how she first acquired a good knowledge and accent in French, and she used to read aloud to me from French children's books and that again was a very, very strong memory

because I think multilingualism is something which is much, much more widespread than people realise and part of the emotional life, even if it is a question of dialect or a question or hearing nursery rhymes or prayers. The things that children have read aloud to them, they are something that form part of how you feel about the world, so I remember about learning about colour names and flowers from this beautiful French children's book. Then the other thing is my father used to read aloud, but his grandfather was Hindu Pundit and so trained in Sanskrit, and my father used to sit in the rocking chair and read aloud from a memorised text in his head, so that was an oral tradition – he'd be doing Sanskrit or medieval Hindi chanting, which I didn't understand perfectly, but it made me then be willing to experience reading aloud in terms of rhythm. [...] Reading aloud for me is also a place where people of different traditions and accents can make a unified whole, the idea of reading aloud as a shared thing, not just something you do alone, is very important in my life.

(C1765/33)

There is a lot here to unpack – a feeling connected with the sounds of French, Sanskrit and (medieval) Hindi as family activity and identity, but also the idea of the 'shared thing' of oral reading (and reciting from memory, which we will return to in Chapters 8 and 9) across, as well as within, cultural traditions. I am reminded also of interviewee GK and her reading aloud of Welsh poetry to be close to both her mother and her native language (see Chapter 5, pp. 75–76).

Class may be a particularly British concern, but many contexts will share a sense of being joined with, and excluded from, others through a mixture of socio-economic, regional, cultural, religious and/or ethnic factors. Interviewee RH remembers working within a community whose voices had been ignored through a process of class-based political oppression. He describes how they found a way to 'write-back' and regain, through reading aloud and listening, their voices and their stories:

people are finding the urge to really tell their story, and I think round here it started in the miners' strike, for instance, when people used to put the news on, put the BBC on, and see a report from their community which was completely counter to what had actually happened [...] so people could see [...] lies being told about them and they need to tell their story.

(C1765/13)

This telling, he goes on to explain, happens through the writing and (oral) communal sharing of texts, their own texts. Another interviewee, PN, speaks about class and exclusion, noting that she rarely feels connected with the voices on audiobooks:

I can't listen to many talking books because if I don't relate to the voice instantly, I can't listen – I can't bare it. And there's not a great diversity of voices and accents in the books that are read aloud [...] it's usually middle-class Southern accents. [...] for me, it's a real big issue of class, it's just the lack of diversity.

(C1765/63)

Conversely, two members of a London Caribbean elder's group and reading circle (interviewees RC and PW) explained to me the closeness they feel reading aloud and talking together from a position of shared cultural heritage.

Family

Instances of reading aloud within families feature heavily within each data collection strand of the RABiT project, just as they dominate cultural discourses of reading aloud in many countries (see, for example, Gurdon, 2019; Lynx Qualey, 2018). There is no denying the huge number of mentions of adults reading to children and the emphasis on reading aloud as part of taking on the role of parent or grandparent. When asked what she reads aloud, a questionnaire participant writes simply 'children's books – *I am granny*' (my italics). Interviewee DL expands:

When I visit my grandchildren in the north, one of their favourite things is to bounce into my room about seven o'clock in the morning, each clutching about three or four books that they expect me to read from cover to cover [...] It's just part of the tradition. If Grandma's in town, we have to be in her bed. I mean four of us in the bed is quite a squash but with the books as well, but that is, it's our, it's our tradition now, I can't go there without that happening.

(C1765/28)

Here, reading aloud is core to being 'Grandma' and part of their shared grandmother-grandchildren 'tradition.'

The picture of reading aloud with children presented by the RABiT data is overall one associated with forms of tradition or security. One questionnaire participant explains '[reading aloud] is an extremely deep-rooted and richly meaningful part of my formation and extended family and cultural traditions.' Another, with no children yet, notes 'I really look forward to reading aloud to my children in the future. I miss having those shared stories in a family and it meant so much in my childhood,' while Observer F39 writes:

I don't have children, but the thing I most looked forward to doing with my children was reading stories to them. It is one of the few things now that I have accepted childlessness that can still make me cry. I have missed out on something that I treasured in my own child-hood as a very special memory. I was read to as a child. It is a strong, pleasant memory. I remember once when I was a child the electricity being cut off and my mum reading to us by candlelight because, obviously, the TV was off. She read Ted Hugh[es]'s *The Iron Giant*. I bought it, years later, to read to my own children, it was such a strong memory.

Reading aloud as a way of being together in families is something lived, loved and mythologised.

And yet, family reading, in and out of the RABiT data, is much more varied. The first thing we can note is that parents, grandparents and other carers have many different reasons for reading to or with children, and children may find oral reading appealing (or not) for different reasons. Interviewee SB explains that her son liked reading with her for the stories, while for one of her daughters, it was both the stories and getting to spend one-on-one time with her mother that was important (see Chapter 5, p. 73). Questionnaire participants also note reading to children in order to calm, entertain, develop language skills, share stories and/or induce sleep.

Alongside this variation in purposes, reading aloud in the family is also multigenerational and multidirectional. It is not just adult family members reading to children but children reading to adults, children reading to other children, and adults reading to adults. We see children reading to adults to practise their reading, and children (both young and grown-up) reading to parents and grandparents because their parents and grandparents enjoy it, cannot read or do not have their glasses. We have examples of children watching their parents or other adults reading to each other and of children reading with cousins and siblings:

> My first memory of reading aloud was trying to teach my little sister to read. She was desperate to learn. When I went to school, I used to take her to wait behind the air-raid shelter. The book was *Alice in Wonderland*, and the first line (in case you've forgotten) is 'Alice is sitting on the bank...'
>
> (MO F83)

> I read when I was a teenager to my grandmother who was, her sight was suspect, and we used to love, she used to love hearing me read *Little Women*. And we did an episode of that most nights and I think we both looked forward to that and we got to know those characters, whose names I've forgotten, but I think one was Meg and one was – I can't remember now, that was over, how old am I, 86? That was probably when I was about fourteen so that's quite a long time to

remember, but I know [...] we'd really look forward to those reading sessions.

(TC, C1765/01)

The texts that are read are not always stories or novels either:

> My dad & I read aloud from a 1930s house brochure. We read out what we each felt to be funny, even though we were sat next to each other and could easily read everything in our heads. It was a big part of the interaction, reading aloud and laughing together, and I know I got a kick out of making him laugh. It also led to further discussion about the house he grew up in and my memories of it. I think that's rather nice.

(MO F45)

This is reminiscent of Kalman's study of literacy in Mixquic, Mexico, where we are told that one of her adult participants, Gudelia, reads aloud religious texts with her father, something they both enjoy a great deal (2005, p. 71).

Nor is this reading necessarily 'for pleasure'; interviewee LL discusses reading aloud with her mother and others to address her son's specific needs:

> We would perhaps research something or google something as we do nowadays and then we might read that back to each other to, to try to get to the bottom of something or the best solution [...] My son was recently diagnosed with ASD, so my mum might look stuff up and you know and relay it to me and vice versa [...] – sharing information in reports about my son to my family or then with external professionals as well, so that's like trying to sort of absorb information, and you know that you're actually taking it in and understanding it so you can then be making the right decisions.

(C1765/74)

While it is certainly true that reading aloud is one of the ways people can join together as families, these practices of family togetherness are far more diverse and nuanced than 'parents reading to children.' And yet despite the range of what actually seems to be going on in families around the world, there remains a message within wider cultural discourses that reading to children is something a parent *should* do. One Observer reflects:

> My mum used to read to me when I was younger, but she wasn't confident at reading aloud. She was scared she would get a word wrong and, because my reading age was quite advanced from a really young age, I think she was a little embarrassed that I may be able to read a word that she couldn't. So when I was able to read alone,

I would read my bedtime stories myself. Due to this, I don't remember bonding over books with my family as they are not very bookish, which can mean that I feel a little isolated from them. Also, I didn't really have that theatrical and playful experience of using different voices and excitement while reading aloud at a young age because the experience was so full of angst, worry, and nervousness for my mum.

(F27)

This is a haunting piece of writing, a daughter's expression of what she feels she missed out on, and her experience of her mother's fears. Another Observer writes

I don't remember my parents reading aloud to me. I suspect that my mother may have done. Well, I hope she did but I have no memory of it. My father entertained us with stories and songs but he made them up himself and did not read them out.

(F69)

'I hope she did'. Could this 'hoping' represent an internalisation of the idea that mothers *should* read to children, despite the stories and songs she remembers from her father? These strains of the *should* – the *I didn't really have*, the *I hope* – could tell us something about wider judgements about what parents – arguably, particularly mothers – and carers *should* be doing.

Mace (1998) argues that many literacy campaigns (in different parts of the world, including Britain, the United States and Nigeria) have focussed on the importance of improving the literacy of mothers in order to improve the literacy of their children and, by implication, the nation as a whole. She highlights how these campaigns often position mothers as the main person responsible for their children's literacy development and present the importance of a woman's literacy learning as mainly or solely in terms of their children, rather than being of potential importance in other aspects of a woman's life, a point also made by Cuban and Hayes (1996). Mace further notes that such campaigns may also suggest that being able to read herself is the only way for a mother (or anyone else) to support a child's literacy. She draws on six points made in Barton's influential 'Exploring family literacy' article (1994) to rebut these positions and sum up her own argument: that literacy is more than reading certain types of books; that family is more than mothers; that home literacies are not necessarily the same as school literacies; that family literacy involves different generations interacting in a range of ways; that different people take part in literacy practices, including those more *and* less confident or skilled in forms of reading and writing; and that there are a range of ways to support literacy development (beyond reading to children or explicit teaching).

Twenty-six years later, these are still points that need making. They also lead us nicely back to the ways that some RABiT participants experience reading aloud in the family. An Observer reminds us that there are different ways for families to support children's literacy:

> When I was learning to read my parents used to ask me to read to them
> [...] when I was able to read properly they gave me a present – a little
> Bible brought back from Jerusalem by my uncle, which had mother-of-
> pearl covers. I loved it and my reading has never looked back!
>
> (F77)

Similarly, within Gebre et al.'s (2009) *Everyday Literacies in Africa*, the artist Ayelech explains that she herself is 'illiterate,' but she encourages her children to 'read for me and I enjoy hearing it' (2009, pp. 101–102). The RABiT data and other studies certainly suggest that reading aloud can be part of together-ness in families and can indeed be a way to support children in their literacy learning, but this is not necessarily about a parent reading to a child. The rea-lity seems more varied and interesting.

Friends, lovers, partnership and marriage

> I used to read a newspaper aloud with a friend every day as a routine,
> as well as papers or letters either of us has written. It was very
> important to both of us.
>
> (questionnaire)

Oral reading is also part of friendship, something people do for or with those close to their hearts. Another questionnaire participant notes 'fan fiction read aloud to me is my FRIENDS reading to me and that's the best thing. I love it' (their capitalisation). Whether these are friends reading aloud in person/online or someone else reading the words of fellow fan-fiction friends may be ambig-uous, but the importance of 'FRIENDS reading to me' is clear. This resonates with Finders's (1997) study of the 'hidden' literacies of teenage girls in the United States and her examples of girls reading aloud together from magazines, in person and over the phone, sharing interesting bits of text as part of what we might see as friendship rituals. It may be that few(er) read from print magazines these days, but many of us have observed (or taken part in) similar interactions with online news or social media – that is, the same crowding around the text, the same excited or comic voices, and outraged or amused commentary.

Similarly, reading aloud as part of romance may seem to fit best with our ideas of times gone by, of handwritten letters read aloud by the writer, reci-pient, horrified parent or even behind-the-scenes Cyrano figure, but the RABiT data suggests that oral reading is still a part of romance. This includes practices that are very much deliberate, such as forms of serenade, the reading of love letters and poems, partners reading novels to each other in bed, as well as those which may be barely noticed, such as the reading of 'snippets' of news, social

media or other texts over the breakfast table to a partner who could be interested or may not even hear. Interviewee DL explains that she rarely reads
poetry herself but that poetry has nevertheless played a large role in her life:
'my husband was, he was a very, very keen reader of poetry [...] he wooed me
via the metaphysical poets' (C1765/28). Interviewee JSP (C1765/88) speaks of
always having read out loud with friends, family and boyfriends, though her
role has shifted, from being the person most read to, to being the reader. Also
aware of shifting lives and shifting practices, a questionnaire participant writes,
'When I was in a long-distance relationship, I used to read book chapters out
loud every evening over Skype. Now we live together and I don't read out loud
so often.' Continuing the thread, Observer M19 records:

> On Wednesday [...] I was reading aloud to my girlfriend in bed as she
> was upset. Being in a long-distance relationship reading to her like this
> tends to calm her down when she's upset when I otherwise can't
> because we are talking over the phone.

Can voices replace physical contact or provide another sort of intimacy? In
2012, Chloe Angyal reviewed Lauren Leto's book, *Judging A Book By Its Lover:
A Field Guide to the Hearts and Minds of Readers Everywhere*. She titles her
review 'In praise of the lost, intimate art of reading aloud' and ends her second
paragraph by noting that she was surprised, in a book that is 'a love letter,' to
find no mention of oral reading. She goes on to share memories of being read to
by family members and then by lovers, before making a more explicit connection between reading aloud and falling in love:

> Leto is right that for people who love to read, love and reading are
> often intertwined. And it is true that you can tell a lot about a person
> by what's on their bookshelf. But you can fall in love, or in my case,
> fall further, with a person by listening to them read from what's on
> that shelf. Some things – love, a great book, your hilarious voice for
> Mr. Collins – are too good to keep to yourself.
>
> (Angyal, 2012)

We will return to ideas of intimacy, and to love, later in this chapter and turn
now to marriage and partnership. Oral reading is part of state and religious
marriage ceremonies all over the world, most often when the magistrate, or
religious leader, reads aloud text that the couple must repeat word for word –
the voicing of particular words in a particular order acting as the magical spell
that can call the marriage into being (see Chapter 7 for more on this). There are
also a great many mentions in the RABiT data of partners or married couples
reading to one another different sorts of texts, as exemplified by this questionnaire participant: 'most often I read aloud to my fiancé about recipes,
horoscopes, and some interesting articles we have found.'

There are instances coming from shared interests or activities: visits to a museum (with one person reading the placards), cooking or building flat-pack furniture together, reading aloud to share or write family greetings cards, or reading favourite novels or poems. Other examples seem more about creating bridges between the quite different interests or lifeworlds of each partner. Observer F75 writes 'Quite often I will read extracts of my book to my husband. I will also read to him extracts from my diaries,' while interviewee PO explains that he and his wife often sit side by side reading their separate books silently,

> but sometimes we'll, you know, I'll say what I'm reading and she'll read something. She likes reading stories, novels, but about real things, stories about, say, in Birmingham or in London how kids were then or in Ireland, so she likes reading things that are based on fact but still a story, whereas I like reading science fiction, so she often reads things that are really interesting, so she'll probably tell me bits more than I'll tell her things because what happens in 2095 doesn't really interest her.
>
> (C1765/67)

There are also many examples of routines developed as a couple. One of the participants in Mace's (1998) study of mothers and literacy remembers:

> Many years ago there was a daily newspaper called the Daily Graphic, it has more photographs of daily events than any other paper by far. They purchased this paper daily price 1 1/2d (pre-decimal). Grandfather looked and studied all the pictures and then grandmother would read out the captions to him and I thought that was a very good arrangement.
>
> (p. 111)

Observer (F65) shares a similarly 'good arrangement': 'My husband and I usually have a lazy start to the day when we can get away with it, being retired. We read the papers in bed ... We often share titbits.' And as we heard in Chapter 5, interviewee AL regularly reads his partner's messages to him while he (his partner) is driving.

Other practices may be reactions to the non-routine. 'My husband once read Lord of the Rings to me when we were camping' (questionnaire), or new routines developed to cope with new challenges:

> Sadly in 2005 my husband had a severe brain haemorrhage and lost his ability to read or write. So since then I have been reading aloud to him every day!! Any letters we receive I read to him.
>
> (MO, F87)

> Oddly enough, I still read to my wife from time to time for a very strange reason. She often becomes quite constipated [...] Somewhere

along the line we discovered that the sound of my voice makes her relax! It may have been when I was away and speaking to her on the phone that we discovered this. So from time to time I suggest I read something, either from a book I am reading or whatever comes to hand; the summary of soap opera plotlines in the TV magazine or the blurb on the back of a bank statement. It doesn't matter what, it must be the dull monotone of my voice that does something, and it works nearly every time!

(MO, M51)

This last example also brings us to changes to routines over time, also noted by these questionnaire participants, 'My husband used to read out loud to me but now we go to bed at different times' and 'Had a short-lived habit of reading to my wife at bedtime,' as well as by these Observers:

As a young married couple – perhaps like many – we tried reading to each other in bed, a new chapter on successive nights. A short-lived experiment; I can't really remember why, but rather less on grounds of 'performance' than a joint decision to engage with our own choices of books!

(M72)

Twice this week I have read aloud programme information from the TV on-screen guide to my husband at his request. This was a little more irritating as he could have read it himself. [...]. As I get older I expect to read aloud more especially with or to my husband because things that are difficult to understand are often made clearer read aloud & shared. Produce instructions etc.

(F63)

Interviewee LC also reflects on changes over time and what she sees as 'co-dependency':

Now, my husband doesn't like wearing reading glasses, so I am his reader when we are out – sometimes at home because he likes to cook so he looks at recipes – he'll say, I can't read that, so then I have to read it out loud to him. I know it's a really weird example, but it's becoming more obvious to me that I've become his reader because he can't be bothered, or he's forgetful or he's broken them, so you'll be out shopping and I'm having to read things, or you'll be in a restaurant and I'm having to read what the food is out loud [...] instructions, maps, all those sort of things I've found myself more and more reading those out loud to him, and it's like a co-dependency, so the more I do it, the less he uses his glasses I suppose.

(C1765/48)

As I have talked about the RABiT research to people in different countries (Britain, Chile, Finland, Ecuador, France, Hungary, Estonia and Ethiopia), many have offered examples from their own hetero- and homosexual partnerships, and are all remarkably similar to the examples already given. Sometimes their examples suggest adoration and at other times irritation (that fine line in any partnership), but there is always a sense of oral reading as something quietly important in the ways we can join and live our lives together. Observer (F83) captures this powerfully when she writes of her late husband: 'For a wedding present, we were given a cheese board adorned with the legend *Please help yourself*. He read it aloud every time it was used.'

Domesticity

Many of these examples of reading aloud in marriage or partnership also tell us something about what we could call domestic life (and here I am using the term domestic and domesticity to mean in and of the home). From Chapter 5 we may remember interviewee JR discussing the centrality of reading aloud in his married home life, with him and his wife reading aloud to 'negotiate shopping,' read newspapers or magazines together or read aloud emails to organise seeing family, 'everyday stuff' (C1765/04). Similarly, in his reading aloud diary, Observer M79 writes: 'My wife read to me (while I chewed my dinner) an article by Hilary Mantel about Princess Diana and the 20th anniversary of her death,' while another (M63) records: 'Sun 3, My wife was serving rhubarb crumble and custard for Sunday dinner and I read out a short letter from the previous day's newspaper,' and a third starts her reading aloud diary with:

Day 1: In the living room with my husband and dog whilst having coffee, reading from the Times newspaper to my husband – Article on Clothing optional research group who suggest that theatre goers are dared to go naked a musical show!

(M70)

These provide colourful (if perhaps old-fashioned in the gender roles they suggest) pictures of the domestic. We have people reading aloud at kitchen tables, in the bath, living rooms, gardens and beds.

We can also see the domestic as a range of activities associated with the safety of this home space. A number of instances involve cooking or eating. Observer F37 remembers: 'I was read aloud to by my Mum [...] She used to read a story to us when we ate tea. I remember eating sausages whist listening to a story from a series called 'Blackberry Farm',' while interviewee SB recalls,

> We made pumpkin cake last week [...] I read out the instructions, so I tell her to measure 50 grams, yeah because she likes to do rather than read it out [...] so I read out the instructions and then she would be weighing the stuff and mixing.
>
> (C1765/07)

And questionnaire participants echo with 'I read recipes to my boyfriend, my Mum or my Grandma when we're cooking together' and 'when first married my husband and I read aloud novels as the other one cooked'.

Yet cooking and eating are certainly not the only domestic activities that feature, as the Observers remind us: 'In my third pregnancy I was into knitting Aran jumpers and my husband read all the Jane Austens and Trollopes to me and George Eliots' (F84) and 'During my married life of 30 years, there were times when my husband would read to me after breakfast, sometimes in Spanish or Italian, of which I had a basic knowledge. While he read I embroidered or worked on tapestry' (F90). An academic I met at a conference in Finland explained: 'I read my husband detective novels while he cleans the cooker. It seems to be the only way to get it done.' Here we have domestic oral reading as something both practical and imaginatively sustaining, a form of togetherness elevating the domestic from the 'ordinary' drudgery of cooking, cleaning or sewing to the 'extraordinary' of George Eliot, detective fiction or the Italian language.

Intimacy, service and death

A great many of examples we have seen so far in this chapter of families, friends and partners reading aloud together are examples of oral reading in or as domesticity: oral reading in the physical space, activities and routines of the 'inner' world of the home as opposed to the 'outer' world(s) of the public sphere. Another way of thinking about this 'inner' is offered by ideas of intimacy, by which I mean an interpersonal or emotional closeness. A great many of the instances of reading aloud already explored within this chapter are also examples of forms of intimacy: grandchildren bundling into their grandmother's bed for an early morning story or partners reading aloud to alleviate their other halves' pain. We can also see intimacy in the recording of voices: the voice made gift. A mother writes, 'When my daughter was very small and I was away for work, I made a recording of me reading some of her favourite books' (MO, F41). Another shares, 'My partner has created several talking books of my favourite childhood stories' and notes the emotional nature of 'My partner investing so much time to recording books for me – the ability to hear his voice when I'm away from him' (F54). A third remembers

> As a child my mother's father recorded a number of the Thomas the Tank Engine stories to cassette for me, though I have not remembered

this for many years. 'Duck the Diesel Engine' was my absolute favourite. My grandfather was a Yorkshire man, softly spoken, he read, as I recall, at a very consistent pace.

(M44)

As with the earlier example of a young man reading aloud to his partner over the phone to comfort her, there seems to be something particularly intimate about the voice in these examples. Anne Karpf starts her extraordinary examination of *The Human Voice* (2011) by noting the links between the voice, forms of identity and emotion, the ability of the voice to communicate love and generate trust, and how 'the voice lies at the heart of what it means to be human' (p. 3). With due awareness that not everyone has the same uses of voice and ear, and are of course no less human for it, Karpf's point nevertheless resonates with much of the RABiT research and the challenge of expressing (perhaps even more so in writing) what it is that the voice brings or does, particularly in relation to oral reading as acts of intimacy. Observer F24 tells us something important and relevant to this challenge when she writes, 'When I'm depressed it's a lot harder to read aloud, because there's something quite raw and vulnerable about it.'

The above examples of oral reading, live and recorded, are intimate – gifts of the voice and of time as a pilot study participant noted: 'it feels like you are being given a bit of a gift I think when somebody perhaps reads to you.' Interviewee JV provides a powerful illustration:

I had a recent experience where my partner was not well and it sort of, it ended up being not quite for medicinal purposes, but lie down and I'll read you a story, and it brought back, not quite memories – it was an adult story, I was reading a novel – so, but that quiet, calm, someone not well, it was soothing, it was lovely, it was just a time to be together, it was a time to be calm, that was a new experience [...] He felt poorly, and I thought, actually it would be good – lie down, in bed, and so I'll read you a story, the idea came from just lie down in bed – and I thought, well I'm here, let's – instead of me chatting, because we could chat for – but he was tired, and he was poorly, and he just needed quiet time, and I thought well that might sort of help to make you feel better – you've got nothing to do apart from listen – you don't need to respond – you don't need to acknowledge anything – just lie down and listen, and it will be nice. Yeah. So yeah, so I read the *Old Man and the Sea*, and interestingly, you know, it was [a] wee book, [...] it was an afternoon of let's just calm down, and about – the whole thing took probably about 4 and a half hours but it – it just – it flew in – and afterwards we thought, wow – we talk about it now – but wow. It was just a time to do something that could last that long, on one thing [...] it was quite a bit emotional moment, actually, where the engagement of one reader and one listener was dead interesting I think.

This may remind us of how many of the practices in this chapter are acts of intimacy of service, of helping others with gifts of voice, text and time, like the questionnaire participant 'Reading to my elderly blind mother,' interviewee TA reading to his grandmother as she could not read, interviewee PO reading to his wife after her stroke, interviewees MG and KB reading to their elderly mothers and Observer F26 reading poetry to her dying friend. Another Observer (F65) regularly reads in a hospice:

> Another of the first people I read to, I should so love to write his name [...] I went in one Christmas Eve and he had died. His relations had just gone, and the nurse said to me, 'would you like to go to see him?' I said, 'well he won't want to read will he?' [...] I wasn't being face-tious, just shocked and don't really know where that came from. In retrospect, I really wish I had read to him, right then. I wish I had given him my voice in his passage even after life had left him, out of respect, private respect, and thanks for what we had shared. I did thank him, but I didn't read.

Forms of reading aloud associated with death may be the most intimate of all. There is certainly reading aloud at funerals, including of eulogies and poems. This is a common literacy practice if we think of the 'common' as the culturally prevalent rather than the frequent in the lives of most individuals (as discussed in Chapter 3). Reading at funerals is also discussed in Chapter 4 in relation to the Mass Observation data, but here I'd like to present the thoughts of three participants in relation to the intimacy of this form of reading. Pilot study participant M50s recalls:

> At my mother's funeral, I read a eulogy, and that was a pre-prepared written text. I wrote it and I read it, and I'm not sure how much I was reading because I knew the text pretty well, and I remember I had tears in my eyes, and I couldn't see the text particularly well anyway, so that was an odd hybrid between reading aloud and reciting.

Interviewee MB explains something of her experience:

> You cannot afford to catch the eyes of anybody. Because normally if you are reading or telling a story of whatever, at a concert, you are looking at the folk because you want the feedback, you want the reaction, so you can really feel you are there and sharing, but at a funeral it's quite different. A friend asked me to do the eulogy at her funeral [...] and I found it extremely difficult to write it and very hard

to actually read it, and I think you usually get to within one sentence of the end and you've held yourself together, you've got yourself standing properly, proper stance and able to do it and then it's about the last sentence you crumple, and you feel, well I did it [...] if you are asked to do something like that, you cannot say no, but it is very stressful. I always think one of the really important things about doing something as emotional as that is to stand properly, get your back straight, get your feet apart, kind of make yourself as physically strong as you can be for actually reading [...] You're still looking about the room as you'd always do, but you're just not catching anybody's eyes. At my friend's funeral, I was asked to read two poems, and it was a small church, it was in Fair Isle [...] and I looked up, when I was reading, and I just saw one of her daughters, who was a teenager, who was wearing her mam's beautiful clothes at the funeral and for a moment I nearly lost it.

(C1765/83)

And DL, who, as we heard earlier, was wooed by her husband with the metaphysical poets, speaks of his funeral:

One of his favourite poems was a Dylan Thomas poem called 'Do Not Go Gentle Into that Good Night,' which was really, he was addressing to his father when he was dying and [my husband] used to read it to me, and you know, a long, long time ago. But when it was his own funeral, I decided I had to read that poem at the funeral. I read the whole eulogy, and I finished the eulogy with that poem [...] there are contrasts in the verses, sort of, telling his father to rage because he'd always raged against everything and fight this, fight this death, but then there are other verses which are not as strong somehow, there's a great contrast [...] because I had rehearsed it, I was able to really make the people I was reading to in that congregation really think about those words.

(C1765/28)

In different ways, these three people tell us something of the difficult but important intimacy (and service) of reading aloud for the dead and those they leave behind. Finally, the memory of this Observer (M, age unknown) helps us see that it is not only at funerals that we see lives – and love – expressed or contained within oral reading:

The only instance I can recall in reading aloud was at school for my English Oral exam, and we had to select a book and a chapter from it to read to the teacher. The chapter had to have meaning/drama, and the book you selected it from had to mean something too. I picked a

Reader's Digest book called *Collision Course* [...] I selected this book as it was my Father's book [...] It means a lot to me now as I haven't my Father but I still have the book and think of the times we spent together reading.

Mediation

In this chapter, we have explored practices where the most important thing seems to be the ways that different people use or experience the vocalisation of written texts as ways to be together, as larger and smaller groups, as couples, family members, and as people physically alone and yet in communion or fellowship with distant others through texts shared and voices heard. There is, though, something else going on, at least some of the time. Sometimes the oral reading is part of a linking, translating, relocating, re-contextualising or reframing between outer worlds of strangers, work or public affairs and inner worlds of domesticity, intimacy and established relationships. This, I am arguing, is a form of mediation.

Within literacy studies, the term 'mediation' has been used for acts of brokerage or service, when literacy 'mediators' support others with forms of reading and writing; for example, in unfamiliar genres, registers or languages (Baynham, 1993; Baynham & Masing, 2000; Papen, 2010). These forms of mediation – for example, scribes in Mexican plazas (Kalman, 1999) or youth workers helping young people in Quebec with healthcare literacies (Thériault, 2016) – can involve people reading or writing for or with others, incorporating aspects of informal learning and the challenging of power structures. Building on this understanding of mediation, Rockwell (2013) writes of the 'oral mediation of literacy' in her study of teachers' uses of textbooks in Mexican school classrooms. She notes how teachers use oral questioning and discussion to 'mediate,' recontextualise or scaffold understanding of what they want students to gain from these texts, stressing how teachers shape students' experiences of their textbooks through forms of 'oral interventions' (Rockwell, 2013, p. 187) including reading aloud. Like the earlier examples of literacy mediation, teachers are supporting their learners in accessing a form of literacy (a textbook) by bringing something external and challenging (and potentially alien) into the realm of the familiar. The teachers are also, though, controlling the key messages that the students take from the texts.

The RABiT data is full of examples of the reading of extracts from newspapers and social media posts, the selective 'bringing in' of news from the outside world into the inner sphere of the domestic or familial: the breakfast table, the fireside, the bed. Someone reads the news aloud, often on a small hand-held device (conjuring the outside in) and so it arrives in the domestic space already 'translated' into a familiar voice, with an interpretation or verdict expressed through that voice (distressed, amused or something else); in this way, the external news is presented or packaged for intimate consumption. I am arguing that this too is a form of mediation, not because the person being read to could not read it for themselves but because the oral reading is an act of bringing something external (local, national or international news) into the familiar (the home, the family, the relationship), with the reader's selection, voice and commentary supporting a particular understanding of, and reaction to, the text, for both reader and listener. Questionnaire participants indicate that they read 'Social media posts – to share their content with family or friends in the room with me.' Interviewee MG explains her desire to read news aloud to her husband as about both a sharing of the shocking and a form of checking her own understanding:

> I do probably the most annoying reading out loud, which is to my husband, when I'm reading something from the papers that has incensed me [...] it's always, almost always because I feel very cross and I want to share it with him, I want him to know, just in case he's missed this, and I think it's really important [laughs], and I think it's just a way of expressing, expressing how I feel about it. It's no good just reading something I think is awful, to yourself, it's that feeling that it needs to be shared with someone else to find out how they're feeling about it – am I overreacting to that? Was – have I read it – have I understood it even correctly? [...] say it's talking about homelessness, like localised homelessness or the, something you can directly relate to [...] it does generate conversation.
>
> (C1765/47)

As in Rockwell's (2013) example above, this mediation can be seen as both support and control, with the reader supporting access to, as well as filtering, messages from the outside world. It is also, as emphasised by MG above, a form of self-support, facilitating the processing or managing of particularly striking news – whether funny or horrific or incomprehensible. The reader may also be managing how the read text relates to other language practices; for example, using it to start or slant a particular discussion. A questionnaire participant reports reading aloud driven by 'outrange/despair at depths of stupid politics (Trump, Brexit). Esp[.] from younger co-workers who can't believe what is going on. Usually a prelude to a discussion,' and another reads out 'newspaper articles when I want to share the story. I typically do this because I want to engage in discussion.' Here the mediation may be mainly for the benefit of the reader, who wants to talk about it, rather than the listeners.

Crucially, control over or mediation of written texts (a form of exercise of power) may be unwanted. Observer F55 remembers:

> An ex-boyfriend used to read out the information by each item in [a] museum, which I found deeply embarrassing because people can read the plaque for themselves when they get to the relevant section. It

seemed to suggest a lack of awareness [...] Maybe even a bit patronising to suggest that they or I needed him to read it.

In Chapter 7 we will also look at examples from work and prison contexts of power wielded by those who read for others.

Conclusion and love

This chapter has argued that reading aloud can be a way of being with others – and that 'being together' takes many forms: as members of communities, as family, as lovers, partners and spouses. It has argued that this relates to ideas of domesticity and intimacy and the polarities of public and private that both domesticity and intimacy suggest, as well as that oral reading can be used as a form of mediation between these spheres. Within these arguments is the idea that reading aloud has something to do with not only power but also love. We have examined many examples where the time together, the physical proximity, the voice(s) and the content of the text itself may be expressions or enactments of love. Observer M79 remembers:

> As a child, I was always chosen to read aloud to the class, a result perhaps of my early love of reading, which was a brief escape from an unhappy childhood. To a person of low self-esteem, being read aloud to forms a temporary feeling of being some value after all, and worthy of this spell of attention from another person.

Interviewee NS explores what reading to a child has in common with religious reading or the reading aloud of poetry, and in doing so arrives at love:

> What I think is in common is the joy of sharing language with another human being or other human beings, and that of course is different to reading silently. What is different is that with a child, that's a very intimate, nurturing situation, so it's likely to be one to one, unless other members of the family are around, but essentially it's one to one, and it's really starting from before the time the child can understand what you are saying, so the whole context of it is physical warmth and nurturing and sound and growing up as sound as something associated with being loved. [...] in the church service I hope there would be some context of loving and being loved because that's something that takes place in an accepting community; in the reading poetry aloud, it's a common attention, and that's, that is a kind of love.

(C1765/38)

I also remember a woman in the Glasgow Women's Library *Story Café* group explaining that throughout her marriage she used to read to her husband and now after his death continues to read to him.

References

Angyal, C. (2012, October 10). In praise of the lost, intimate art of reading aloud. *The Atlantic*.

Barton, D. (1994). Exploring family literacy. *RaPAL Bulletin*, 24(Summer), 2–5.

Baynham, M. (1993). Code switching and mode switching: Community interpreters and mediators of literacy. *Cross-Cultural Approaches to Literacy*, 294–314.

Baynham, M., & Masing, H. L. (2000). Mediators and mediation in multilingual literacy events. *Multilingual Literacies: Reading and Writing Different Worlds*, 189–208.

Byatt, A. S. (1978). *The Virgin in the Garden*. Penguin.

Cuban, S., & Hayes, E. (1996). Women in family literacy programs: A gendered perspective. *New Directions for Adult and Continuing Education*, 1996(70), 5–16. https://doi.org/10.1002/ace.36719967003.

Duncan, S. (2012). *Reading Circles, Novels and Adult Reading Development*. Bloomsbury.

Finders, M. J. (1997). *Just Girls: Hidden Literacies and Life in Junior High*. Teachers College Press.

Gebre, A. H. (2009). *Everyday Literacies in Africa: Ethnographic Studies of Literacy and Numeracy Practices in Ethiopia*. African Books Collective.

Gurdon, M. C. (2019). *The Enchanted Hour: The Miraculous Power of Reading Aloud in the Age of Distraction*. Hachette UK.

Kalewold, A. I. (1970). *Traditional Ethiopian Church Education*. Teachers College Press.

Kalman, J. (1999). Writing on the plaza. *Mediated Literacy Practices among Scribes and Clients in Mexico City*, 5.

Kalman, J. (2005). *Discovering Literacy: Access Routes to Written Culture for a Group of Women in Mexico*. UNESCO.

Karpf, A. (2011). *The Human Voice: The Story of a Remarkable Talent*. Bloomsbury Publishing.

Long, E. (2003). *Book Clubs: Women and the Uses of Reading in Everyday Life*. University of Chicago Press.

Lynx Qualey, M. (2018, January 18). On the great joy of reading aloud. *BookRiot*. https://bookriot.com/2018/01/18/reading-aloud-joys/.

Mace, J. (1998). *Playing with Time: Mothers and the Meaning of Literacy*. UCL Press.

Nafisi, A. (2004). *Reading Lolita in Tehran*. Fourth Estate.

Papen, U. (2010). Literacy mediators, scribes or brokers? *Langage et Société*, 3, 63–82.

Rockwell, E. (2013). Preambles, questions, and commentaries: Teaching genres and the oral mediation of literacy. *Literacy and Numeracy in Latin America: Local Perspectives and Beyond*, 184–199.

Thériault, V. (2016). Literacy mediation as a form of powerful literacies in community-based organisations working with young people in a situation of precarity. *Ethnography and Education*, 11(2), 158–173. https://doi.org/10.1080/17457823.2015.1101384.

Woldeyes, Y. G. (2017). *Native Colonialism: Education and the Economy of Violence Against Traditions in Ethiopia*. The Red Sea Press.

7

WORKING LIFE

My work gets sent to me via email [...] my work is for health and
safety reasons, so every 12 months the stuff has to be checked
[electrical portable appliance testing, PAT] so sometimes when
I get to the place I have to be at, the people don't know that I'm
supposed to come for the job; they are not aware that I'm
coming, and then I have to tell them, 'well Ma'am, all I can say is
I got an email [...] this is the email,' then I read wherever I'm
supposed to be, this is the amount of tests I'm supposed to do...

(pilot study participant M30s)

In these years of researching adult oral reading, when anyone asked what I was
investigating and my explanation included the words 'reading aloud,' a
common follow-up question was 'oh, you mean with children?' or sometimes
'ah, reciting poetry and things?' or 'like at church?'. These seem to be the adult
oral reading practices that to many people come to mind most easily. No one
has ever responded with 'oh, like the bits of reading aloud I do for work?' And
yet, in all three strands of the RABiT project, as well as in the pilot study,
reading aloud at work features heavily. These workplace reading aloud practices can tell us something about not only the roles of oral reading in adult life
but also about how literacy more generally features within different workplaces,
how it might not be self-evident what exactly different employees are expected
to do with the various screens, bits of paper, files or posters at play and how
these acts may relate to forms of workplace power or control. In this chapter,
we will also look at six types of working roles where reading aloud seems
particularly central and explore what it means in each case to be reading aloud
'professionals.'

Ubiquity and diversity

As a local councillor, I often read letters and emails that people from
my ward have written to me aloud during council meetings.

(questionnaire)

Thursday – on a phone call with a colleague, amending a paper we are both writing, reading sentences I had drafted that he couldn't see.

(MO, F48)

I used to work in social welfare and had to give presentations, so, yes, reading aloud but reading my own words really [and] perhaps reading bits about the Children's Act [...] or reading for changes in legislation, reading those out to people [...] I think because it's quicker [...] I feel we do take in information better if we hear it, rather than, reading it can be a bit slow. And to be honest, the books were usually quite expensive, so we didn't have that many copies of them, and if you've got 20 members of staff and 3 copies of the book, or a particular piece of legislation, it's much quicker to read it out loud [...] you can high-light paragraphs or sections and read it out. So that's what I would do.

(KB, British Library, C1765/11)

Before job interviews, I write memos and read aloud to get familiar with what I would be saying.

(questionnaire)

My workmates read out emails to me. I also attend readings as part of my job in publishing.

(questionnaire)

I read lists of apologies and sometimes my own written reports to committees when I'm being their secretary.

(questionnaire)

The range of forms of oral reading in or for the workplace is striking: an electrician reading emails to confirm PAT testing appointments; a film executive leading script development readings; shop assistants reading backs of products for customers who cannot see or cannot read the small print; physiotherapists (and other medical practitioners) reading doctor's letters with patients to recap a history or process; a cleaning company manager reading health and safety information to those they manage; a clothes shop manager reading appraisal forms with shop-floor staff; and air traffic controller 'read-backs.' We can find teachers, volunteers and teaching assistants reading to children (and listening to them read); colleagues reading emails to each other from computer terminals; religious leaders reading prayers and other forms of worship; a translator reading aloud the Welsh of their translation; therapists reading 'relaxation scripts' to or with clients; and an admissions officer reading aloud admissions codes. Work colleagues read aloud while writing communal emails or when what they are writing concerns someone else in the room; colleagues read emails they have received to others who are not at a computer or screen; an advisor reads tax forms or regulations to clients at the Citizens Advice Bureau; florists read back messages for flower deliveries; and nurses read their notes to patients. Workers of all sorts read and listen to meeting minutes; writers and poets read to audiences or to themselves when writing; waiters read back orders from notepads – the list seems to have no end.

The above examples come from the RABiT pilot and project, and readers may be able to recall instances from their own lives (whether observed or taken part in), both in Britain and other parts of the world. Anecdotally, I have heard others talking about oral reading as part of stock-taking in a pharmacy in Moscow; notaries reading aloud to clients in Chile; professional marketplace form-fillers reading aloud to their clients in Ecuador; a waiter reading aloud specials in New Orleans; and a Berlin-based translator reading aloud (in both languages) as she translates from Russian to English. This seeming ubiquity of workplace oral reading may lead us to reflect on what this means for someone who is not a fluent reader, not confident reading aloud or not confident reading in the language of workplace texts. One (speculative) answer to the question of why some adults seem to be less aware of the oral reading that they perform regularly may be that confident, fluent readers are less likely to notice these instances of oral reading, while someone less confident will be more aware of these instances and may experience requirements to read aloud, whether at work or for other life functions, as a struggle or barrier.

We could also consider the various degrees to which oral reading is central to the job in question (what would happen, for example, if someone did not do the reading aloud that is asked of them, or if they asked a colleague to do it instead?), as well as how individuals perceive the nature and requirements of their work. A customer-service employee in a supermarket who is often asked to read from pro-duct packs to customers may see this as central to their role or, equally, may see this as something completely outside of it. This difference has the potential to impact on both job satisfaction and ideas of appropriate vocational training. And we could consider the ways that forms of oral reading are intertwined with workplace power-relations. In Chapter 5 (pp. 74–75), we heard interviewee PO describe the oral reading he does in his role as a cleaning supervisor, reading aloud health and safety and other training information to members of the cleaning team because 'English is very often not their first language or they might not be able to read themselves.' He is describing the work of a responsible supervisor working with his team, an act of supportive literacy mediation, and yet (remembering the discussion of mediation in Chapter 6), this is a position of power, of control over texts, their messages and potentially aspects of working life; a role that could be abused by a less honourable supervisor.

The professionals

Oral reading is a part, then, of many different work roles and relates to workplace power relations. It is also true that reading aloud is more central to certain work roles than others, and these we could call the reading aloud 'professionals.' Here we will look at six groups: editors and writers; actors; broadcasters; religious roles; magistrates, judges and registrars; and librarians and teachers.

Editors and writers

The RABiT data contains many examples of editors and writers reading aloud as part of their editing and composition processes, to share with audiences at events or performances, and as preparation for such events. The questionnaire responses contain examples of each of these, including an editor who writes of the centrality of oral reading to her editing processes and a poet who stresses two distinct forms of oral reading central to his role: as part of creating his poems and, at a later stage, to publicise his work through public readings. A Mass Observer writes of his role as a script editor and the importance of the 'first read through,' orally and communally, while interviewee MT explains three different forms of reading aloud central to her working life as a novelist: refining her writing, reading aloud at events and preparing to read aloud at events:

> I'm the author of a series of crime mysteries, and I've also written a history of women's suffrage in Shetland and a couple of ones on historical topics [...] and I find reading out loud a very, very useful tool; obviously if I'm doing events and I would read out loud for that and that has to be practised beforehand, but also when I'm writing the book then it really helps you to get a feel of how your prose is going, whether a sentence is clunky.
>
> (C1765/80)

In his *Paris Review* interview, American novelist and story-writer Sam Lipsyte speaks about the potentially exposing nature of public readings:

> you have to create a persona that's not noticeable to others but is you going out and reading your work. With that persona, the effects of your fiction can be realized live [...] if you write something good it will sound good read aloud, if you write something bad it will sound bad read aloud.
>
> (Doten, 2018)

Writers of all kinds stress the role of oral reading in their working lives, including composition and editing as well as performing, publicising or sharing the finished product. We will return to literary creation in Chapter 9.

Actors

Interviewee JR considers oral reading absolutely central to his life as an actor (as we can read in Chapter 5, pp. 72–73). He describes reading aloud to learn audition pieces 'so that you are connected to it,' 'so that it becomes habitua-lised,' 'part of you,' 'you keep reading it out loud, going back to it' (C1765/04). He also describes reading aloud as part of the rehearsal process, as well as of understudy work to 'keep it fresh.' He expresses shifting relationships between actor and text at different phases of the work of an actor, highlighting how oral reading is both a vehicle for an inward movement of 'connecting to it' and 'keeping it fresh,' and also at other times a projecting outwards: at an audition, to a director, a group of fellow actors or an audience. Observer F53 adds two further examples of the diversity of actors' oral reading:

> I'm a theatre practitioner/director so reading script is always an out loud thing – the first day of any production is the 'read through' where the script in entirety is read by the cast to grasp its arc and meanings and structure before it is intensely taken apart/segmented to be rehearsed [...]
>
> I've worked with actors with Learning Difficulties, and one of the strategies to support actors with literacy issues is to produce a tape of the text for them to learn from. Important in producing these is to ensure the punctuation informs the reading, but otherwise it is as neutral as possible so that the reading does not inform the actor's characterisation of the role and they are able to develop this for themselves in rehearsal. These readings are taped or put on CD.

Broadcasters

Interviewee GW reads scripts for the *Island Voices – Guthan nan Eilean* film series (Island Voices, 2020):

> Over the past few years, I've been collecting, making and collecting a bunch of videos which I've put online and recording interviews and in fact making short documentary- type things. So for those, then, for the documentaries I would put a voice-over on them – and that is [a] question of putting together a sequence of pictures, a picture sequence and then scripting something to go with it and then speaking it and recording it, so that it, it becomes part of the film, so I've done that in, mostly in Gaelic and English but sometimes in – [...] I've done one in Hindi, for example, so I guess that is reading aloud; it is me looking at the script and saying aloud what is written there on the page in front of me.
>
> (C1765/53)

Interviewee SG, a journalist and broadcaster, remembers presenting a radio programme where he would read aloud letters (often of complaint) sent in by the general public.

At one time, there was somebody who once thought that every letter I read, I read out, was my opinion, my opinion personally, even though I did tell him that it wasn't. But I saw that maybe as a compliment, you know because I sounded as if I believed what I was reading out, even though it was often very far from what I personally believed in. But when I was reading it out I would tend to put on [a] slightly, you know, entertaining performance. I wasn't reading it as if, as if it, you know, deadpan, as if news. I was putting expression in.

(C1765/82)

Is this an example of reading aloud so 'well' that the listener thinks that these were his views, his ideas? Or is this a story about a listener missing the subtle mark of tone that indicates that these are not the broadcaster's words, however full of expression?

Another interviewee, MB, reads aloud as part of her role as a broadcaster, including reading literary extracts on her radio books programme and recording Shetland dialect poems. She also remembers a further strand of her professional oral reading:

And I've just thought of a completely different kind of reading that I did, which was for Jarlshof, which is the big archaeological site. I was asked to do the commentary for the guiding yourself around [...] and that was really weird because you are giving folk instructions and reading really complicated extracts and things. [...] press the blue button, or is it press the red button, I'm not very sure [...] and it's quite surprising the number of folk I meet who say 'ah it was you.'

(C1765/83)

She also recalls:

When I first went to work at BBC Radio Shetland, I was told you are only talking to one person, whatever you're doing, there's only one person sitting listening to that radio or whatever, so I kind of got, I thought about my Auntie Mary because I knew she'd be listening, so, whenever I'm reading, I've got Auntie Mary in my mind.

(C1765/83)

Two other RABiT participants were also taught (one in Somerset and one in South Africa) that to read aloud on the radio you must imagine that you are reading to one single listener, suggesting this is fairly common advice, and potentially something we could consider a key element of broadcaster professionalism.

Religious roles

Chapter 8 will examine reading aloud for religious purposes in more detail, but here we will briefly think about those whose professional lives relate to religion. In Chapter 5 (pp. 76–77), I included a conversation between two women in a Roman Catholic religious community. One woman starts by noting the oral reading she does in their Chapel, for their community and a wider public, and then mentions the reading aloud she does as part of work as a spiritual director. This is the very beginning of her answer to the question of when she reads aloud. After this, she goes on to discuss the oral reading she does for her 'own prayer life,' but it seems significant that her answer begins with the examples core to her professional life, or vocation of service: facilitating the worship of others and spiritual guidance/teaching.

Interviewee NS explores one aspect of this work as an Anglican priest, explaining how he and lay readers do the work of reading Bible passages to a listening congregation:

> It's a great art and much underestimated, because for reading in church, it's not the same thing as an actor reciting a speech [...] because I think it's actually harmful to the process when the reader imposes too strong a meaning – that's my view, others might differ – but I think the reader needs to have internalised a meaning so the reading is coherent but not too strongly to stress a particular way of putting the text over so that people feel under pressure, as it were, to read it in a certain way because with the reading of scripture you want it to be open to people's own interpretation from where they are – that is to say, not that it can mean anything but that it might mean quite different things to different people, so for instance if you take the parable of the prodigal son, [...] if you are a young man you see it one way, if you are an elder brother you see it another way, if you are a parent and things have happened in your family where things have gone wrong, you see it in another way. [...] It's important to read it so that it can be heard from those different perspectives, which means that clarity is important, pace is important, an understanding of the text is important, but it must be read with an openness to understand that people will be hearing it from very different contexts in different lives.

(C1765/38)

Here we have an explanation of the 'art' of this type of reading, which is quite different to the reading aloud of an editor ensuring clarity of phrasing, a novelist reading her work to an audience, an actor either 'internalising' or projecting lines, or a broadcaster reading to their single imagined listener, despite some communalities.

A different sort of 'professional' religious reading aloud role is represented by interviewee AN, who supports children with their Hebrew reading to prepare for their Bar or Bat Mitzvah in Judaism:

> In the past, I've worked as a Hebrew teacher, and I would read aloud then, teaching children their Bar or Bat Mitzvah portions [...] these are British children and some were American [...] They wouldn't know any Hebrew. They would be taught it in Sunday School, which we'd call Religion School or Cheder; we would teach them in a phonetic kind of way the Hebrew alphabet and how to read, and then by the time they are 11ish, they would be expected to read Hebrew sentences in preparation for their B'nei Mitzvot, which would be when they are 13, and then they would be expected to read [aloud] a whole Parsha, a whole portion of the Torah, which would usually take them about 15 minutes.
>
> (C1765/64)

These examples can help us see religious roles as reading aloud professionals in ways which both overlap with and differ from the other professional roles we are exploring in this chapter. We will return to religious reading in Chapter 8.

Magistrates, judges and registrars

'My job requires me to read aloud as I conduct marriage ceremonies and read out evidence in court,' explains a questionnaire participant. Magistrates, judges and registrars (these titles, and others such as notary, vary from country to country, but here I am looking more generally at those who work in these sorts of official legal roles) perform acts of oral reading which carry significant legal, as well as social, weight. Two powerful examples come from the Mass Observation data, as noted in Chapter 4. Observer M79 explains:

> Having served as a magistrate it was necessary for me to read aloud in court. This involved official warnings, court verdicts with reasons and statutory declarations. As a new magistrate I was nervous at first but quickly grew into the routine, remembering that it was important to look at the person I was reading aloud to as much as possible. If I did not make eye contact with the person being read to, it negated the importance of what was being read.

Observer F71 is similarly aware of the particular rules of her professional role:

> Conducting a wedding involved a certain amount of reading aloud, although in due course I came to know all the words by heart [...] The object of the exercise was, primarily, to comply with the law, so no

deviation from the set text would have been permissible. In addition, everyone in the room needed to be able to hear everything, so clear pronunciation and sufficient volume were necessary.[...] At the same time, regard had to be paid to the fact that the bride and groom were often nervous; also it had to be borne in mind that this was a very special occasion in their lives [...] It was important therefore to strike the right manner; too much informality was inappropriate, but a certain warmth and sincerity had to come through in the voice, if possible.

In these two examples, the professional reading aloud central to these roles involves careful attention to eye-contact and tone of voice in order to reflect the nature of what is being enacted with these words (whether a marriage, a custodial sentence or something else).

Librarians and teachers

Though in some ways less obvious reading aloud 'professionals' than poets, actors or clerics, many librarians and teachers (in and out of the RABiT project) identify their roles as necessarily involving a great deal of oral reading. Questionnaire participants and Observers frequently start their responses: 'I'm a teacher so,' 'I'm a librarian and,' 'I'm a lecturer...', 'I'm an ESOL teacher and therefore...'

A questionnaire participant specifies 'I am a librarian and I often read information about books and library services to my customers.' Another writes, 'I read information from a computer screen to answer a customer enquiry – face-to-face & over the telephone – frequently during my working days (2–3 per week).' Interviewee GD expands on the range of different forms of oral reading central to her role as a librarian:

Because I work in a library, we do reading aloud. When I was at the public library we used to have reading groups, and you would read to children and perhaps – and at the university library where I work now we have library skills sessions for students and they come along; we've got, it's mostly stuff from the website, but you've got a presentation, you've got PowerPoint and you've got the words up on screen and you have to read what's there to them and try to explain things and wait for their questions.

(C1765/25)

Other library-based questionnaire participants note, 'I run a read aloud group at a library,' 'I work in a library and take weekly story time,' 'I share books with children and adults at library storytimes' and 'I work in a library so hear children's storytimes weekly, people generally reading bits around library, authors and poets at events.' Here I am also reminded of the numerous reading circles I have observed in libraries, and the reading aloud (whether of tiny extracts or longer passages) that many involved, often facilitated by librarians themselves (Duncan, 2012, 2014), and of the nineteenth-century (US) Kalamazoo Ladies Library Association and where librarians and other group members would read out selected texts related to the topic of the weekly self-education-focussed meeting (Jackson, 1999). Having to read out loud is seen by many librarians as core to their work, if for slightly different reasons. Interestingly, another questionnaire participant highlights the *listening* she does as a librarian: 'My manager at the library where we work reads children's stories to her staff while we work (we love it).'

Chapter 11 will examine uses of reading aloud as a teaching tool, but here we will look briefly at some of the ways that teachers (including university lecturers) use oral reading for a range of non-teaching purposes (while recognising that it is not really that easy to separate out the 'teaching' from 'non-teaching). For example, a questionnaire participant writes of reading aloud 'Paperwork as part of my job as an Adult Literacy Tutor,' while others note oral reading as part of exam invigilation, reading daily announcements to learners and reading aloud at staff meetings. Teachers, teaching assistants and volunteers report listening to children read, while university-based academics in both the questionnaire and MO note reading aloud academic articles, including their own. One questionnaire participant shares: 'Academic historians regularly read their work aloud to each other so this is a regular thing.' Bringing in yet another purpose, ESOL (English for Speakers of Other Languages) teacher interviewee JI explains that he reads aloud as he edits newspaper articles to create external assessments:

> I run an exam called National 5 ESOL, which is taught at upper intermediate level, so I work for the Scottish Qualifications Authority, and what's proved time and time again is that however well you think you are reading silently when you are editing a text, taken typically from the Guardian for a reading test, you miss things that you don't miss if you, if you read out loud.
>
> (C1765/20)

These library and teacher forms of oral reading – to present or provide information, to entertain and encourage children and adults, as part of author events, to create materials, read and write academic texts – may all be quite different, but to these participants, each is core to teacher or librarian professionalism.

***

We can see that for each of the above groups of reading aloud 'professionals,' oral reading is a significant part of working life. And yet what it means to read aloud well or effectively depends, in each case, on the particular professional role: whether what matters is delivering a strong interpretation or leaving room for interpretation; whether this means being as loud and joyful as possible or using tone to indicate the gravity of a verdict; or whether this means modelling a form of reading for children and parents, or conveying instructions as unambiguously and uniformly as possible (as in the case of exam invigilators). To return to Shove et al.'s (2012) terms, the competences required, and valued, differ, as the materials and meanings of the professional roles vary. A broadcaster reading aloud a poem as part of an arts programme may be imagining they are reading to one person, one listener. This might be part of the 'meaning' of some radio arts programmes, an intimacy between reader and listener. Recording, amplification and transmitting equipment, the materials, allow for this illusion of intimacy; no need for the reader to project their voice like a head teacher trying to reach the back of a large assembly hall. Projection isn't a key competency here, but pacing, pausing, use of tone and expression of emotion may well be part of what makes a good reader in this particular professional example. A registrar conducting a wedding is reading aloud within a different set of meanings, around the legal binding of two lives, around personal commitment and public display, acknowledgement and witness. The materials are different, a printed script which cannot be departed from, a room of a certain size perhaps, which may require projection, as well as precision and clarity, so the words are heard by all in the room and able to be repeated by those getting married. The 'manner' as the Observer notes above, is important – formal but warm and sincere. This is a different type of 'good' reading. We could also think about a librarian reading aloud at an under-5s story time in a busy library, an actor reading in early rehearsals, a priest reading aloud to a listening congregation, or an editor reading aloud to edit an article, and each time we could map slightly different meanings linked to slightly different materials and slightly different competences. Whether or not these competences are developed through more formal professional training (or not) is another matter and one that will be taken up in Chapter 11.

Wrapping up: public life, protest and prison

Oral reading can be quite 'a different beast' across different workplaces, work roles or even aspects of the same role: carrying different meanings, using different materials and requiring different competences. It is a small part of many different jobs and a larger part of a few. It is bound up in workplace protocols, relationships and power structures. We can also think about oral reading and power in a different way and recall instances where the more 'powerful position' may be to seem as if one is not reading at all but rather talking confidently and eloquently; for example, television newsreaders and politicians 'making' (rather than reading) speeches. In other instances, potentially those of the magistrate or clergy, to be clearly and obviously reading aloud from a written document is the more powerful position, as the power comes from reading these particular words, in this order, from this particular document, established by tradition and the higher authority of God or law.

The other side, perhaps, of the above look at working life, is to think about the systems of organisation, law or administration that we deal with as citizens. When doctors read aloud from patient's notes or receptionists read out appointment information, we as patients listen (and interrupt, and ask questions…). In courts of law, we have to listen to, and sometimes read out loud ourselves, written statements, as pilot study participant (M50s) recalls, 'as an asylum seeker I had to read aloud one statement to the judge […] to give the story of my life to the judge […] it was my own writing, what I had written myself.' We may have to read aloud voting information for an elderly relative with a postal vote, and most of us have listened to a news bulletin or politician's speech read aloud on the television. Many of the ideas in this chapter about working practices can also tell us something about the place of oral reading in public life.

There are two aspects of public life I'd like to finish with. The first is political protest. Interviewee JH stresses the uses of communal writing and reading aloud among communities whose stories had been suppressed or subverted, where the reading aloud is a form of regaining control over the presentation of a conflict (see Chapter 6, p. 86). Working and public life involves political protest, sometimes in the form of gatherings, strikes and marches, and sometimes involving forms of oral reading. Observer (M50s) writes of reading aloud vigil readings for an HIV/AIDS benefit, and one of the RABiT sound recordings is of a group of striking university lecturers taking turns to read out pieces of writing they have chosen as they stand on a very cold and windy picket line (C1765/52). Instances of oral reading at picket lines and political rallies are common around the world (including the Hong Kong and Climate Change protests of 2019 and the Black Lives Matter protests following the death of George Floyd in 2020). On protest marches, too – as slogans are written on placards, shouted, chanted, recited, repeated and adapted, we can see forms of oral reading as togetherness, as power or demonstration of energy, as 'fight back', as identity, as the creation of a unified voice or embodiment of a movement.

Finally, this also seems the place to reflect on prison, which is the daily life of many adults around the world. Famously, the US and Russia have the highest numbers of their populations incarcerated, with, according to BBC figures (2020), 737 and 615 people (respectively) locked up out of every 100,000. South Africa, Poland and the Ukraine are also at over 200 per 100,000, with England and Wales at 148 and Scotland 134. Prison life highlights some of the contradictions within how we talk about literacy more generally and reading aloud specifically. In many countries, there are resources or initiatives which aim to improve the lives of those in prison through reading, such as prison libraries, reading groups (see for example, Billington, 2011; Hartley, 2020) and initiatives such as *Storybook Dads* and *Storybook Mums* (*Storybook Dads* runs in the

UK, US, Australia, Denmark, Hungary, Poland and New Zealand; see, for example, Crawford-Smith et al., 2015; Storybook Dads, 2020), where oral reading is used to relieve much of the inhumanity of prison – as a way to connect with fellow prisoners, family members and the worlds of different written texts.

Members of a reading group I visited in an English prison explained to me the forms of oral reading that some of them take part in – including religious worship and peer literacy teaching. They also spoke of the reading that some of them do for others who cannot read, including reading personal letters from home (another example of literacy mediation, see discussion in Chapter 6). These men shared their understanding (and in one case his previous personal experience) of the frustration and anger of those who have to rely on others to read for them in this way, about the loss of power and increased vulnerability. As in any context, the joys that reading may bring need to be understood alongside the dangers of creating contexts which make life harder for those who cannot read.

Forms of reading aloud are present in larger and smaller, more and less obvious, ways across our working lives and lives as citizens. What it means to be a 'good reader' (or good 'read-aloud-er') is at least slightly different in each case, as purposes, priorities and contexts vary, as do power relationships and the ways in which written documents are used. These practices may be part of serving customers, writing, running meetings, arranging dental appointments and protesting injustice. They may provide a great deal of satisfaction and joy, and they may also intimidate, threaten or exclude.

References

BBC. (2020). World Prison Populations. *BBC News*. http://news.bbc.co.uk/1/shared/spl/hi/uk/06/prisons/html/nn2page1.stm.

Billington, J. (2011). 'Reading for life': Prison reading groups in practice and theory. *Critical Survey*, 23(3), 67–85. https://doi.org/10.3167/cs.2011.230306.

Crawford-Smith, J., Mahy, D., Radwan, J., & Smith, L. (2015). *Evaluating changes in literacy and social connectedness as a result of a Storybook Dads programme*. Evaluating changes in literacy and social connectedness as a result of a Storybook Dads programme.

Doten, M. (2018, Winter). Sam Lipsyte, The Art of Fiction No. 242. *Paris Review*. https://www.theparisreview.org/interviews/7289/sam-lipsyte-the-art-of-fiction-no-242-sam-lipsyte.

Duncan, S. (2012). *Reading Circles, Novels and Adult Reading Development*. Bloomsbury.

Duncan, S. (2014). *Reading for Pleasure and Reading Circles for Adult Emergent Readers: Insights in Adult Learning*. National Institute of Adult Continuing Education.

Hartley, J. (2020). Twenty years behind bars: Reading aloud in prison reading groups. *Changing English*, 27(1), 100–108.

Island Voices—Guthan van Eilean. (2020). https://guthan.wordpress.com/ [accessed 4 June 2020].

Jackson, M. L. (1999). 'A delightful entertainment': Study groups as part of the Kalamazoo Ladies' Library Association. 1–18. [Annual Meeting of the Popular Culture
   and American Culture Association (San Diego, CA, March 31–April 3, 1999)].
Shove, E., Pantzar, M., & Watson, M. (2012). The Dynamics of Social Practice: Everyday Life and How it Changes. Sage.
Storybook Dads. (2020). https://www.storybookdads.org.uk/ [accessed 4 June 2020].

8

RELIGION

My grandmother was a member of a group of men and women who took part in group recitations of the Quran and other supplications at events in the town that she lived in. After my grandfather died, I think she found it difficult to live without him. I'm sure she was a little lonely. I believe that joining the group and taking part in the events gave her some company and also purpose.

In Malaysia, Muslim family and religious events are marked by a celebration called a 'kenduri'. However, these are not just for what we would consider happy occasions. There were kenduris for when people died and for remembrance too. Generally, kenduris are to celebrate and ask for blessings for events such as births, engagements, starting school/university, weddings, birthdays (though not so often), moving to a new area/house and wishing someone safety in their travel overseas. Also, kenduris are held for religious observations such as finishing a number of Quran chapters (khatam Quran) and special religious dates. I went to many kenduris in my grandmother's town and the nearby villages when I was a child. In many cases, I couldn't tell what the event was actually for – I was more interested in the mouth-watering spread of food!

During these events, it was usual to have separate groups of women and men sitting cross-legged on the floor reciting Quranic verses or 'tahlil'. Tahlil is a pattern of religious verses and surahs (or chapters) from the Quran. Although my grandmother did not take part in these when I was young, after my grandfather's death, she started getting more involved in a group. She was in her 60s, and I was in my teens. The group was generally led by a religious leader – either a man (ustaz) or woman (ustazah) – and I think they were given donations by people who were holding events. The belief was that the recitation could be gifted as 'sedekah' to others and everyone jointly asked for blessings for the occasion.

Her social life was soon very busy. I remember her telling me that she had at least one event a week, and in the busy months during Syawal (the month of Eid) she sometimes had up to three engagements a week.

The act of the recitation itself involved all of the group following a practised set of verses and surahs, which many learnt by heart, through initial reading from the Quran and booklets of surahs. Many had been taught by their own parents, and perhaps variations in the patterns were decided by the religious leaders. These days, you can go online and see a guide of how to recite tahlil. Many of the surahs recited were from the early part of the Quran, Chapter 36 called 'Yasin' and the 'Qursi' verse, which is a highly revered verse. Although the recitation was not timed, members of the group would all recite together, and so they were not reciting the Quran as individual Quran readers. The style was different. Whereas with individual Quran reading there is an emphasis on volume, accuracy and individual style, with group reading, the focus is on keeping pace with each other and maintaining a low and steady volume, like a discernible hum. You are able to recognise what the group are reciting and can join in if you want, but no one in particular is highlighting themselves. The beauty is in the joint recitation. I guess the best way to describe it is like people chanting together. To me, it was usually a calming sound.

More recently this practice has reduced in metropolitan areas. However, the recitations still take place in mosques and in areas in towns and villages.

(personal memory kindly shared by Nafisah Graham-Brown)

*****

CO: The fact that the words on the page are being verbalised, it gives them a different, a different resonance, it gives them a different meaning [...]

ST: There's a double dimension, isn't there. I would agree with what you are saying. It's something to do with your body, something to do with your voice, the ownership of the word widens completely, and I think there's something quite mysterious, actually – it's a bit like what you're saying, when you actually make this word public, you let go of it, I think that's important, that becomes a much wider dimension and not just the individual, and for others to hear your voice, too, is something, maybe for your children, too, that's quite something. They hear, they hear their own voice, so it's 'I am', you know, so I think it's a very, it's a letting go of me to something much wider, I think. I find that quite mysterious [...] it's something about ownership yourself of that word before you make it public

119

CO: I was just going to add to that, saying there is the ownership, but there is something about living in the text [...] how am I going to let myself go and let myself enter in that, in a way that I'm attentive in a way to what's being said and that in that split second I can bring it to life and I can own it, yeah. [...] I think it's an inner disposition; it's about being calm and being still.

ST: Which I would agree.

CO: You know when I arrive in the chapel, I like to arrive early if I know I'm going to be reading [...] and have everything ready so it's, it's, yeah that exterior disposition that leads to that interior space, where that's all that exists in me in that moment, in some sense, is that text, and that's what my entire being with, I guess, in our context I would add, with God, but our entire being with God is, is living at that moment. Even if it's a secular text, God, I think, for me, God is still there.

*****

We as a family normally recite this once; we normally have a sit down and recite [...] typically once a week, and during that time we try to read from the Arabic, and then we try to understand the English, sometimes we will actually translate the English and read the translation – if not, we will look at what the poet is actually trying to tell us, perhaps look at, read the commentary and discuss the commentary and perhaps look at related stories or instances that occurred with the Prophet Mohamed, Peace Be Upon Him, from which we can learn from, so for us, reciting this poem, not only is it an expression of love for Him, Peace Be Upon Him, but it is also a way that we can learn more about him and a way that we can teach our family about Him, Peace Be Upon Him, so it's quite an intimate, it's quite an intimate gathering that we have, whenever we sit here, we make sure that the room is clean (normally it is not), we burn some 'bahur,' which is a scented, fragranced wood, we burn that on charcoal so we have a, we create a lovely ambience, [my son] sets up the microphones so that we have good acoustics, we try to do some drumming because we just love to get into the spirit of the whole recital. We are quite musical in this family as well.

(SM, British Library, C1765/49)

*****

Prayer experience is different for every person [...] I mean what draws them into the place of worship in the first place, it might be that they just want to be with community [...] they've got something going on in their lives that they just want to be part of a group, so they are just letting it wash over them. Other people will be really fervently thinking about the words [...] If you've got a, say, 200 people in a room, everybody probably has a different reason.

(DL, C1765/28)

These are the words of five different women (two we have heard from before, in Chapter 5, but here we move into a different part of their conversation), representing three different religions: Islam, Christianity and Judaism. These women each tell us something profound about oral reading – about celebrating, sharing, healing, voicing, calm – and at the same time they tell us something equally profound about religious practice – about taking part in something larger than the human self, about service, dignity, spirituality, the 'interior,' community and diversity.

Chapter 6 explores reading aloud in relation to how people are connected with others, and what they (we) are to others, while Chapter 7 looks at how oral reading can be present in the daily structure of working life. Another way that adult lives may be structured, and another way that we may spend time with others and take on roles in relation to others, is through religious identi-fication and observance. The aim of this chapter is to examine the roles that reading aloud can play in this dimension of adult life, to explore as many dif-ferent forms of religious oral reading as possible, from the perspective of indi-vidual participants and as part of the overall endeavour of trying to understand the breadth and meanings of reading aloud in adult life. This chapter is not trying to be a work of theology or a sociology of religion; I am not writing as a specialist in religion. I am, rather, writing as a literacies researcher who has, through the course of a project, noticed that religious practice plays a large part in some adult lives and yet is absent from others. Like many of the oral reading practices we are exploring in this book, forms of religious reading aloud may be largely invisible to those outside of these traditions; in this way, this chapter may help us understand the reading of (some) others a little better.

Reading aloud for religious purposes: the range

There is not one form, type or typical manifestation of religious oral reading but many. One challenge I have wrestled with in writing this chapter is how to convey this diversity of practices with some sort of coherence. Another chal-lenge is to avoid suggesting that all of these religious oral reading practices are either more or less the same (not true), or that they are all completely different (not true either). In this section, I aim to illustrate the extent of the range of practices by highlighting five categories of difference, before, in the next section, examining three elements of communality which run through many of these examples.

Different religions, different systems of belief

The most obvious way that religious oral reading practices differ is that they belong to different religious traditions, with distinct systems of belief and uses of sacred texts. In Gregory et al. (2013), we see songs to the Lord Ganesh sung by Hindu children and the Hail Mary recited by Catholic children, in keeping with the belief systems of each tradition, while the reading aloud of meeting minutes is just as deeply linked to Quaker beliefs (Mace, 2012) as the chanting of poetry to (Islamic) Sufi beliefs (Cancian, 2019). Yet the more interesting, and potentially fundamental, differences may be not between religious traditions but within them.

Formations

Adults read aloud for religious purposes in a range of formations, including completely alone, as one voice reading to a group of listeners, in unison and in varieties of 'call and response.' Interviewee SB describes reading the Quran alone at home every day so that it is 'on your lips' (C1765/07), just as interviewee MA reads her Baha'i prayers (C1765/23,24) and ST reads aloud religious poetry as part of her 'prayer life [...] because I like to hear the resonance of sound and expression and it becomes much more alive for me.' These three women, however, also read aloud for religious purposes communally, and this communality takes different forms. RABiT participant CC reads Gospel passages in Tamil to his wife (C1765/79), SD trains clergy to read to a large Cathedral congregation (C1765/72), ST and CO read prayers, reflections and Gospel passages to smaller gatherings in their community chapel and DL reads passages from the HafTorah to her synagogue study circle (C1765/28).

In the above examples, what is read is often prepared or decided on in advance. Interviewee HAE, however, describes something different: 'This is a moment here. A moment of truth. That's my truth,' he says, pointing at his *Quaker Faith and Practice* book. He explains that in his Quaker meetings 'it depends on if you feel, feel the calling from it. Yesterday I read out that particular passage because it, well it just sang out to me. That was it, it just came out.' When I ask how those he was reading to reacted, he explains:

> Some would respond; some would just hold the quiet. What we do, for an hour on a Sunday, we sit in silence and during that silence, if anybody is felt called to, to say or to read something, then you did.
>
> (C1765/09)

This illustrates quite a different type of religious reading aloud from others, as does the example from Malaysia that opened this chapter. Still another formation is illustrated through 'call and response' models, where one person reads, sings or recites a line or lines to a listening group which then repeats back this line and/or another in response. This is part of a tradition shared by Judaism, Christianity and Hinduism (and no doubt other traditions), and a Skye church group can be heard preparing for Gaelic psalm call and response on recording C1765/54.

Perhaps the most obvious example of communal religious reading, though, is reading in unison: a group of people reading aloud as one voice. Examples from the RABiT recordings include SM's family reading and singing Islamic poems, with drums, every week in their living room (C1765/49) and the Taizé chanting within a religious community in South London – the words of Taizé chants sung from books by a mixed group of Sisters and members of the public, sometimes with guitar accompaniment (C1765/48), replicating (on a much smaller scale) the multilingual chanting tradition of the Taizé community in France, where during the busiest months there may be six thousand people seated cross-legged, chanting, reading or singing in unison (Taizé Community, 2020). Texts are sung, chanted, read and recited from memory in places of worship, homes, community centres and elsewhere by Jews, Muslims, Christians, Buddhists, Hindus, Sikhs, Baha'i, Jains, Zoroastrians (and other religions) across the world, and there are those who do not live near others of their religion but join in with communal worship through the internet, like Baha'i interviewee MA(C1765/24). In all of these cases, we have many voices becoming one.

Physicality: bodies, objects and spaces

The use of individual voices or voices in unison is one aspect of the physicality of oral reading. Uses of (the rest of) bodies, objects and spaces are others. Forms of religious oral reading differ in their uses of the voice (different volumes, styles and rhythms) and body: as participants are seated on benches, cross-legged on the floor, prostrate or standing, still or moving around, alone or in larger or small groups of other bodies, holding hands or linking arms or not, reciting from memory with faces tilted upwards, eyes open or closed, reading from texts displayed high up on screens or gazing skyward, faces bent down in prayer or to read from texts held in hands. Griffiths writes of wooden holders created to hold palm leaf Buddhist manuscripts in India for a seated reader or teacher to comfortably read from (1999, p. 121), reminding me of interviewee LC's explanation (in the context of drama and voice work) of the importance of the position of the head and torso: 'the minute you put your face down to your book to read, it does change the way your voice works' (C1765/48).

The position of the body affects the sound of the voice, as does the place where the reading happens – whether in a small room at home or in a huge place of worship, newly built or hundreds of years old, wooden or stone, with a sound system or not. Architecture, candles, cloths, artwork, statues are all part of the physicality of oral reading and all affect how a voice is experienced by both readers and listeners. Lukkala's (2019) research into the 'soundscapes' of Finnish Orthodox Christian worship is helpful here. She argues that 'praising God with voice' through 'words that are being read or sung aloud and heard' is key to Orthodox teaching and its emphasis on communal worship. She defines a 'soundscape' as 'everything a person can hear in a given place and time' and stresses that 'the concept of soundscape includes subjectivity. What people perceive and pay attention to as well as the meanings people give to different sounds vary, and so do their experiences of soundscapes' (Lukkala, 2019). A 'soundscape,' in this view, is at least partly subjective and relates to what participants find personally and culturally meaningful. The 'soundscapes' of Orthodox worship are formed not only by voices and the acoustics of architectural space but also by physical objects:

> The metal cup hanging on chains that the deacon is holding and swinging in certain parts of the service is the *censer*, with incense inside. Swinging it makes a jingling sound that can be quite loud, especially if there are bells attached to the chains [...]. Censing is an example of a part of the soundscape of Orthodox worship that is not a human voice. Thus, the worship sounds include sung and read biblical texts, prayers and hymnography, the alternation of voices of different people, the alternation of reading and singing, different melodies and musical styles used, other sounds of liturgical action, and possibly other sounds, more or less related to the service itself.
>
> (Lukkala, 2019)

All of this, she argues, contributes to the experience of Finnish Orthodox worship, and each of these elements – bodies, objects and spaces – are ways that acts and sounds of religious reading aloud can differ, echoing the messages from the RABiT data.

Texts

We can also see religious oral reading from different types of text. There are several dimensions of difference here. The first we could describe as how the text relates to the religious activity. Both Tusting (2000) and Rosowsky (2008) provide examples of newsletters (from a Roman Catholic Church and a Mosque, respectively) which may contain a combination of practical community information as well as more devotional elements. These, or parts of them, may well be read aloud, but this reading aloud has a different function to other instances of oral reading that are part of the worship event or gathering (more practical or organisational, perhaps, than devotional). Other types of texts read aloud for religious purposes in the RABiT data include prayers, poetry, passages of Holy Books and hymns or songs. In each case, we could think about who the reader is reading *as* (the subject position or persona of the reading voice) and *to whom*. For example, a hymn may be sung *as* a community voice and *to* both each other and God; a prayer may be read *as* an individual *to* God; an item from a newsletter may be read on behalf of a local community to other members of that community; interviewee NM (C1765/55, 56) reading Gospel passages, in Scottish Gaelic or in English, to a congregation may be reading *as* the Gospel writer and *to* the congregation (as a conduit between the two); while the Islamic or Catholic creeds may often be understood as read by each believer as a vow to her- or himself.

A second dimension of difference around texts is their difference as physical objects: books or photocopied sheets? Phone screens or large screens? This is partly a difference again of body positioning but also about ownership: is someone reading from their own personal copy of a text (like the mother-of-pearl covered Bible received by Observer F77 as a present from her parents for learning to read) or reading from a shared text? Interviewee MG speaks of large screens in Ethiopian Orthodox churches in London, providing both English and Amharic translations of Ge'etz (C1765/76), and in a church in Skye, I saw screens where English translations of Gaelic readings were provided. Sánchez Tyson reports a Mayan speaker using a Mayan language Bible app to read from her phone (2021) and Cuban (2019) notes Haitian women in Chile reading Bible extracts in Haitian French to each other from their phones.

Here we can also think about whether 'the text' is a physical text at all, or whether the text is internal, something recited from memory. The RABiT recordings include three examples of psalms: NS (C1765/40) and NM (C1765/56) both chose to read Psalm 23, NS in English and NM in Scottish Gaelic. Both men are reading from the written text (that is, with the text in front of them, looking at it) though they have read this psalm many times before. LH, 103 years old, recites Psalm 91 from memory (C1765/35), just as, he told me, he did at his brother's funeral. LH is blind and explained that he started to recite the psalms from memory long before he lost his sight, as part of what he remembers as the tradition of the Jamaica of his boyhood. The Malaysia case study which opened this chapter is also about reciting from memory, with 'the text' internalised (and we will come back to reciting from memory later in this chapter).

Languages

The fact that we can find different languages used within different religious traditions and different parts of the world is of course no surprise. Within the RABiT data, we see reading aloud in Scottish Gaelic in a Gaelic-speaking community in Skye, reading in Tamil in the Tamil Catholic community in London and the Arabic-speaking MA reading in Arabic for Baha'i worship in Glasgow. What may be more surprising are the uses of different languages within the same traditions, contexts and even instances of worship. Rosowsky (2012) describes observing a Mosque school in an English town where the Imam moves between Arabic, Urdu, Punjabi and English, reflecting both the multilingual community the Mosque serves and the specific purposes each language takes on in individual and community lives. In the above-mentioned Taizé community in France, multiple languages are used in each service, including French, German, English, Spanish, Portuguese, Polish and Cantonese, all languages of the community and its visitors. The weekly 10AM Sunday mass in my local Catholic church in South London is an English-language service but contains some lines of Latin and New Testament Greek. There are dozens of languages spoken within the congregation, and at times the Our Father, Hail Mary and the Creed (elements which are likely to be spoken from memory) are recited by individuals within the congregation in the languages they *feel* these words best in; for example, a Colombian reciting in Spanish or a Hungarian in Hungarian.

We can also look at the RABiT data and beyond to remind ourselves that a great deal of religious reading aloud happens in languages that participants only use for that religious purpose (and this may be a language they can speak and/ or understand or it may not be). There are two examples of this in the pilot study data: a Hindi- and English-speaking Muslim man who explains that he does not understand many words in Quranic Arabic and an older Catholic English-speaking man remembering occasional masses in Latin, where again, he did not understand many words but like the Hindi- and English-speaking Muslim has a wider understanding of the text and rituals. The range of languages used for religious oral reading, therefore, reflects the histories and beliefs of specific religious traditions (including their internal debates and schisms) as well as the paths that individuals have taken in their lives – all this can be audible in religious practice.

Exploring communalities

We will now turn to exploring what all these instances of religious reading aloud may have in common, looking at three themes: *memory, meditation and meaning; meeting places*, and *the fixed and the fluid*.

Memory, meditation and meaning

Many of the forms of religious reading aloud discussed above involve acts of memory. This includes concentrated attention to committing texts to memory, such as the formal process within the Ethiopian Orthodox Church described by interviewee MG, where children first learn the Ge'ez alphabet and then to decode written scripture with a teacher correcting their pronunciation, and then, for those interested:

> everything has to be memorized [...] To do that, they need to read it aloud to themselves and to the teacher or the clergy to hear it and [...] they are reading this one in the day time; in the evening they will recite what they have learnt, without the book [...] It could be, I mean the whole of chapter of, for instance, the book of St Paul or St John [...] They recite all that, they read, they recite and they have read it aloud to memorise it [...] has to be done, as I said, piece by piece [...] and they need to do it time and time again.
>
> (C1765/76)

We can also find examples in the accounts of three of the co-authors of Gregory et al. (2013): Ilankuberan being taught the words of Avvayar to sing to Ganesh at a Hindu Temple, Kwapong's description of Ghanaian Pentecostal children being taught Psalm 23 in the Twi language, and Choudhury as part of her Islamic religious education:

> Mesab (the Sylheti word used during Arabic classes to refer to the Arabic teacher) would test the children every week, being particularly fussy with the length of time taken to prolong certain words. As I recited to him each week in my nervous, soft voice, he would listen attentively; looking down on the floor would mean his ears were poking up facing me. [...] Reciting it too fast would mean he would stop me and ask me to repeat. Repeating meant I had made a mistake. Making more mistakes meant he would recite in his deep, loud voice.
>
> (Gregory et al., 2013, pp. 35–36)

We can also find examples of religious texts committed to memory through constant hearing and repeating, or reading and repeating, as part of regular religious practice. Thinking about to what extent she has memorised the prayers she recites at her Synagogue, DL notes, 'it's the same prayers week in week out, so it does become an automatic' (C1765/28), and the final Gregory et al. co-author, Woodham, describes Polish children learning the Zdrowaś Maryjo (Hail Mary) through regular bedtime and church reciting:

> Polish children from Catholic families learn The Hail Mary Prayer from their parents when they say prayers at home, usually at bedtime. [...] It is a moment of calmness and intimacy, a moment of reflection on the day that has ended [...] At the Polish School attached to this Church, the Hail Mary Prayer together with the Lord's Prayer and the Prayer to the Holy Spirit are said each Saturday morning at assembly time. The priest stands on the stage with hands put together and the children, parents and teachers turned towards him say the three prayers in unison in Polish language. It is a very powerful shared statement of cultural and linguistic belonging as the words of the prayer sound immediately familiar to everyone present.
>
> (Gregory et al., 2013, pp. 43–44)

Whether memorisation happens through specific training or rather through repeated engagement in religious practice; whether we call these instances of speaking, chanting or singing words from memory 'reciting' (or not); whether the 'readers' in each case have a written text in front of them (or not) and whether a definitive written version exists at all are points of variation. But what strikes me here is that 'the text' is something which has often been internalised – it is something and somewhere inside each of these people. Interestingly, interviewee JR, who speaks about processes of internalising text as an actor (see Chapter 5, pp. 72–73), noted, as I was packing up my recording equipment, that he used to be a Quaker and feels that religious experience (like acting) can also involve internalising texts, 'making them part of you.'

Crucially, though, these processes of memorisation and recall, repetition and recitation are not experienced (at least not always) as something robotic or mechanical, the way we may sometimes talk disparagingly about 'rote learning.' Rather, across different religious traditions memorisation and recitation are associated with forms of meditation, creativity and the accessing of deeper meanings or understandings. I came across three examples during the RABiT project. The first was in Addis Ababa, where I met a theologian who took me to observe some Ethiopian Orthodox church groups, teaching me about the reading and poetry schools within this tradition and explaining that the progression from reading to memorisation is then followed by the creative composition of poetry or theological texts. He noted that this is based on the idea that it is from the meditative experiences of reciting from memory that both wisdom and creativity are born (see also Belachew, 2013; Woldeyes, 2017).

The second example comes from one of the RABiT interviews, where a ST explains the tradition of Lectio Divina:

> Going right back in history [...] it's exactly what it says, sacred reading, so it was when very few people could read, and it was mainly going back to the past, far in the past, when a monk or the head monk had all the other monks sort of sitting there and he would read a passage out loud and usually it was read more than once, and then when one of the monks felt touched or moved [...] he would leave the actual place where they were meeting and then he would return to his cell to repeat that and see what that word means to him. A way of sacred reading, sacred praying.

A tradition from the third century AD, Lectio Divina is also central to a new practical guide for those leading prayer produced by the (London) Southwark Spirituality Commission, where its four stages are expressed as: Lectio (reading and focus on literal meeting), Meditatio (meditation 'Chew it over. Listen to the inner message of the word'), Oratio (pray 'Savour the essence. Talk to God about it') and Contemplation ('Let the Word quietly penetrate and nourish your being') (Archdiocese of Southwark Spirituality Commission, 2019). As in other analyses of Lectio Divina (see, for example, Casey, 1996), this guide emphasises the internalisation of text, allowing for words to settle within and 'nourish' one's being as part of a transformative and creative prayer experience.

The third example comes from an event I attended in March 2019, 'Juz Amma, The Qur'an in public', where a group of women, including members of the Inclusive Mosque Initiative (IMI) and Madinah Javed of the Female Reciters campaign, discussed (amongst other things) the meditative and aesthetic qualities of Quran recitation and whether or not reciters (or listeners) need to understand all or most of the Arabic. There was general agreement that there are different forms of meditation and meaning which come from the sounds, rhythms and sacredness of the recited text, as well as the meaning of the words. A woman in the audience noted how a Sufi sage had told her that even if she does not understand much Arabic, she should recite the Quran 'as if you have a piece of gold in your mouth' because the act of recitation has 'healing properties' (a podcast of this event is available as *All The Ways We Could Grow*, 2019).

This is not to say that the Ethiopian Orthodox, Lectio Divina, Sufi and other Muslim recitation traditions are the same, or to ignore their specific points of emphasis. And this is certainly not to say that these are the only examples of recitation used or understood in this way. Rather, these are examples which demonstrate the belief that recitation from memory can be something meditative, creative and transformative.

Meeting places

With Quakerism [...] the Society of Friends, that's its other name, [...] it is like speaking closely with friends, in the true sense of the word.
(HAE, C1765/09)

When I go to bible study groups we tend to take it in turns to read sections from the bible, or read a verse each. It is as if reading aloud is a way of bringing us together as well as focussing our minds.
(MO, F30)

I used to go to the synagogue where I would hear the Rabbi read aloud.
(questionnaire)

I like to hear the Bible and prayers being read in French. I sometimes go to a French church to hear this.
(questionnaire)

Not only do we do this weekly as a family, which is just us and our children, but we also hold a monthly recital at our community centre [...] it's just something that we've always found really, something we do as a family that we really enjoy and that brings us together.
(SM, C1765/49)

A key theme, perhaps *the* key theme, running across religious oral reading is the idea of reading aloud as fellowship with other people and with God/s. This can be a togetherness in a physical place (the synagogue, French church or community centre above), it can be a togetherness in voice and language, and it can be a togetherness in time. Lukkala's (2019) above-mentioned research into Finnish Orthodox 'soundscapes' not only links the importance of 'common prayer' with the sounds of oral reading (and other sounds of communal worship) but also makes another link:

> Worship as sanctification of time, as it were, is related to the physical ephemerality of sounds. People must set apart a certain period of time to go to a divine service, to listen, to sing, to pray together.
>
> (Lukkala, 2019)

Religious worship has a particular relationship with notions and experiences of time, and, as Lukkala highlights, its sounds (including the sounds of oral reading) are central to this. On one hand, this is 'time' as we often talk of it: people need to make time in their lives to worship, and in worship, people make and hear sounds and 'the physical ephemerality' of these sounds is part of the experience of that present moment. Yet also, religious worship itself is something which questions or resists everyday notions of time and invites participants instead to think about 'being present' to and for different things and with different people and to recognise (in some traditions) past historical moments as present reality. Taking Lukkala's point forward, we could argue that oral reading in particular brings together all these notions or experiences of time. A woman in Finland reading aloud a certain prayer is, in that present moment of saying and hearing, united not only with those she can hear worshiping around her but also with those others who are reciting that same text across the world at the same time, and with all those who have recited that same text in the past and will in the future. This idea echoes how interviewee NS views the reading of psalms:

> They are the backbone of the daily worship, and they are poems, and they were made to be chanted, so they chant very well, and there's a particular way in the Anglican tradition that each verse is said slowly and meditatively with a break in the middle so it has a rhythm to it as you go through it [...] and that's very important, and even when you are reading on your own, you have the sense that others elsewhere are doing the same reading, so it's linked with being together to read these texts which are thousands of years old and [...] which are about living and loving and being loved and hating and being angry and being hurt and feeling lost and all life's conditions [...] it's still the same funda-mental texts, and it takes you right back through three thousand years, and of course it's something which is going on all around the world too, so, and it also, it links you with the experience of Jewish people, if you are Christian, with Jewish people, so that's an enrichment because these are shared texts, they do bind people together.
>
> (C1765/38)

Here, he links the rhythms and messages (covering 'all life's conditions') of psalms with how their recitation connects people across geographical space, time and religious traditions. I am borrowing Barrs' (2000, p. 54) idea of the text as 'meeting place' between writer and reader (which we will examine further in the next chapter) and using it to suggest that the present moment of reading aloud, and/or hearing, sacred texts is *a meeting place* for worshippers past, present and future. This meeting place is present in the memorisation, meditation and meanings of the previous theme and within the dynamism between the fixed and fluid of the next.

The fixed and the fluid

This third theme is a tension, or perhaps dynamism, which runs throughout many descriptions of religious oral reading: between texts that are fixed (and unchanging, whether existing in written form or not) and texts which co-exist in multiple variations. Rosowsky (2012) borrows Fishman's (1989) term 'religious classical' in his analysis of the relationship between the deliberately unchanging liturgical or sacred languages (and their texts) and the 'other' languages used in and around religious practice which are ever-changing, shifting and cross-fertilising. Both forms of language, Rosowsky argues, are central to the identities of members of religious communities and their 'translocal and transnational linguistic repertoires.' The fixed nature of the texts in or of the 'religious classical' is key to their cultural role and how they function as a 'meeting point' (remembering the last theme) across space and time, unifying readers across the world who are reciting exactly the same words, in the same language, in the same order. Yet, alongside reading or reciting texts in the religious classical (such as Quranic Arabic or Biblical Hebrew), Rosowsky's participants use other languages (such as Punjabi and English) to pray, read and talk about their religion. We can see an example of this dynamism in the home worship of SM's family, as they read the Quran in Arabic and other devotional texts in Arabic, Urdu and English.

> For us, it's very important that we not only read the Arabic but we also read the English, so we try to make sure that whatever we read we have an English translation too because my parents are from Pakistan and so are my husband's parents, and we have, our mother tongue is Urdu [...] a lot of the vocabulary from Urdu is similar to Arabic, so for us when we read things in Arabic, it resonates with us [...] but for our children, who are here, and are British, they are not fluent in Urdu unfortunately, and their mother tongue is English, so for them they don't have that connection, so we always try to make sure that we have an English commentary and an English translation to what we are reading and reciting so we can make sure that we involve them and encourage them.
>
> (SM, C1765/49)

All three of these languages hold a place in the religious lives, and oral reading, of the family.

Interviewees CO and ST discuss their experiences of reading the same religious texts in English and French:

CO: for me it's a completely different experience, two texts, the same text in two different [...] there's a whole different way. Each language, I think, has its way of being and of doing and of encountering the world [...]

ST: Both of us have lived in other countries at other times and the language of our congregation is French [...] it's very interesting because I lived in France for 20 years, and I'm now going to move to Belgium, where I'll speak French again, and I'm speaking about only body and ownership. For me, the visceral part of a language is something that needs to be explored much more, I think [...] if I'm reading in French, I quite like reading in French [...] but my body is not quite engaged in the same way; it doesn't touch my intestines if you like or the deeper part, so saying something about the reading out loud, it's not just vocal, an articulation, it's something about my whole, my whole being engages.

This is a slightly different form of tension between the fixed and the fluid or varied. Here they are comparing the experience of reading the same fixed text (the Christian Bible) but now in two different (still 'fixed' to a certain extent and certainly 'authorised') languages, and it may well be the 'fixedness' of both the French and English texts that allows such a direct comparison of the experience. We can also (in some religious traditions) find examples of different versions of a text in the same language, as Observer M51 notes:

Often we will have more than one translation of the Bible. There is always a variation in the arrangement of words between say, the King James, New International, or Good News translations of the Bible. For example, the Gospel of St John 3:16 –

King James Version:

For God loved the world, that he gave his only begotten Son, that whosoever believeth in him should not perish, but have everlasting life.

Good News version:

For God loved the world so much that he gave his only Son, so that everyone who believes in him may not die but have eternal life.

New International Version:

For God so loved the world that he gave his one and only Son, that whoever believes in him shall not perish but have eternal life.

Reading one version and hearing it in another is an interesting exercise in how the brain processes information. It is almost as though you are seeing two sides of one thing at the same time or getting two different angles on an object.

(MO, M51)

Interviewee CD reflects similarly on differences in Scots and English Bibles:

> I've got a Scots Bible at home, and I sometimes read that, and it's just a different way of the same thing, and it gives you a different view. [...] 'the skies were filled with the heavenly host,' I think it says in the English. 'All of a sudden the heavens were festooned wi angels'.
>
> (C1765/57)

Both identify the experience of reading two versions as providing 'different angles,' 'a different view.' Another interviewee, CO, expresses this as both 'curse' and 'blessing':

> I guess one thing that might change a lot in sacred reading is that from one translation to another, you're going to have different words, different verbs, different sentence structures that are used, and that can be interesting in itself; it's like, 'oh I thought I knew this text and oh, oh, they used this word here, ok ok,' that's interesting [...] it's also kind of a trap because you know I've found myself sometimes babbling on and it's like oh, oh wait, no it's a different translation, read the text for what it is [...] at the same time it's a blessing and a curse [...] a text that you know that well, how to be attentive to it, to the point where you can hear something new, and you can hear it said in a different way.

In these examples, the tension or dynamism is between different versions of sacred texts – whether these different versions reflect different languages, religious traditions, time periods or publishers – and, to use CO's terms above, the 'curse' is potential confusion or disorientation, while the 'blessing' is the new 'view' or 'angle,' a defamiliarisation which allows renewed 'attentiveness' to words and meanings.

As a final thought on the different forms of the fixed and the varied, the Sisters also felt that even the very same text can become different over time because we, as readers, become different:

CO: For me, it's never a repetition [...] it's always different, and that's going to depend on a lot of things, it's going to depend on what I'm living, especially if it's a sacred text, on what I'm living in that moment, things are going to speak to me differently [...]

ST: So it will depend on where you are now.

CO: Yes, what I was saying about living that text, it's all part of it, where am I, where am I now, and that's going to influence how I read that text, even if it's one that I could, you know, recite almost by heart.

ST: So it will always be new [...] I think the word 'repetition', it doesn't mean just repeat [...] it means to go back to that, to savour and to chew that word.

Conclusion

This chapter was not an attempt at a theological or religious ethnography; it has not been written by an expert in religion, and it simply could not include all of the religious traditions of the world (however wonderful this would be). Rather, it aimed to capture some of the diversity of religious oral reading, the themes or meanings expressed and the questions raised. Some of these themes and questions – for example around repetition, meditation and meanings, and the idea of the 'meeting place' – will be picked up on again in the next chapter when we think about literary reading.

References

All The Ways We Could Grow: Juz Amma, The Qur'an in Public. (2019, March). https://soundcloud.com/free-word/atwwcg-juz-amma.

Archdiocese of Southwark Spirituality Commission. (2019). *Ways into Prayer Leader's Guide: Praying with the Bible: Lectio Divina- Sacred Reading*. Southwark Spirituality Commission.

Barrs, M. (2000). The reader in the writer. *Reading*, 34(2), 54–60.

Belachew, T. (2013). From Abba Salama to King Lalibela: Christian traditions in Ethiopia are among the oldest in the world. *Christian History Magazine* (105).

Cancian, A. (2019). Sufism. *British Library Discovering Sacred Texts*. https://www.bl.uk/sacred-texts/articles/sufism.

Casey, M. (1996). *Sacred Reading: The Ancient Art of Lectio Divina*. Triumph Books.

Cuban, S. (2019, June 27). *Mapping immigrant women's journeys for education and opportunities*. Informal Literacy Discussion, UCL Institute of Education.

Fishman, J. A. (1989). *Language and Identity in Minority Sociolinguistic Perspective*. Multilingual Matters.

Gregory, E., Choudhury, H., Ilankuberan, A., Kwapong, A., & Woodham, M. (2013). Practice, performance and perfection: Learning sacred texts in four faith communities in London. *International Journal of the Sociology of Language*, 2013(220), 27–48. https://doi.org/10.1515/ijsl-2013-0012.

Griffiths, P. J. (1999). *Religious Reading: The Place of Reading in the Practice of Religion*. Oxford University Press.

Lukkala, T. (2019). The soundscape of Orthodox Christian worship and participants' experiences – at the start of fieldwork. *Music and the Sacred*, 41(2). http://musiikinsuunta.fi/2019/02/.

Mace, J. (2012). *God and Decision-Making: A Quaker Approach*. Quaker Books.

Rosowsky, A. (2008). *Heavenly Readings: Liturgical Literacy in a Multilingual Context, Vol. 9*. Multilingual Matters.

Rosowsky, A. (2012). Performance and flow: The religious classical in translocal and transnational linguistic repertoires. *Journal of Sociolinguistics*, 16(5), 613–637. https://doi.org/10.1111/j.1467-9841.2012.00542.x.

Sánchez Tyson, L. (2021, projected). Literacy for life and work? Exploring an Indigenous bilingual education programme for adults in Mexico. Doctoral dissertation, UCL Institute of Education.

Taizé Community. (2020). https://www.taize.fr/en [accessed 5 June, 2020].

Tusting, K. (2000). New literacy studies and time. In D. Barton, M. Hamiton & R. Ivanič (Eds.), *Situated Literacies: Reading and Writing in Context* (pp. 35–53). Routledge.

Woldeyes, Y. G. (2017). *Native Colonialism: Education and the Economy of Violence Against Traditions in Ethiopia*. The Red Sea Press.

9

LITERARY LIFE

Production, performance, experience and the *Wordhord*

What exactly is a literary life? Do some people have a literary life – perhaps those who work in publishing or go to book launches and read literary papers in extended kitchens while chatting on the phone to their poet uncle about the latest gossip from the playwright who used to live with their mother-in-law – while the rest of us do not? Does a 'literary life' have to include such (potential) agonies as:

> My first reaction to this topic was to recall the end of Evelyn Waugh's novel *A Handful of Dust*, where the hero, stranded in the Amazonian rainforest, is rescued by a strange eccentric. The latter is illiterate and in return for saving the hero's life makes him read the complete works of Dickens aloud day after interminable day, a fate, we are invited to think, almost worse than death.
>
> (MO, M50)

Or rather does a 'literary life' mean a creative and story-alive life, awake to the experiences of others, whether reading, writing, singing, hearing, watching or imagining them? I am arguing the latter, that each person has a literary life, the side of our lives concerned with, or captivated by, forms of literature and storytelling (which I'm defining fairly openly and loosely as stories and songs, plays, novels and poems), for example:

> I belong to a poetry reading group. I write poems and also perform at 'open mic' sessions regularly in pubs and cafes.
>
> (questionnaire)

> Sunday 22nd: My partner C and I both enjoy spending around an hour in bed early on weekend mornings, reading books over a cup of tea. On this morning I was reading an Icelandic crime novel in translation and read aloud to C a couple of sentences about the breakfast eaten by one of the characters in the novel – porridge and liver sausage – as to

English tastes this seems an unlikely and alarming combination and I wanted to share with him this strange discovery.

(MO, F46)

I often read the words to songs which I am trying to learn (in particular Latin, French, German, Russian, Italian and one time in the past year Swahili and Hebrew).

(questionnaire)

Robson (2012) starts her study of the decline in school poetry recitation in Britain and the United States by addressing several 'schisms' relating to trends in public, school and university treatments of poetry in the nineteenth and early twentieth centuries: 'Of these schisms, I direct particular notice to the chasm that yawns between ideas about poetry within the university and those that pertain elsewhere,' (2012, p. 20). The 'elsewhere' is where her (and my) interest lies, which, crucially, is not a lesser or simplified idea of literature but one which focusses on the place of poetry in a range of different adult lives. This, extended to other literary forms, is the perspective underlying this chapter. The literary is part of most adult lives, to a greater or lesser extent, though it may look different in different instances. Across the RABiT data, we have people of all ages, linguistic, cultural and educational backgrounds reading (aloud or not) poems, plays, stories and novels and listening to others reading them, live or from audiobooks or the radio, or writing poems, novels, stories and plays, alone and with others, and often sharing these with writing groups large and small. Participants at the five RABiT regional community events also talked about storytelling around fires in Ghana, Ethiopia and Scandinavia, poetry on the underground in London and New York, the Wall Poems in the Netherlands, book groups organised for refugee children in Jordan, teenagers painting poems on walls in Bolivia, and women's Buqualah poetry in Algeria. These are more examples of literary lives.

The importance of sound

While recognising that not everyone is able to speak or hear (and that literary experience includes far more than the spoken and heard), it is nevertheless important to note that the ear and voice are often considered to play a large role in literary experience, and to acknowledge perspectives such as, 'all real literature is addressed to the mind through the ear not the eye' and 'poetry, like religion, must be experienced to be understood and to be experienced, it must rightly be heard' (Eaton, 1913, pp. 151–152). These words were written over a hundred years ago, at a time when their author already thought that such a reminder was needed (a time when previously strong traditions of memorising and reciting poetry had significantly weakened in both the UK and US, as analysed by Robson, 2012). Eaton was writing about poetry in particular, and his

137

PART 2

full discussion examines ideas of metre and rhythm and their relationships to meaning, as well as the links between this oral/aural 'experience' and ways of understanding poetry. This may remind us of the discussion of recitation, meditation and meaning in Chapter 8. It also calls to mind Eliot's 'auditory imagination' and the sense of sound and rhythm in poetry communicating something deeper or even more 'primitive' than conscious thought (Eliot, 1964; Pullinger, 2017, pp. 21–22). It is certainly echoed by RABiT questionnaire responses such as 'I read poetry aloud because part of the meaning is in the sound' and 'Poetry NEEDS to be read aloud to get the rhythm and feeling of the words. I read striking texts aloud to absorb them.'

Eighty years later, in 1989, and thinking about the short story rather than the poem, Margaret Atwood provided a similar reminder, arguing that the 'the voice of the story' means

> something more specific: a speaking voice, like the singing voice in music, that moves not across space, across the page, but through time. Those little black marks on the page mean nothing without their retranslation into sound [...] Perhaps, by abolishing the Victorian practice of family reading and by removing from the school curriculum those old standbys, the set memory piece and the recitation, we've deprived both writers and readers of something essential to stories. We've lead them to believe that prose comes in visual blocks, not in rhythms and cadences; that its texture should be flat because a page is flat; that written emotion should not be immediate, like a drumbeat, but more remote, like a painted landscape [...] When I asked a group of young writers, earlier this year, how many of them ever read their own work aloud, not one of them said she did. I'm not arguing for the abolition of the eye, merely for the reinstatement of the voice and for an appreciation of the way it carries the listener along with it at the pace of the story.
>
> (Atwood, 2005, p. 71)

Atwood ends this essay with the further reminder, 'From listening to the stories of others, we learn to tell our own' (2005, p. 79), a statement which carries a meaning more precise than the idea that we learn from others, as we will explore later in this chapter.

Another decade later, Brown's edited collection *The Pressures of the Text: Orality, Texts and the Telling of Tales* (1995) examines relationships between printed literature and oral performance, with a particular focus on African and Caribbean traditions. The collection opens with a line from poet (and psychiatrist) Femi Oyebode: 'the text only lives through the human voice' (Brown, 1995, p. i), an idea threaded throughout all the contributions in this collection, providing another reminder of the potential roles of the voice and ear in literary experience. We could imagine some RABiT participants responding to Brown, Oyebode, Atwood and Eaton, explaining that they do read poems out loud,

138

they do read their own stories aloud as they write, that their voices (and ears) are indeed appreciated and not about to be forgotten. And yet in 1913, 1989, 1995 we may well have needed, and may still need in 2020, reminders that literary life, for some at least, centres on the voice, ear and forms of oral reading.

'Role-taking' and 'the meeting place'

Dorothy Heathcote, in a seminal 1970 paper 'How does drama serve thinking, talking, and writing?' states that drama in education has 'two significant aspects and aims. One of these we can define as "creative work," the other as "coping-work". Both are significant areas of experience in the developing person' (1970, p. 1077). She poses the question 'How does role-taking help in these processes of coping and creating?' and discusses the ways that any of us may 'act out,' rehearse or prepare ourselves for a difficult situation by identifying with others and 're-living' or 'pre-living situations of importance' (p. 1077). Barrs (1987) takes on Heathcote's idea of 'role-taking' as central to the experiences of both drama and reading (the text 'lives through us') and notes that the link between reading and role-taking is particularly acute for oral reading: 'if we consider what is involved in reading aloud, the links between reading and enactment are apparent' because when we read aloud we 'lend the text not only our consciousness, but, actually, our breath' (Barrs, 1987, p. 209). Reading – particularly oral reading – is a form of role-taking.

Heathcote ends her 1970 article with seven aspects of 'the teacher's role in employing drama in education,' the last of which is 'To understand that drama is *not* stories retold, but confrontations between individuals standing up, lived at life-rate' (1970, p. 1080). Similarly, from the aforementioned Brown collection, Nanton (1995, p. 88) stresses 'an essential characteristic of oral performance has to be the present tense, a story is a life event happening now. The recipient literally has to be within earshot.' Heathcote writes of drama and Nanton writes of oral performance, and yet I would argue that the use of the voice and ear in reading aloud extends this idea of the 'present-tense' 'life-rate' 'happening-now'-ness to a wider range of literary experience (and sometimes religious experience, as discussed in Chapter 8) because oral reading creates a physically embodied, spoken and heard, moment in time. The reading of literature, particularly out loud, is not the retelling or repeating of the same thing, the same story, the same work, but always the unfolding of something new, the story or poem lived again, now in the act of reading (this may remind us of some of the ideas about religious reading towards the end of Chapter 8). In a later article, Barrs (2000) uses the term 'meeting place' for this present-tense place where reader and writer are united through not only the literary text but, when read aloud, through oral enactment in a specific place and time. I am arguing that the concepts of 'role-taking' and 'the meeting place' can help us understand the role of oral reading in the literary life.

PART 2

Literary life: production

We could call one aspect of this literary life *production*: how people produce or create, compose or write literary works. This includes those who see themselves as writers or poets, who make a living from their work and/or are published, as well as those (many more) who write or compose without seeing themselves as 'real writers' or even sharing their work. RABiT participants write poems, stories, plays and novels, for themselves, family members and friends, writing things they share or never share, alone and in different sorts of writing groups (including an Observer who included in his submission a long and beautiful piece he had written for his father), those who write in their spare time, and as those for whom writing is the day job. Each tells us something about the possible relationships between oral reading and acts of literary production.

Reading aloud as role-taking to edit

In Chapter 7 we explored 'writers' as one group of 'reading aloud professionals' – that is, those who use oral reading as an important part of their work. We looked at how writers and editors read text aloud to help them notice errors or awkwardness and make necessary adjustments. Observer M50, for example, notes 'sometimes when I'm writing something, I will read it aloud to see if it sounds right rhythmically.'

A pilot study participant, a singer and songwriter, speaks of reading aloud as part of her creative composition and revision processes and the double role this involves:

> When you are writing something and as you're reading it [aloud], there is a different word that comes into this place that is better [...] it's like someone else presenting it because you have a double facet kind of thing, double position, you are the writer and at the same time also the listener, so you are reading and listening and you are hearing it [...] I change it because it fits better than what I had written previously.
>
> (F70s)

Similarly, interviewee CS discusses her uses of reading aloud for hearing and 'testing' her poetry:

> Sometimes it's to test out whether something that I think is occupying a space on a page also occupies a sound space. I think a lot of poets do it to see what something sounds like because there is a relationship, it seems to me, with what is verbalised and what is written [...] you are finding out whether it is what you intended it to be, if that makes sense. [...] I see it as testing, testing whether it needs to be adjusted, written, to what it sounds like spoken.
>
> (British Library, C1765/10)

Interviewee AL writes short fiction and speaks of how supportive he finds writing groups, valuing both 'listening to everyone reading stories aloud' and the opportunity to hear someone else reading his draft work: 'I prefer someone to read it out for me so I can listen.' Someone else takes on the role of reader, while he takes on the role of listener. Returning to Barrs' take on role-taking, we can see this as a writer taking on a 'sense of the reader' (Barrs, 1987, p. 209), taking on the role(s) of listener, audience or judge in order to 'focus on what it sounds like' (AL).

Reading aloud as taking on the role of writer

Oral reading as a form of taking on the role of judge, listener or 'other' is the most common way the relationship between oral reading and writing is expressed in the RABiT data. Yet, there is another way that oral reading relates to role-taking and writing, as suggested by the closing line of Margaret Atwood's essay discussed above: 'From listening to the stories of others, we learn to tell our own' (2005, p. 79). Barrs also examines how reading, and particularly oral reading, allows the reader to become or take on the role of a writer. Through reading aloud and listening to others reading (that 'meeting place' between writer and reader), the reader gains 'a sense of the author's voice,' taking in rhythms, patterns and structures of language and thus becoming able to write in a similar way: 'Writers who are also readers are people with a large number of tunes and structures in their heads' (Barrs, 2000, p. 55). Reading aloud allows us to take *in* examples of writing and therefore take *on* the role of writer. Barrs' own research with children's writing development demonstrates that 'reading aloud seemed to be a particularly helpful way of foregrounding the tunes and rhythms of a text in a way that subsequently influenced children's writing' (2000, p. 59).

This form of oral reading as role-taking is less obvious in the RABiT data, apart from the striking observation that those participants who say that they write also report doing a great deal of oral reading; for example, interviewee GD, who attends poetry groups where participants read and discuss published poems as well as groups where they read and discuss their own work in progress. A questionnaire participant also reports reading aloud 'To try to remember a style of language so I can later imitate it (both in my native language and in languages I am trying to perfect).' We could also remember the many high-profile writers who talk about the importance of reading, or listening to, the words of other writers. Stephen King, in his *Paris Review* interview, is asked 'What did you learn from writers like Faulkner, Dreiser, and McCullers?' He replies 'The voices. I'm reading All the King's Men again now, but I'm also listening to it on CD. [...] You hear it and you say to yourself, Oh man, that's the voice! It just clicks in your head.' (Lehmann-Haupt & Rich, 2007, pp. 488–489).

Reading aloud: walking, talking and claiming spaces

The RABiT interviewees say two more things about reading aloud and literary production. Interviewee GD explains:

> I like haiku, and I write haiku, so I like to go on a Ginko, a haiku walk, along the river, but I speak it as I am walking, and walking and speaking at the same time you get a rhythm, I think. Sometimes when I'm out, I might see something that might inspire a haiku, and other times [...] while I'm walking it kind of falls into place, but I have to be talking while I'm walking.
>
> (C1765/25)

She is describing a very particular composition tradition and also saying something about ideas and sounds 'falling into place' while talking and talking. This is a different relationship again between the oral and poetic composition – with the actual process of composition coming from an oral/aural and physical walking process. Finally, another thought on poetry composition from CS,

> Sometimes I'd speak it out loud, just say it, to, even if no one else was ever going to hear it, sometimes I just read out loud to claim a space for myself if you like, or to, to be heard in the world, well, you know, to, to breath that air, to have spoken those words out loud for the sake of myself.
>
> (C1765/10)

This is also oral reading and production, but this time the reading aloud is not to edit or to gather banks of others' words and sounds with which to write, or part of a moving rhythm; rather, it is part of a reason for wanting to compose in the first place: to be heard.

Literary life: performance

Preparation and performance

Reading aloud can be used as a way to perform stories and poems to audiences of different sorts and can also be a way to prepare for, or rehearse, such performances. Interviewee SD talks of the importance of reading aloud to rehearse: 'I do poetry programmes and poetry readings professionally and so you have to, obviously, rehearse that aloud to get the cadences and the language.' Novelist MT, as we heard in Chapter 7, reads out loud to both prepare for and perform author readings: 'If I'm doing events and I would read out loud for that and that has to be practised beforehand [...] I would tend to do that on my own or with an audience of cats.' Then, when she is in front of audiences:

it's like an acting job. I do a fair bit of am-dram, and I'm trying really to throw myself at the story and make it come alive [...] I tend to be reading from the page. What I do do is print it out big so I don't need my reading glasses, so I can read it and still be able to see people's reactions. [...] I need the audience feedback, it feels very strange you know, reading and not being able to glance up and see if they are enjoying it, see if they are listening, seeing if they are smiling at the funny bits.

(C1765/80)

Performance and 'the work'

In the example given by the novelist MT above, her public readings are to publicise her work (and, as she notes, to get a sort of feedback). These readings, though, are not 'the work' – her 'work' is the novels themselves, published pieces of writing (or audiobooks) that audiences buy or borrow from the library. This distinction is fairly clear. Similarly, at the other end of the spectrum, a play is nearly always understood to mean the live performance; the written version is merely the play script. Here we have a set of poles, two ends of a spectrum to do with whether what is performed is 'the work' or a version of 'the work,' or whether the performance is a showcasing of a work which is predominantly defined as something else, a published novel, for example. Pullinger and Whitley (2016) introduce a research project exploring memorised poetry with the question 'Where does poetry naturally live?' This is a good question; where *does* a poem live? On a page? In performance? In a person? One answer is that this depends on the views and traditions of the poet and those experiencing the poem, as interviewee CS discusses:

There's a lot of spoken word stuff that I have been to or slam poetry is very much, doesn't involve the book or something clearly visually present as the written text, it seems very much to be a verbal [...] then you go to poetry readings, other poetry readings where people are very much reading from the book or from a text [...] I think it's certain conventions at work [...] I mean there are all sorts of conversations about distinctions between page poetry and spoken poetry.

(C1765/10)

She then returns to the idea of a space, that a written poem and a performed or spoken poem can be thought of as *spaces*: 'I think of them as a space really, and space that occupies a place on a page and a space that occupies a place in my head, and also occupies a sort of sound space.' A question remains, perhaps, as to whether the written poem (if one exists) or the performed poem (if it is performed) is the 'definitive' version and who decides. At the RABiT event at the Scottish Poetry Library with poet Vahni Capildeo in February 2019, we discussed these questions and ruled out the idea of a simple answer:

Is a poem an oral/aural 'thing' (that can later be 'recorded' with written words on a page)? Or is a poem a written text (that then becomes something else when it is read, either silently or aloud)?

Do we consider a poem in terms of its composition, as 'arriving' or being created as sounds or rhythms, or as a voice with a particular origin (gender, region etc.)? Or do we consider a poem as performance, where it is not a singular thing 'to get right' but rather exists only as experienced by readers/listeners? What difference does this make?

(Duncan & Capildeo, 2019)

A note on audiobooks

I'd like to end this section with a reminder that 'performances' are not just live and that people all over the world listen to audiobooks, other recordings or radio programmes of literary works read aloud: '*Poetry Please!*, there are poems that almost bring tears to the eyes, the words are so beautiful' (MO F71), poetry podcasts such as *The Verb*, or the *DUAL Poetry Podcasts* from the Poetry Translation Centre, and '*Book of the Week* and *Book at Bedtime*; I find them very relaxing and often use them as a way of getting to sleep' (MO, M56). Numerous international examples include Cape Town's *Balidisha Poetry* Radio, France's *France Culture 'Fiction Littérature'* and *'Fiction Poésie'* podcasts of novels and poems read aloud and Radio Ambato's *Al Morir De Las Tardes*, a popular radio programme where Ecuadorian novels and poems are read aloud.

One thing that seems clear is that people listen to such recordings for different reasons: to enjoy the sounds, voices and stories, to pass the time on long journeys or while cooking or cleaning (I met a librarian in Skye who listens to detective story audiobooks when cleaning but never reads detective books). Some reasons are more practical, as a way to access a text that you might otherwise prefer to 'read yourself' but are unable to; for example, as explained by Observer F74: 'I love talking books, which my next-door neighbour, B, registered blind, introduced me to. They have enlivened many an hour of ironing and were a life-saver when I was without spectacles for five months owing to eye surgery.' For others, the appeal is the experience of the aloud:

Some things need to be read aloud to get the full meaning, so voices are important. Some are squeaky or rush things or just generally irritate. Others are a thing of beauty. I could have listened to the late Alan Rickman reading a bus timetable and it would sound beautiful. Likewise, I find Huw Edwards mesmeric.

(MO, F78)

[I] would prefer to be the listener as I find it extremely relaxing, especially when the reader has a soft, mellow voce. Being read aloud to makes the hairs stand up on the back of my neck and gives me a feel-ing almost of paralysis [...] Being read to brings book characters to life, adds someone else's pace and suspense to a story that you might not have had if you had read the book to yourself.

(MO, F49)

You've only got to listen to Richard Burton read Under Milkwood [...] It's just something about the timber of their voice and the way they can read out, the way, the passion they put into it, the emphasis they put onto certain words. Hearing Roger McGough reading his poetry out loud. Or even, you know, an old crackly recording of TS Eliot; it's just something about the nature of the human voice I think that either turns you on or turns you off to listening to what they are saying, and some people have got a real gift for it and others haven't.

(KB, C1765/11)

Interviewee TA also provides a useful reminder that audiobooks and radio performances are not the only, or even the main, ways that people access read aloud (or recited) performances digitally:

In the last couple of years, in Addis Ababa, there have been [...] poetry programmes, and many youngsters are writing poetry to express themselves, so I listen a lot through [...] the social media, so it's interesting, they read out loud because there are lots of emotions in it, it's mainly political, social, a reflection of their life [...] The beauty of the language but also the message [...] I mean you listen to politicians and it's dry. Poetry is much more complex, and it has beauty. It expresses life in a very amazing way, in a way that I like to listen because I can relate to that.

(C1765/62)

We will return briefly to audiobooks in Chapter 10, when we think about reading aloud alone.

Literary life: experience

A third way we can look at reading aloud and literary lives is through a focus on literary experience: how and why people read and listen to literary texts (something we have started to do above, with audiobooks).

Reading for pleasure?

One way this is often talked about, particularly when thinking about literary experience outside of formal study, is the slightly strange phrase 'reading for pleasure.' It can be hard to unpick exactly what this means, and one of the odd things about this phrase, to me, is the fact that it is mainly used within formal educational or advocacy contexts to try to describe a type of reading that happens outside of these formal contexts. It is also a phrase which can make reading sound much less appealing than it actually can be. What is meant by 'reading for pleasure' is the idea that reading, particularly (but not exclusively) literary or fictional texts, provides various possible pleasures, including pleasures of escape, distraction and entertainment, of feeling less alone, and of moral or other instruction (see Duncan, 2014). The main pleasure, though, in 'reading for pleasure' remains reading because *it pleases you* – that is, reading *because* you feel like it, *when* you feel like it, *what* you feel like reading, and, thinking about oral reading in particular, *how* you feel like reading (as articulated very well in Pennac's *The Rights of the Reader* (2006)), whether aloud or silent, reading to someone or someone reading to you, whispered, murmured, chanted or screamed.

Individual and communal

We can find examples of individuals enjoying reading literary texts aloud alone:

> And I did it [reading aloud] to a bit of *Tess of the D'Urbervilles* the other day, which, you know, reading out loud makes something come alive, so there's a bit where Tess says goodbye to Angel, who she's just married, but she is in trouble because of her history, and you know you read that out loud and it gives it tremendous colour that you don't get when – you know.
>
> (JI, C1765/20)

> I'm usually pretty quiet [reading], but then [...] you are reading it out loud but you are not realising that you are reading it out loud, if you know what I mean, because you are engrossed in the characters.
>
> (ME, C1765/73)

> Sometimes in bed when I'm reading, if I think how does that sound or if I want to do an accent [...] if somebody writes something and you can just hear in your head that Irish voice or that Scottish voice [...] and sometimes I might [...] just try a little bit to see if that does sound right [...] sometimes something will take you and pull you up and you'll think that's a bit odd, and you'll read that bit out loud and see if it makes better sense.
>
> (LC, C1765/48)

> Fiction or poetry which I read daily, I read aloud sections that I found particularly atmospheric, beautiful or powerful.
>
> (questionnaire)

I find I can hear the personalities of characters differently when I read aloud.

(questionnaire)

And not quite alone:

For pleasure I read aloud to the dog because she likes the sound of my voice and enjoys falling asleep on the sofa as I read to her.

(questionnaire)

Chapter 10 will return to the idea of 'aloud alone.' And we can find just as many examples of communal reading for pleasure. Describing being part of a poetry reading group, interviewee GD notes the benefits of a shared, aloud experience of poetry:

I think it just makes you feel that you are part of a group, and you are much more in touch with what you are reading, I think, if you are hearing it, especially poems because if you are reading them on the page you get a different, a completely different feel, and when they are read aloud you get more of the rhythm and you hear the rhymes in different places [...] and the way the rhythm changes, and some people when they are reading they take something different from it, and they read more quickly or in a different [...] and it can change the meaning completely. It's lovely.

(C1765/25)

Two members of a reading group of Caribbean elders in South London discuss:

RC: We say what we think, what the story is about. We get the books and we share it and everybody give their own opinion, depending on the story, it makes it quite interesting. [...]

PW: People have got different opinion about the, the subject, the people that's in the book, you know like, a friend, might have a brother or a sister, or a parent or something, and so we talk about 'oh the mother was like this or like that' or 'oh the sister, she was very nice to the brother,' something like that, we discuss. [And] we just read [aloud] so that other people can hear us.

RC: [...] So the other person can follow on and see what's going on. [...] It's being together, and you get to come out, isn't it? [...]

PW: Yes that's it, and we have a little laugh and a chat –

RC: A chat and a cup of tea and you know [...]

PW: [...] And each person have their own opinion of whatever the story is saying. I find it very entertaining.

RC: Everybody find it very entertaining and interesting.(C1765/36)

Similarly, members of the *Drama Queens* play-reading (C1765/18) and *Story Café* (C1765/17) groups at the Glasgow Women's Library talk about the ways that reading aloud and discussing plays, poems and stories together, as a group, provide a mixture of deeper understandings, insights, challenges to thinking and social interaction (these issues of oral reading and reading groups are also discussed in Duncan (2012) and Jones and Harvey, 2015).

Intersubjectivity and the meeting place

The experience of novel reading (and potentially other forms of literary reading) can be described as one of 'intersubjectivity,' where readers take on new identities or personas, 'becoming' the narrator or characters as they read. This is very much related to Heathcote and Barrs' concepts of role-taking and the meeting place. Working through Poulet, Barrs (1987) creates an explicit link between reading aloud and the intersubjective experiences of taking on a new identity 'as if it were a cloak held ready for us to put on, a temporary identity, in other words, a role [...] we assume the voice of the text, tuning our own voice to its demands' (p. 209). The 'usual' acts of role-taking or the intersubjectivity of literary reading are intensified by the use of the voice, as the reader 'tunes' their voice to the new identity.

The idea of 'the meeting place' comes into play here, too, as writer and reader(s) meet across time and space in the moment of the oral reading – as roles are taken and words are said and heard. Interviewee BL exclaims of his love of reciting poetry: 'Oh, I love the idea that you are in the presence of the poem and poet' (C1765/44), while interviewee VC shares a particular memory that can help us see another dimension of this 'meeting place':

> I was hit by a police car when I was 20, when I was a student, and I woke up on the road, and there's a massive hole in my head, and I was bleeding and in a lot of pain and shock, and I put my hand to my head, and I took it away and there was blood. It was fascinating because the blood was in strings, like stings of proteins because it was so much blood, and I had been doing Shakespeare, and the first thing I started doing was quoting *Macbeth* because I needed to make sense of what was happening, and I couldn't make any sense of, of lying on the road with a hole in my head, and my brain kindly produced for me a long piece of *Macbeth*, which [...] it just kind of came up, and that was interesting because that was reading from the text of memory. It was reading aloud again from the text of memory [...] I always get very pleased when metaphors turn out to be naturalistic as well as imaginative. I was thinking Duncan's 'silver skin laced with his golden blood' because when the blood comes out in strings and clots it glistens, and it was in the evening that I woke up on the road, so it glistened in the night lights, and it did look like silver and gold – ah, it's

naturalistic, it's not just stylised. Shakespeare must have seen blood – people always fighting and they were stabbing each other in Shakespeare's streets; it was very stabby.

(C1765/33)

This incident tells us something about 'reading aloud from the text of memory' (something we will come back to), but it also tells us something about the voicing of texts (whether remembered or read) as a meeting place between potentially vastly different times and places, a meeting between the world of the writer and the world of the reader. In this case, it is a meeting of Shakespeare's 'stabby' streets, where (VC realises) Shakespeare probably would have regularly seen blood looking like golden lacing, and the world of VC's university life, which, until this accident, had not taught her that blood webs or looks metallic. At the previous meeting place between VC and this text, recently at university, she had read the description 'laced with his golden blood' as 'stylised', and now at this particular meeting place, lying in the road watching her blood web and shine like metal, VC realises the description is 'naturalistic' (we could also relate these two different 'meeting places' or readings to CO and ST's conversation in Chapter 8 about how rereading the same text is never an exact repetition because we, the readers, have become different). VC's real-life world became, in this accident, a little closer to Shakespeare's, and this created a new meeting place – and one which brought those words from *Macbeth* back from wherever they had been waiting.

Conclusion and the *Wordhord*

This chapter aimed to capture the roles of oral reading in our literary lives, first by examining what we could mean by literary lives and then by looking at oral reading within acts of literary production, performance and experience. We have looked at different ideas of how the ear and voice can be central to the literary and at how sound relates to meaning and emotion. We have taken Heathcote and Barrs' idea of 'role-taking' to explore how reading aloud can allow the taking on of the roles of first writer and then later listener or judge to edit that writing, and have examined thoughts from RABiT participants on walking, rhythm and composition, and oral reading and writing to 'claim a space' in the world. We examined how reading aloud relates to 'reading for pleasure' and returned to Barrs' concept of 'meeting places' (first explored in Chapter 8) to look at meetings between writer and (oral) reader and, reflecting on interviewee VC's memory, at meeting places between not just writer and different readers but also between the same reader at different points in her life.

All of this brings us to an idea introduced to me by interviewee BL. BL recited songs that he had last heard well over half a century before (C1765/45,46) and then, after our interview, told me about the Anglo-Saxon idea (featuring in several Old English poems, including *Beowulf*) of the *Wordhord*. [1] He used this

149

term to talk about the 'treasure-trove' of words, phrases, lines or poems inside each of us, the banks of texts we have memorised or internalised, that we can 'unlock,' draw upon and that, as we have seen, connect us to others. This understanding of the *Wordhord* adds to our developing picture of how the texts we have read aloud in the past allow us to take on the role of writer. It can also help us imagine where all those memorised or internalised texts *go, wait* or *live*, where they are stored and how they are carried around with us. Before recounting the story of her accident, VC ponders:

> My parents also had a colonial education, so they had both been made to memorise things at school, and that's interesting because then they would use them either at moments that nowadays people experience as boredom or stress, so people would be checking their phones or have their earphones in, which is quite passive really in some ways, but when they were washing the dishes, or in some sort of stressful – my parents would more likely be reciting bits of poems, and I do wonder about First World War soldiers who carried poems in their kit bag, and also wondered what else they were carrying in their heads.
>
> (C1765/33)[2]

BL's use of the *Wordhord* allows us to consider the remembered as both a very personal accumulation of the texts we have experienced, heard, loved or hated and as that which connects us with others in the multiple meeting places of reading aloud and reciting. Bayley (2016) expresses this idea beautifully in his exploration of poetry and memory:

> I am suggesting that remembered poems are active in our mind like memories are. [...] Though much of the power of poetry is in its imagery, for me the indelible fact is that it is the words that I remember. [...] Language is not just any old dwelling. [...] To possess in my own mind the exact words chosen by a poet is to have a small room in the house of my being that contains that most invaluable of human productions, poetry, the words given to us by a poet. Words with which I can look out from my room on to my past and on to the world around me.

Notes

1 The modern spelling is 'word-hoard' (with hord/hoard meaning a collection of something), but the modern word 'horde' (meaning a crowd or rabble of people or animals) also seems apt, conjuring images of all those people, characters, voices grappling, hustling, bustling (or sleeping or snoring) inside us.
2 She also goes on to explore how 'memory banks' fit into uses of racist language: 'And I've also been thinking of it more after this so-called Brexit Advisory Referendum,

which has caused me to experience a lot of racism at personal street level, also in work, and I often wonder when people shout things at me or say certain things whether the language they are speaking is original, you know, is this racisms spoken with conscious intent or are they in a way reading a script from memory [...] where does it come from?'

References

Atwood, M. (2005). Introduction: Reading blind: The best American short stories 1989. In *Writing with Intent: Essays, Reviews, Personal Prose 1983–2005* (pp. 68–79). Caroll & Graf.

Barrs, M. (1987). Voice and role in reading and writing. *Language Arts*, 64(2), 207–218.

Barrs, M. (2000). The reader in the writer. *Reading*, 34(2), 54–60.

Bayley, N. (2016). 'A long-legged fly upon the stream': Poetry, memory and the unconscious. *Changing English*, 23(4), 387–395.

Brown, S. (Ed.). (1995). *The Pressures of the Text: Orality, Texts and the Telling of Tales*. Centre of West African Studies University of Birmingham.

Duncan, S. (2012). *Reading Circles, Novels and Adult Reading Development*. Bloomsbury.

Duncan, S. (2014). *Reading for Pleasure and Reading Circles for Adult Emergent Readers: Insights in Adult Learning*. National Institute of Adult Continuing Education.

Duncan, S., & Capildeo, V. (2019). RABiT discussion, reflection and next steps with a poetry focus. *UCL Institute of Education*. https://discovery.ucl.ac.uk/id/eprint/10080085/.

Eaton, H. A. (1913). Reading poetry aloud. *The English Journal*, 2(3), 151–157.

Eliot, T. S. (1964). *The Uses of Poetry and the Use of Criticism*. Faber and Faber.

Heathcote, D. (1970). How does drama serve thinking, talking and writing? *Elementary English*, 47(8), 1077–1081.

Jones, S., & Harvey, K. (2015). 'He should have put them in the freezer': Creating and connecting through shared reading. *Journal of Arts & Communities*, 7(3), 153–166.

Lehmann-Haupt, C., & Rich, N. (2007). Stephen King: The Art of Fiction. In *The Paris Review Interviews: Volume 2* (pp. 462–500). Canongate.

Nanton, P. (1995). Making space for orality on its own terms. In S. Brown (Ed.), *The Pressures of the Text: Orality, Texts and the Telling of Tales* (pp. 83–90). Centre of West African Studies University of Birmingham.

Pennac, D. (2006). *The Rights of the Reader* (S. Hamp Adams, Trans.). Walker Books.

Pullinger, D. (2017). *From Tongue to Text: A New Reading of Children's Poetry*. Bloomsbury Publishing.

Pullinger, D., & Whitley, D. (2016). Beyond measure: The value of the memorised poem. *Changing English*, 23(4), 314–325.

Robson, C. (2012). *Heart Beats: Everyday Life and the Memorized Poem*. Princeton University Press.

10

SOLITUDE

Aloud alone

I listen to stories on the radio, but only when I'm alone.

(questionnaire)

I read a lot, most of the time silently, but when I'm alone I read aloud.

(pilot study participant, M30s)

It helps me focus on the words when it's not practical/possible to drown out noise with headphones. I read aloud recipes when I'm cooking to keep it in my head more easily/for longer. I read aloud to get a better feel for foreign words.

(questionnaire)

What is done alone is mainly hidden. Even the most seemingly mundane aspects of alone-time can be hard to share, hard to talk about, mysterious to others. For some, forms of oral reading play a role in the experience of being alone. Do some people read aloud alone because there is no one to hear? Or because there is no one to listen to them? The rest of this book includes many examples of oral reading done completely alone, from reading aloud to edit journal articles to praying, from reciting poetry to reading out recipes while cooking. Why, then, devote a chapter to it? One answer is that for some (perhaps simply those who do not do it), it is the reading aloud that happens alone that is the most surprising. It can be easy to assume that oral reading is communal reading: something done for or with others. Historical studies of reading sometimes explain the shift from reading as predominantly oral to reading as predominantly silent in terms of changes in the proportion of a population that can read; the more people who can read themselves, the less need for others to read to them, and therefore (the story goes) less oral reading takes place (see, for example, Pugh, 1978; Vincent, 2000). Similarly, nowadays we may hear of parents ending the habit of reading to their children once those children can read for themselves and therefore no longer 'need' it. The idea is the same: reading aloud (in this view) is something that is done for those who cannot read, or do not have books or glasses. And this may often be the case; oral reading can be a service performed for those who are unable to read (as well as a service to, or communication with, those who can read for themselves). Yet, if we consider someone reading aloud as she sits, completely alone, and writes a story, checks an index or enjoys Syrian poetry, whatever her voice is doing, it is not serving or communicating with others.

From the questionnaire

The RABiT questionnaire asked its participants about the formations in which they read aloud ('just to yourself,' 'to one other person,' 'to several other people...' etc). 570 people responded to this question. Of these, 30% say they *never* read aloud 'just to yourself'; 20%, though, read aloud to themselves 'about every day or two'; 15% 'about once a week' and 15% 'about once a month'. If we group monthly, weekly and daily together, we find 50% of participants indicating that they read aloud to themselves regularly. Later in the questionnaire, participants were presented with the open question: 'Why do you read aloud rather than silently?' 396 people responded, and 186 of these responses refer to practices which seem to be done alone or are at least expressed in terms of individual purposes. I am reproducing twenty of these here, in no particular order, and invite readers to think about what these responses tell us and how these could be grouped or organised.

- Reading aloud to myself helps me to visualise and create pictures. It allows me to connect what I am hearing to other information or pictures I have in my head about connected topics.
- Aloud rather than silent because it retains in my memory better if it's something I will need to recall later.
- To fix instructions in my head or for comprehension of tricky language.
- Can get you into a book quicker than just reading it, helps 'paint the images.'
- For greater understanding, to take things in more. The dual acting and reading and speaking out loud reinforces things.
- For instructions/recipes, it makes them clearer and easier to follow step-by-step. If I am reading a book for pleasure when tired, I will read the first few words of it out loud to ease into the story.
- To play around with voice. To enjoy the sounds of the language.
- When I do it due to anxiety, it can be reassuring because it makes me focus on the words rather than possible negative interpretations. Ironically, I sometimes read aloud for pleasure to enjoy the different meanings suggested by words as well as their sounds.
- For my work, to help me process things and ensure things make sense. If I am learning a language, I read phrases out loud to also process. Sometimes I read books out loud because I haven't used my voice if I am home alone.
- Prayer is more effective when accompanied by sound.

- For proofreading purposes, reading aloud helps me catch errors that my eyes might slide over otherwise (since I'm forced to physically say the words).
- Hearing the words, the cadence, rhythm, for making sense sometimes. To hear my own voice.
- I read poetry aloud because part of the meaning is in the sound. And I just like it.
- In prayer, I read aloud to concentrate on the words, the pronunciation (in another language) and to retain focus and not get distracted, because I don't always know meaning.
- It can be nice just to hear the sounds of the words.
- Poetry needs to be read aloud to get the rhythm and the mood. When writing I will read back what I have written to check for meaning.
- I read aloud when I'm studying languages because I'm trying to learn to speak as well as read.
- The text has more impact and emotional expression for me to appreciate if it's a good poem or story. I like my reading voice. Reading an email before sending helps me get the tone right, especially if it's a difficult one to write.
- You pay attention to every word and don't skip.
- The ears are more difficult to deceive than the eyes.

Thinking

One group of practices we could identify in the above (and elsewhere) are those which use reading aloud as part of individual thinking work: to write, concentrate, remember, learn, revise, focus or understand something. In Chapters 6 and 9, we examined uses of reading aloud to write, for example, an email or compose a poem. Here we will look at three other sub-categories: focussing or concentrating; memorising or learning; and understanding, unpicking or interpreting.

Focussing or concentrating

Participants across the RABiT study speak of reading aloud in order to concentrate or focus on a text. Several Observers note reading aloud forces them to concentrate on a text when their minds 'start to wander;' for example, during exam revision, when trying to read a book while tired, reading medical notes in a noisy office, creating or checking an index ('otherwise you just start to turn pages over automatically,' M50) or doing 'Sudoku.' Interviewee DN explains that while doing an Open University degree she was not able to concentrate on the texts she was assigned to read unless she read out loud:

> When I was doing, with the Open University, it used to sort of sink in more, so everything I read [...] I had to read it out loud. [...] It seemed to be the only way I could do it, the only way I could read and take in. I suppose my mind used to wander a lot if I didn't.
>
> (British Library C1765/87)

And pilot study participant (M70s) reflects:

> Sometimes when I'm reading quietly my mind goes somewhere, and I find that if I read out loud for a moment or two it brings me back [...] it's just that my mind has picked up a thought and without realising it, even though I'm looking at the words, I'm not actually reading any more, I'm dealing with the subject in my mind, and so by reading out loud, I'm coming back to the book [...] because it forces me to actually acknowledge to myself the words, in an amplified way.

Here, oral reading acts as a sort of anchor or focussing device.

Memorising or 'learning'

In Chapter 8, we looked at uses of reading aloud to commit religious texts to memory. Here, we can see that many participants discuss oral reading as a way to 'memorise', 'remember' or 'learn' chunks of written text, whether Holy texts, poems, study materials or other works. Observer M43 writes:

> I do try to memorize poems and the only way I can do this is by reading them out loud and repeatedly so. You have to be able to hear the sounds of the words to be able to remember them and you can only do that by reading it out loud.

While pilot study participant, M30s, remembers reading aloud as a young person in South Africa:

> That's when I read out loud, when I used to study [...] when I was reading out loud what I was studying, it kind of like tend[ed] to stay in my mind [...] I remember in my grandma's house [...] the lounge area was the quietest, and that's where me and my brother both studied, and I remember my brother also reading out loud, [...] I remember like talking out, reading out so it would stay in my head [...] when I'm reading out loud, then I think to myself, ok, hopefully it stays in my head this time, you know?

Similarly, interviewee LL reads out loud when she needs to remember something for her studies, finding that 'hearing' supports or amplifies repetition:

> I think the fact that you are hearing it out loud can help you take it in more, like repetition of something that you want to learn so that it becomes a bit more second nature [...] for me, it definitely helps hearing it and reinforcing it.

(C1765/74)

Pilot study participant M70s goes on to compare reading aloud to 'writing something out' in terms of remembering and 'discipline':

> I think if there's something particular you want to indeliblise in your mind, you may read it out loud to yourself a couple of times to make sure you remember it. Sometimes we all do that, don't we? [...] You try to commit something to memory – it's a bit like [...] why very often writing something out helps you remember it [...] I think in different ways they both help you to remember what you are [...] because the fact that you are reading out loud means you literally read every word and it is – and it becomes a harnessed discipline.

This idea is shared by participants who explained how important reading aloud is for learning languages, as we will examine in Chapter 11.

Understanding, unpicking or interpreting

> Sunday – Read recipes aloud under my breath to make sure I understand all the steps/have all the ingredients.
>
> (MO, F27)

The questionnaire participants also suggest that oral reading can help to understand complex text, to 'unpick' tightly bound clausal structure or unfamiliar phrasing and, potentially, (linking back to Chapter 8's discussion of memorisation, meditation and meaning) to enable 'deeper' or simply different interpretations. This includes those who read aloud to better understand written recipes or instructions (flat-pack furniture, knitting and gardening are common responses) and the many who note that they sometimes read aloud to understand 'difficult,' 'technical,' 'legal,' or 'academic' writing, such as the Observer who recalls:

> I read out loud to myself and a cat on Saturday AM – I was trying to grasp a complex idea in an academic book, and I couldn't really get it in my head, but it made sense out loud – I suspect I do this a lot more than I realise. I'm heading into the last year of a PhD and read a lot of stuff that is beyond my grasp, that I 'slide off,' so reading out loud forces you to acknowledge the punctuation and the writer's intended meaning.
>
> (F53)

A pilot study participant explores why oral reading might help understanding and concludes:

> If it's a bit that's hard, if it's a bit that I'm not quite understanding, then I would read it out loud then. I'm making myself sound really

silly, aren't I? I suppose you are hearing it like someone else is saying it, it's not just you saying it, it's coming out of your mouth and back into your ear again, isn't it?

(pilot study M40s)

Interviewee PN adds a link back to memory:

I read out loud very frequently when I need to understand documents. [...] I've never found reading, the act of reading, easy, and if I need to really take on complex information or want to remember something I have to read it out loud, and I listen to myself – that's what I remember, I don't remember what's kind of coming in through my eyes, I remember what I hear.

(C1765/63)

And Observer M57 to slowing down and 'pay[ing] greater attention':

I find that when I read out loud, it provides a sense of reality in that the words actually have some meaning. When reading, say, a passage in a book, it is very easy to let the words slip by without actually fully understanding or interpreting the meaning intended. Reading aloud also allows one to slow down and pay greater attention.

Summing up

These are variations of a similar message: reading something aloud alone can help understanding. *Can* remains the key word, as the overall message from the data is that everyone's experiences are different, and *alone* is also important, as some participants note that reading aloud a new text to others, with pressure on performance or clear communication, can make it harder for them (the reader) to understand. Pilot study participant F60s explains:

I find, though, when I read aloud, I am so intent on getting what I am saying right that I am not taking it in [...] that's what I find when I am reading aloud – to other people, mind – it doesn't penetrate the mind as much as reading silently.

Reading to other people, she reminds us, is quite different in this respect from reading aloud alone. Other participants noted that with repetition oral reading can also help commit something to memory and it can help readers gain or regain focus. Participants offered explanations for why that were to do with slowing down, emphasis on each word, and the repeated double- or triple-ness of seeing, saying and hearing. These ideas are widely shared across the RABiT data and were also offered by others I spoke to about this project – including those in the otherwise quite different cultural and linguistic contexts of Finland, Ethiopia, Chile and Skye.

When I have presented these ideas at conferences, psychologists and applied linguists have mentioned the work of Paivio on dual-coding: the idea that the use of visual information (images) alongside verbal information (words) can aid learning, for example, in learning new vocabulary in a foreign language (see, for example, Paivio, 1971, 1986; Sadoski & Paivio, 2013). Paivio's work was not about oral reading, and yet the more general idea of 'double input' aiding memory may potentially be relevant and certainly resonates with participants' thoughts about the value of saying and hearing (or seeing, saying and hearing) the same words. Similarly, we may be reminded of Hallam's (1997) work on the triple visual, aural and kinesthetic input of musicians' memorisation strategies. Another name that often comes up is that of Mary Carruthers. In her work on medieval memory techniques, including emphasis on image association, 'places' within the mind, visualisation and numbering techniques, Carruthers notes that memorisation of longer texts was also achieved through the division of texts into smaller chunks, the copying of texts and their repeated recitation (Carruthers, 2008; Carruthers & Ziolkowski, 2004). This is echoed by the work of Sabki and Hardaker (2015, 2013) and Boyle (2006) in relation to memorisation through repeated reading aloud and recitation in Islamic pedagogy, including the idea, as noted in Chapter 8, that memorisation is not the opposite of comprehension but, potentially, its first step.

Feeling

Looking back at the example questionnaire responses, though, participants read aloud alone to do more than write, focus, memorise or understand. Some of the examples are about feelings. Once again, I'd like to think these through in three categories: spirituality and enjoyment; identity; and voices, comfort and company.

Spirituality and enjoyment

Many of the religious practices explored in Chapter 8 are performed alone, including forms of chanting, singing and reciting holy texts. We could also remember the description of reading poetry alone given by a pilot study participant in Chapter 2:

> I think it's an emotional thing you get from it, it's spiritual as well [...] it's like shouting at the wind, you know if you are at the top of a mountain and you shout, it's a feeling of power and it's expressing myself [...] it's a spiritual, emotional experience.
>
> (M60s)

Others describe their individual reading aloud in terms which move between the spiritual and forms of enjoyment or pleasure, including exclamations of the importance of reading poetry aloud, of the beauty of the sounds of different languages, of the exhilaration of voicing or hearing words. Interviewee NS speaks of the joys of chanting poetry:

> I think chanting is very close to the routes of what poetry is [...] this is pretty close to what happens with magical incantation, and it's pretty close to dance in which there are repetitive phrases, whether they are musical or whether they are verbal – but *again* and *again* and *again, tomorrow* and *tomorrow* and *tomorrow* or *never never never never never* [...] the poetry that you hear gets inside you [...] and then you can't shake it off [...] a love of poetry starts with the kind of poetry that can be chanted.
>
> (C1765/38)

Others report enjoying 'doing voices' when reading aloud alone or 'getting into' a story or novel through oral reading, as noted in Chapter 9.

Identity

Some of these pleasures or experiences are related to what we could see as threads of identity. We have already met interviewee GK, who reads aloud Welsh poetry alone to – amongst other things – connect with the language she spoke with her mother (see Chapter 5, pp. 75–6). Similarly, MM recites South American poetry from memory, accompanying himself on guitar (C1765/61). This is something he has done for decades, and now, as a South American living in London, something that connects him both to his cultural heritage and to a different era of his life. Interviewee CK reads aloud in French, not to con- nect to her heritage (which is not French speaking) but to connect to an earlier time in her life:

> Sometimes I would read aloud something in French [...] I was looking at something yesterday, and I did read that out just because I think I just wanted to practise and hear it [...] I think it's one of the things that I don't get to use much now because we don't go to France [much anymore].
>
> (C1765/69)

For these participants, reading aloud alone is about connecting to a person they once were or a person they want to be.

Voices, comfort and company

On first reading the Mass Observation responses, I was struck by one Observer writing, 'I now live alone so there is no point in reading aloud,' while another wrote, 'Occasionally I read aloud to myself if I have been on my own all day without speaking which makes me feel alienated and strange sometimes.' For some participants, living alone means that there is no need to read aloud: Observer F91 writes, 'My experience of this [reading aloud] is very small, and now, living alone, I find opportunities do not arise.' In almost direct contradiction, for others, reading aloud is something they do precisely because they live or spend a lot of time alone, like these two questionnaire participants: 'Sometimes I read books out loud because I haven't used my voice if I am home alone,' and 'I live alone – maybe the sound of my own voice breaks the silence. I read to my imaginary friends (sad:-))' and the other, who comments, 'Occasionally I read aloud to myself if I have been on my own all day without speaking which makes me feel alienated and strange sometimes.'

Reading aloud to pets is another way to use one's voice (more on this later), while audiobooks and reading on the radio provide a way to hear a reading voice while otherwise alone. In Chapter 9, thinking about literary performance, we looked at audiobooks/reading on the radio and their pleasures of stories, language and/or voices. These are also, though, ways that voices are brought into solitude. Observer M93 writes of listening to Russian short stories and Arabic reading on long-wave radio, remembering these voices as a form of 'intense' and 'mesmerising' company from afar. Interviewee KB, and Observer (F45) by contrast, convey a more domestic form of comfort:

> I like radio adaptations of books; I think there's something quite comforting about being read to [...] I just think it's a very comforting thing, and it's also very relaxing. If I'm ironing or doing something that you don't really need to think about, you know, some sort of repetitive household chore, you can have the radio on and listen to say an adaption of *Jane Eyre* [...] well it makes me feel relaxed and comfortable, and quite happy with the world.
>
> (British Library, C1765/11)

> Tuesday – listened to reading on the radio
> Wednesday – listened to reading on the radio.
>
> (MO, F45)

Summing up

Some people, then, read aloud when completely alone for spiritual or identity reasons, for enjoyment or the comfort or company of using or hearing a voice: a particular voice or perhaps any voice. Karpf's (2011) exploration of the human voice contains many ideas that resonate here: that our reactions to voices (including our own) are emotional; that voices are related to both individual and group identities; and that voices may need to be exercised so they don't 'rust up and creak' (Karpf, 2011, p. 124).

A different sort of echo comes from the Pennsylvanian 'Book Buddies' scheme (Animal Rescue League of Berks County, 2020), where children are invited to read to cats in shelters. There are similar programmes elsewhere, including Australia, and the shared idea is that children get the chance to practise their reading with a non-judgmental audience (as one child says, 'if you are reading to a cat and you mispronounce a word, it really doesn't care'), while the cats get used to children and enjoy plenty of attention (ABC, 2018).

Conclusion – and overlaps

We may never get the chance to observe others doing it, but the RABiT data and other accounts tell us that some people do indeed read out loud when completely alone (as well as to animals), and this act is often described in terms which make it seem a cognitive tool, to achieve acts of writing, concentration, memorisation and understanding. It is also described in terms of spirituality, enjoyment, identity, comfort and company, of feeling present or not in the world, heard or not. Many practices fit into fairly neat categories (to write, to understand, to enjoy the sounds), while others do not. When interviewees HM and AL discuss their uses of oral reading for both study and across their personal lives (see Chapter 5, pp. 77–78), they use the word 'reinforces' to describe the way oral reading allows them to memorise *and* understand *and* write *and* check ingredients and cooking steps. When interviewee JI describes how he reads aloud alone to make *Tess of the D'Urbervilles* 'come alive' and also to edit articles into assessments for use with students, he considers both to be about 'feeling the force of words' (C1765/20), and when the questionnaire participant who reads to imaginary friends writes about reading aloud to 'break the silence,' they follow with 'It does help me concentrate, though occasionally I will read out aloud and not at all remember what I just read – must be on autopilot.'

This provides at least two important reminders: that we cannot really separate out the affective and the cognitive, and also that none of these ideas about what reading aloud can do are always true. None of these 'alone' practices will help or appeal to everyone. And reading aloud alone is not something that even the most ardent participants feel that everyone should do. It is certainly not something everyone does. It might not even be something that 'most people' do. It is, though, something that at least some people do and greatly value, but it is seldom talked about or observed by others.

References

ABC. (2018, October 16). *Reading to Cats*. https://www.abc.net.au/btn/classroom/reading-to-cats/10448604.

Animal Rescue League of Berks County. (2020). Book Buddies. *Animal Rescue League of Berks County*. https://www.berksarl.org/programs/book-buddies/.

Boyle, H. N. (2006). Memorization and learning in Islamic schools. *Comparative Education Review*, 50(3), 478–495.

Carruthers, M. (2008). *The Book of Memory: A Study of Memory in Medieval Culture*. Cambridge University Press.

Carruthers, M., & Ziolkowski, J. M. (2004). *The Medieval Craft of Memory: An Anthology of Texts and Pictures*. University of Pennsylvania Press.

Duncan, S. (2015). Reading aloud in Lewisham: An exploration of adult reading-aloud practices. *Literacy*, 49(2), 84–90. https://doi.org/10.1111/lit.12046.

Hallam, S. (1997). The development of memorisation strategies in musicians: Implications for education. *British Journal of Music Education*, 14(1), 87–97.

Hardaker, G., & Sabki, A. A. (2015). Islamic pedagogy and embodiment: An anthropological study of a British Madrasah. *International Journal of Qualitative Studies in Education*, 28(8), 873–886. https://doi.org/10.1080/09518398.2014.917738.

Karpf, A. (2011). *The Human Voice: The Story of a Remarkable Talent*. Bloomsbury.

Paivio, A. (1971). *Imagery and Verbal Processes*. Holt, Rineheart & Winston.

Paivio, A. (1986). *Mental Representations: A Dual Code Approach*. Oxford University Press.

Pugh, A. K. (1978). *Silent Reading: An Introduction to its Study and Teaching*. Heinemann.

Sabki, A. A., & Hardaker, G. (2013). The madrasah concept of Islamic pedagogy. *Educational Review*, 65(3), 342–356.

Sadoski, M., & Paivio, A. (2013). *Imagery and Text: A Dual Coding Theory of Reading and Writing*. Routledge.

Vincent, D. (2000). *The Rise of Mass Literacy: Reading and Writing in Modern Europe*. Wiley.

11

ORAL READING AND EDUCATION

If, as Observer F72 notes, 'adults and reading aloud don't go together,' *school* and reading aloud certainly do:

> In thinking about 'reading aloud' it is hard to avoid starting with school, usually in literature and language classes; these instances were distinctly 'standard demands' – rather hated small events in the school day when the dreaded finger of fate pointed my way. There was never any guidance or tuition associated with these events; it was very much a case of avoid it if you can, but otherwise muddle and murmur through it.
>
> (MO, M72)

> Thurs 7: Back at school. Another go at a shared reading of *The Lion and Albert* (different pupil). I also read part of a short play called *Night Fishing* with a new pupil. Listening to them, it's noticeable how pupils adopt a different voice for reading the part in a play to that they would use when reading a school book. The flat delivery is replaced by something much livelier.
>
> (MO, M63)

This book is not about how to use reading aloud in the classroom, just as the RABiT project was not primarily about reading aloud within educational contexts. And yet many people I talked to about the RABiT project assumed that it was, probably because within existing attention to oral reading education looms large. A lot is said about reading aloud as a teaching tool within educational settings or as something done in homes to prepare children for compulsory schooling and its teaching of literacy. Reading aloud within educational contexts or for educational purposes, whether in classrooms or as part of self-study, was therefore part of what RABiT participants, and others, wanted to discuss. Because of this, if nothing else, ideas about oral reading and education are present in the RABiT data. We can also see education as a life domain, as an aspect of life, a context shared by many adults (just as we can see family, work or religion as domains), and like other domains, it contains instances of oral reading which may be different from, or similar to, instances in other domains. For both of these reasons, then, this chapter is devoted to thinking about the relationship between reading aloud and education.

We will investigate the relationship between reading aloud and education in three ways, first looking at how oral reading is used as a teaching tool. This will include the teaching of early and further reading and the teaching of foreign or additional languages, as well as within teaching more broadly, across a range of subject areas and contexts. We will then look at the relationship between oral reading and education from a different perspective, examining how people have been taught to read aloud, including traditions such as elocution training and religious formation. Finally, we will reflect on the possible educational implications of this book's examination of contemporary adult reading aloud practices.

Reading aloud as a teaching tool

Chapter 10 examined reported uses of reading aloud as part of self-study, to concentrate, memorise or understand difficult text or concepts. This chapter will look at how reading aloud is used within what we could call formal and non-formal education – that is, teaching and learning which is planned and organised. I am following Alan Rogers' idea that there are two types of planned learning: 'formal' (often understood to mean within larger, more formalised settings and working to externally set forms of accreditation) and 'non-formal' (often understood to mean learning within the community and other less official settings, and perhaps not following formalised curricula or forms of accreditation) (Rogers, 2014, p. 7), as opposed to the *unplanned* learning which happens informally across our lives. It is this 'planned learning' which is the focus of this chapter. This section's examination of oral reading as a teaching tool is organised into four sections: a) early reading, b) further reading development, c) language teaching and d) other teaching. I will bring in ideas on reading aloud from the wider education literature, as well as the RABiT data.

Early reading

Reading aloud with children is still as much a common practice across most of the world (Duncan, 2015; Street, 2001; Xerri, 2012) as it was in the past (Clanchy, 2012; Gregory & Williams, 2002; Mace, 1998). As discussed in Chapter 6, this is something that happens in various communities, in various ways and for various purposes. It is also something that has caught the attention of educational research. The extensive 'family literacy' literature argues that family literacy practices, including (but not exclusively) parents or carers reading to young children, are crucial to children's language and literacy development, preparing children for the literacy, wider language and sociocultural demands of school (see, for example, Carpentieri et al., 2011; Van Steensel, 2006). In this way, reading aloud within the family so that children can hear stories and see books being used is often seen as a first step in preparing children to learn to read and write.

Once children start school, accepted good practice in the teaching of early reading to children across most of the world involves teachers and children reading aloud texts, sentences, words and sub-lexical chunks (depending on the writing system), teachers reading to children, children reading to each other and to teachers or other adults, children reading in unison (and sometimes chanting or singing), teachers encouraging parents or carers to listen to children read at home, and teachers encouraging parents to read to children. Many Mass Observers commented on memories of reading aloud and being read to in this way as part of their very early school interactions. In Anglophone contexts, there has been well-publicised reporting on the benefits of systematic phonic approaches, involving children recognising and producing phonemes (sounds) and then linking these with the corresponding graphemes (written symbols; for example, letters or groups of letters) and 'blending' to read words. This phonic work nearly always involves both teachers and children reading aloud both whole words and parts of words, in combination with children listening to teachers reading books and reading aloud themselves, with adults listening to children highlighted as particularly crucial in early reading development (Evangelou et al., 2008). Outside of Anglophone contexts, Wu et al. (1999) write of the importance of children and teachers reading aloud and listening to others read in Chinese school reading instruction, while McEneaney (1997) explores pedagogical continuity in Russian school early reading instruction – including recitation, round-robin and choral reading – with the primers or texts used changing with shifts in political regimes. There may be general agreement that there is no single 'right' way to teach children to read, but the use of some form of oral reading does seem to be a staple as children grapple with linking spoken language with its written code, as recalled by Observer F4: 'I remember being called up to the teacher's desk to read aloud from my reading books as a primary school child, so the teacher could check that I was actually reading them.'

Forms of oral reading are also central to the teaching of early or emergent reading to adults. In my own experience in England and Scotland, as well as talking to colleagues in the United States, Australia, Ethiopia, Wales and Holland, adult literacy teachers combine attention to words and parts of words (including sound–symbol relationships) with the reading and writing of whole texts, silently and aloud, including paired and choral reading, and the use of sound-recordings, where learners can follow on in a written text while listening to that same text read aloud (often at a slightly slower pace than normal) (see, for example, Burton, 2007b, 2007a; Hughes & Schwab, 2010). 'Language experience' is also a common approach, where a learner dictates an account, a teacher or someone else scribes it, and then they use this newly created, written text to read together (often both aloud and silently) (Moss, 2000). Interviewee

JR recalls a variation of a language experience approach with a group of young people with learning difficulties:

> I also did work with special needs groups, later taping, editing and typing student improvisations [...] and we'd read, tape, read, read back, discuss and move on, so, it was, to help them with basic reading, so we'd talk about, I don't know [...] just everyday stuff, having a row at home or whatever, and we'd use that as the basis; it would then be taped, their improvisations would be taped, I would write it out, they would read it back the next lesson [...] so it was a way of engaging kids and giving them some investment in what they were doing so that hopefully it would be easier for them to read.
>
> (British Library, C1765/04)

Sánchez Tyson (2020) writes of oral reading as part of Spanish-language adult literacy programmes run by the Mexican government in the US, where reading aloud is both a teaching tool to develop decoding skills and to enjoy longer texts together, as well as something that participants report doing in their day-to-day lives. Several questionnaire participants write about using reading aloud as part of adult literacy teaching, whether reading to learners or asking learners to read out loud; for example, 'I used to work as an adult literacy teacher and encouraging others to read aloud individually and chorally was a regular part of my teaching.' Again, forms of oral reading are core to the teaching of reading, to adults as well as to children, as links are formed between written and oral language on sub-word, word and text levels.

Further reading development

Oral reading also plays a role in what may be seen as the teaching of 'further' rather than 'beginner' reading. Exploring uses of reading aloud with older children (about ages 8 to 11) in their school English classes, Collins (2005) first provides an overview of how reading aloud with this age group has been viewed in England over the past thirty years (classifying it as a transition from approval to suspicion). She then examines oral reading as a tool for engagement and storytelling, to support learners' understanding and enjoyment of written texts, concluding that teacher education courses should prepare teachers better to read aloud. Also examining uses of oral reading within school English classes, and writing of a similar age group but within their US context, Hoffman, Roser and Battle (1993) argue for a move from the 'modal' (that is, a classroom act performed routinely, with little thought and limited effect) and towards a 'model' of effective uses of reading aloud, including the use of small groups, more discussion, and giving children different options in responding to texts. The 'modal' is certainly remembered by Mass Observers, across a range of age groups, and most often negatively, typified by M34's comment: 'I recall lots of examples in school [...] where people would take it in turns to read a sentence or paragraph from a book. [...] I remember finding it quite boring and mechanical.' Another Observer remembers liking reading aloud in primary school but not when older:

> In secondary school, I remember the whole school having to read a sentence or two aloud working around the room. For the experience in primary school I do not remember feeling as anxious as I did during secondary school. Due to the public nature of reading with your classmates and being petrified to read something wrong, or stutter, in front of everyone (and being laughed at because of it!), I often felt anxious during these sessions.
>
> (F27)

Sticking with secondary or high school contexts (children over 11 or 13), Dreher (2003) argues for the importance of teachers reading to their learners, including to

> model independent reading for students. Reading became theatre, as I read and paused to think out loud about something that happened, comparing the text to something else we had read or relating it to a previous scene. Or, I might pause at a word, considering the contexts, verbalising what is usually the silent process [...] Through these activities, students began to develop an understanding of what it looks like to work through a text.
>
> (Dreher, 2003, p. 52)

Here, oral reading is modelling or making visible reading and thinking processes that may often be silent and therefore hidden. It is also, like the approach advocated by Collins (2005) above, a way to share with learners the joys of a good book (even, or especially, with learners who feel they struggle with reading) by 'dragging [them] into the story' as engaged listeners. Likewise, Westbrook et al. (2018), also working in the secondary/high school context, argue of the benefits of teachers reading aloud to their learners: 'Simply reading challenging, complex novels aloud and at a fast pace in each lesson repositioned "poor readers" as "good" readers, giving them a more engaged uninterrupted reading experience' (2018, p. 1). This may remind us of Daniel Pennac, French novelist and teacher, who talks (and writes) of reading aloud to engage previously demotivated young people in the excitement of novels and the imaginative worlds of reading (Manguel et al., 2008), even if they are not, initially, reading themselves, but rather listening. Echoing these messages, Observer M33 is an English teacher: 'I try to read with intonation and emotion to convey to the students the meaning of the text, as well as model to them how to effectively read a text aloud.'

There are several points made across these examples, including oral reading as a way to model a fluent, reflective, interpretative (and perhaps most often silent) reading process; reading aloud as a way to engage learners, as listeners, in stories and storytelling; and reading aloud as a way to share and enjoy a text. We also need to note that these are all projects which recognise, to a greater or lesser extent, that the teaching practices they are proposing or examining are not necessarily common practice. Unlike within the teaching of early or beginner reading, the role of oral reading within the further development of reading seems less certain and less consistent, perhaps because the nature of that further, more advanced or developed reading is less certain, less agreed upon (is it to do with the quick processing of factual information? Is it a silent process of comprehension and interpretation? Is it something else?).

Language teaching

While oral reading is usually a 'given' within the teaching of beginner reading, and seems to be sometimes used, sometimes ignored and sometimes questioned as a tool to further develop reading, its use has been more controversial in the teaching of foreign or additional languages. Gibson (2008) tackles reading aloud in the English language teaching (ELT) classroom by trying to gather up the debate and move the ELT community on from potentially polarised attitudes. She summarises the arguments against the use of oral reading in the language classroom, including: the challenge of being able to understand what one is reading when concentrating on decoding and articulation; that oral reading does not 'aid the development of efficient reading strategies'; and 'reading is usually a silent activity and it is often said that reading aloud is not a skill that many people need; public speakers and broadcasters are in the minority' (2008, p. 30). She then reviews the research and practice literature to compile a list of potential benefits (including developing prosody and writing) and strategies for reading aloud (including encouraging students to read aloud to each other outside of school), concluding that it would be a shame if examples of poor practice or misuse prevented the effective use of oral reading in language development. She does not, though, question the assumption that reading aloud is not a common adult practice.

Working on a research project investigating uses of literature in secondary/high school foreign language teaching, Amos Paran and I observed so many different examples of oral reading that we ended up writing about its use (Duncan & Paran, 2018). We found teachers using reading aloud in various ways to support learners with challenging pieces of literature, classifying these uses into three categories: reading aloud to scaffold understanding; 'reading aloud for close reading or reflection' (2018, p. 254), so everyone is looking at and listening to the same text at the same time; and 'reading aloud as literary experience' (2018, p. 255), where teachers and learners felt certain literary texts needed to be voiced to be experienced (most often poetry and drama). We also found that, when asked about these uses of reading aloud, some teachers felt that reading aloud was something disapproved of or discouraged, echoing Gibson's (2008) and interviewee JI's sense of its controversial nature within language teaching.

The RABiT data also contains examples of oral reading as a tool for learning languages, such as the many examples in the questionnaire where participants read aloud in other languages to practice their pronunciation, get a 'feel' for the language or 'get mouth practice'; the Observer who uses computer software (involving reading aloud, listening and repetition) to teach herself Basque and teach her family Spanish and French (F, no age) and the Observer who attends a French conversation class where they start by reading articles from 'Le Monde' together: 'we take it in turns to read a paragraph and then translate it' (F78). Interviewee JV, an English language teacher of adults and young people, talks through three different recent instances of oral reading in her teaching:

> Currently, I'm teaching a group of literacies, ESOL literacies, students, and I read out loud for a whole variety of reasons, and [the] most recent thing that struck me is to settle them down [...] to quieten them down is quite hard [...] I sat in the front of the class and made everyone follow me, and it just took the classroom down to such a level that I thought I might try this every literacies lesson [...]
>
> The other class I teach is a pre-intermediate class, and there are 26 people in it [...] I get people to, in their pairs or threes, read something out loud to each other [...] people do help each other with the pronunciation, with the hard words [...] and I think the most important part of that is that people who find it difficult to speak out loud in a group get a chance to hear their own voice [...] potentially, quieter students in the classroom sometimes have difficulty getting their voice heard in a class of 26 people, that's a busy environment, there's potential for somebody just not to speak, whereas if they are tasked to use their voice, it just builds their confidence quietly in the background, and reading out loud helps that. [...]
>
> I'm a bit of a singer. And I play the guitar, and when I am teaching I like to read the lyrics first, read them out loud, fit them into the rhythm, and then, so sometimes I teach my ESOL students songs, so we read that, and that's sort of more of a chanting, so we read the song together, and then we phrase it, before we get to singing.

Interviewee GW also shares:

> You are speaking to the proud progenitor of the first ever Gaelic karaoke tape [...] Inspired by my Japanese experiences, we actually produced [...] a cassette tape and a booklet for learners of Gaelic so that they could sing some well-known Gaelic songs in Gaelic.[...] 30 years

later I can still remember the words of these songs from Japan, and [...] it is a way of concentrating on making sounds and making them correctly without necessarily getting too uptight about it, and because you are doing it for singing, which is a different purpose in a sense, it offers you a way out from the potential of, you know, getting totally inhibited about it [...] there is a place for repetition even in chorus; it's not a popular, for a long time it wasn't a popular thing to say in language teaching methodology – everything that you did had to be meaningful, but that, there's a motor aspect to language learning, and it's actually getting your vocal chords used to making different sounds without feeling weird about it.

(C1765/53)

Forms of oral reading (including karaoke), then, feature widely within language teaching as explored by RABiT participants, whether as part of a wider engagement with texts, to remember words or practise language structures or as part of developing pronunciation and confidence with new sounds.

Other teaching

The majority of examples of teachers using reading aloud within the RABiT data do not come, though, from those teaching reading or languages but from those teaching a wider range of subjects (such as biology, ICT, maths, history). Examples come from university teaching, further, adult and vocational education, secondary/high school, elementary or primary school and those doing forms of teaching as part of other roles, such as librarians (as discussed in Chapter 7). Participants speak of reading aloud to give instructions and share information (including at assemblies and using Power Point presentations), to bring learners together in a shared listening activity, to focus on a text being studied (whether it is a history source or a biology table), to share and celebrate students' work, or to quieten or raise the mood. We have teachers reading to learners, one learner reading to the group, reading 'around the room,' learners reading in unison, in smaller or larger groups, paired or choral reading, and reading aloud as part of playing games.

Interviewee MG is an Information and Computer Technology teacher: 'In my daily teaching, for instance, if I want to put some emphasis, even though it is on the board, or if it is on the screen, I might read it aloud, to get their attention, to highlight where the important parts [are]' (C1765/76). TA speaks of his university teaching in refugee studies: 'In my lectures if there are certain quotations that I want to, that probably I read in the classroom. [...] It is to emphasise certain points' (C1765/62), while HAE recalls teaching student nurses:

Above all, it was important to read to students, student nurses. [...] I would get out the book; I would get one of the student nurses to bring their basic book, which they never read. [...] a textbook sort of thing and I would open it up at any page, and I would read a paragraph, and I would then ask the student, what on earth does that mean, and it would force the student to think about it and to discuss it, and it gave added richness to the student's experience of being a student.

(C1765/09)

This presents a similar idea to the work of Pergams et al. (2018) on oral reading as a think-aloud learning strategy for US college-level biology students, to develop thinking skills and to better understand key concepts.

It is hard to say how widespread these uses of oral reading are, to what degree teachers share the same reasons for their usages, to what degree teachers talk to their learners about their thinking and, of course, what the students think. Warner and Crolla (2015) and Warner et al. (2016) investigate when and why reading aloud is used in secondary or high schools and its effects, using student focus groups and a teacher survey. They find reading aloud is used by teachers of a range of subjects, sometimes with teachers having thought carefully about why they were using it and sometimes not. They also found that while many teachers relied on reading aloud as a teaching (or classroom management) tool, few teachers saw it as their responsibility to develop the oral reading skills that these activities rely upon. Learners report not liking reading aloud when they feel it is being used as classroom control, liking it when they can choose what and when to read aloud but often being unclear on why oral reading is being used at all. These are important points for reflection: that it may be important for learners to understand why teachers are using forms of oral reading and that although many teachers may be using reading aloud for different purposes, they may not be focussed on developing or teaching reading aloud itself – and if they are not, who is?

How were we taught to read aloud?

The Warner work (Warner & Crolla, 2015; Warner et al., 2016) asks us an intriguing question: if many teachers use reading aloud as a tool in their classrooms (but do not teach it), who is it that teaches learners (and teachers) to read out loud in the first place?

Working with the Mass Observation archivists on the Reading Aloud directive, we decided to ask this very question: 'Were you ever taught how to read *aloud* in particular? Or did you find a way to learn certain techniques?' Keeping in mind that Mass Observers often decide not to answer particular questions, writing instead about what they find most interesting or where they feel they have the most to offer, it is still striking that only nine (out of the 160) responded to say that 'yes,' they felt they had indeed been taught to read aloud: one as part of professional training as a speech and language therapist, one as part of professional training as a nursery assistant, three in elocution lessons, one as part of amateur dramatics, one as part of lessons in how to read poetry, one in order to read in church ('I was taught that you need to go much slower than you think' F41), and one who responded: 'I was guided in reading out loud in English and French classes. Doing the Read to Lead training it was more about speed and intonation' (F52) (the Read to Lead training is offered by The Reader organisation for those who may be leading their reading groups).

Other responses to this question are telling. Observer F73 writes that she was 'not taught as such but my father, a vicar, did tell me to project my voice to the back of the church when reading the Lessons for Christmas Carols for example,' a process which some, perhaps, consider being taught, but this Observer does not (reminding us that we may have different ideas of what 'being taught' means). Another Observer, who works in finance, comments:

> I don't recall ever being taught to read out loud and up until my most recent job it has always been something that I did casually. But now having the need to do so in my job, I have worked on my technique (just by using common sense) to make sure that I do it well.
>
> (F41)

While Observer F43 expresses a common refrain: 'I don't remember being taught how to read aloud, but I do remember it being expected.'

The interviews also contain examples of those who felt they had indeed been taught to read out loud. When I asked interviewee HAE if he had ever been taught to read aloud, he replied:

> The gentlemen in question is, has died [...] He was our choir master [...] he is still a hero as far as I'm concerned, and he's the sort of person you never ever forget in your life. [...] I was 10 years old, and I was a treble. He was very, very strict with us [...] he used to make us speak the words before we sang them; when we sang well and we focussed on what we were doing not just for our sake but for the sake of everybody listening, he would give us warm, very warm, very warm praise, and that is something I will never ever forget, and so, there you are, he was a good teacher [...] he was teaching us in part to read the words, to understand what we were reading and then to look at the music, the score of music and to sing it [...] and eventually we grew in confidence and with his praise, and we became a very, very, very good choir.
>
> (C1765/09)

For HAE, his choir training was also a training in reading aloud, and one that he feels has supported his uses of oral reading for both teaching and his Quaker faith. Others feel they were taught to read aloud as part of broadcasting or 'talking newspaper' training. In Chapter 7, we heard interviewee MB speaking of being taught to read aloud for the radio as if to one solitary person (imagining that person to be her Auntie Mary). Interviewee SD echoes this, as she discusses working with her team on the Frome Talking Newspaper:

> One of the briefs that certainly my team I tell them to focus on is that although we are recording to go out to quite a lot of people, you are actually only imagining a single reader, a single listener [...] So, you are actually focussing on the one person that you are reading to and that focusses the voice.
>
> (C1765/72)

Her explanation links the imagining of one single listener with a 'focussing' of the voice.

Mirroring the Observers above, interviewee DL recalls:

> I was born in Yorkshire, and the one thing my mother wanted to do which she didn't quite manage was to eliminate the Yorkshire accent, which I've still got. [...] from the ages of, I don't know, 7 till 12, something like that, I went to elocution lessons and you had to learn a poem every week or two poems every week, something like that, and you had to recite them in front of everybody [...] I think that gave me, because in front of a group, and that gave me, that's given me great confidence in reading.
>
> (C1765/28)

For DL, and three Observers, elocution lessons, primarily intended to 'correct' or modify speech, involved training in oral reading.

Likewise, others explain that they were taught to read aloud (or teach others) as part of religious formation or activity. We can remember the accounts in Chapter 8 of the reading and poetry schools within the Ethiopian Orthodox tradition and the training in pronunciation, intonation, rhythm and memorisation involved. We have also heard, in Chapter 7, how interviewee AN teaches children to read aloud in Hebrew for their Bar or Bat Mitzvahs, and in Chapter 8, again, we saw Muslim, Pentecostal, Hindu and Catholic children being taught to read aloud key religious texts, through modelling, imitation and repetition, as part of their religious formation. Thinking of the regular reading aloud that adults perform in Christian churches, interviewee ST feels the Anglican Church is stronger on the training of church readers than her own Catholic tradition:

> I think the delivery of the spoken word is so important, where our churches vary terribly how people, you know – like a Reader in the Anglican Church is a Reader, they have been trained to read, whereas in the Catholic Church it's quite a weak area.

Supporting this view, interviewee SD (from whom we heard earlier on training readers for the Frome Talking Newspaper) explains how she has also trained those in the Anglican Church in both reading aloud and speaking:

> I was attached to the Wells Cathedral for a time to encourage vicars to speak more clearly in churches [...] I'd go to church first of all to hear them, usually without telling them I was coming [...] and then talking to them about it afterwards. The diocese put up money, actually, for them to have voice training when they needed it and so on, which I thought was really quite, you know, quite clever of the Diocese because you do, I mean, I think, if you think of stage vicars they nearly always mumble don't they?
>
> (C1765/72)

The last example of training in religious reading aloud comes from interviewee RH, who reflects on a potential paradox born of his Catholic childhood roles as altar boy and reader:

> I mean, again, I could probably recite a good lump of the Our Father, and I knew it was the Our Father at the time, but I didn't, I didn't know, I couldn't translate word by word probably, you know, but *Pater noster, qui es in caelis, sanctificetur nomen tuum, Adveniat regnum tuum, Fiat voluntas tua*, etc, etc. It were only later when they made you do Latin at school that you could, I could probably tease bits of it out, you know, and I mean I don't know what the hell use was that in life, well, I think it probably did give, it did ingrain into a nervous kid, a shy kid, the fact that I was able to, given the circum-stances, I was able to articulate stuff aloud, I was able to, and nobody – I didn't feel that I'd been trained in it or that it were any-thing special; it was just something that you could do, you know, and I probably kept me mouth shut at school, but at same time, when the priest said get up there and read that, I got up and read it, and I suppose I realised I were quite a good reader as well, so I suppose it gives you a certain kind of confidence; you might be unconfident in many, many realms of your life, but when it comes to reading, you think 'oh well I can do that'.
>
> (C1765/13)

This passage is powerful and noteworthy for several reasons, not least because RH seems to be changing his mind a little or coming to a sort of realisation as he talks: that the church activity of his boyhood, involving reading aloud and reciting bits of text, was something that gave him ('a nervous kid, a shy kid') 'a certain kind of confidence' that he was actually 'a good reader' and could 'articulate stuff aloud,' despite his school experiences. It also takes us back to the question of how we are taught or how we learn to read aloud. He 'didn't feel that I'd been trained in it' and yet he learnt to read aloud with 'a certain kind of confidence' in front of a (very likely) busy church, and this is a confidence in reading aloud he took with him throughout his adult life, as a teacher, writer, activist and folk singer.

While some participants feel that they were taught to read aloud as part of what we could see as specific traditions (elocution; drama; singing in a choir; nursery or speech therapy training; to lead a reading group; broadcasting or reading for talking newspapers; and religious roles), others do not think they were trained or taught to read aloud at all. How, then, have people learnt to do these and other forms of oral reading – reading to a partner in the bath, reading to write or concentrate, reading to children, reading minutes at a board meeting? Perhaps the answer in most readers' minds will be that of Observer F41, who (as we have just read above) felt she had not been taught to read aloud but now has to do it for her job, and so 'I have worked on my technique (just by using common sense) to make sure that I do it well.' Each of us could reflect on how we learn or teach ourselves many things, particularly as new practices confront us, such as learning to use an automatic supermarket till, or learning that in some places one should smile at strangers and in others one should not. The implication of interviewee HAE's suggestion that his choir training taught him how to read aloud, including to read textbooks to student nurses, certainly makes a sort of sense: that we may adapt what we know of one practice to have a go at another, learning and refining in the process. In this way, perhaps I could take what I know of reading to children and use this to read aloud at a board meeting, projecting my voice for the larger room and adapting my tone of voice for the more business-like setting.

This sort of informal learning has been theorised extensively, including through the idea of communities of practice, where people gain more and more experience of a specific context and in this way move from being novices to experts (see, for example, Lave, 1991; Lave & Wenger, 2001) through ideas of modelling, imitation and innovation (as in the workplace learning literature; see, for example, Ellström & Nilsen, 2014). We could also link it to Shove et al.'s (2012) 'dynamics of social practices' as discussed earlier in this book – that practices develop, and participants learn, in the interactions between competencies, meanings and materials. In Chapter 6, interviewee MB, so confident in reading aloud on the radio, describes the difficulties of reading aloud at a funeral and the need 'to stand properly' to cope (pp. 98–99). This is something she has learnt with experience, recognising (we could imagine) that the competences needed to read aloud on the radio could be adapted to face the significant challenges of reading aloud at a funeral, with its distinct meanings (of commemorating a life, providing a service to the family, reaching out to others, focussing grief, providing a show of strength) and materials (a church, a different sort of microphone or none, a text that can or cannot be improvised, a strong stance, the rows of people staring up with eyes that she stresses should not be met). However it is conceptualised, the RABiT data strongly suggests that many of the reading aloud practices which play such large roles in adult life were not taught explicitly but were, rather, learnt somewhere and somehow along the way, as described by Observer M79, who traces his learning from before he started reading aloud for acting or work:

> I first shouted at people when I learnt to cox a rowing boat, and then drilled army cadet force boys. Shouting was part of the activity! For ten years or so later I was an amateur actor and enjoyed simply using my voice in different ways. In the course of my work, I had to address groups of people varying in number from small classroom to large auditorium (before the use of amplification). I found this a pleasure and adapted my voice accordingly, without any teaching.

Conclusion and what all this could mean for education

In this chapter, we aimed to look at the relationships between oral reading and education in three ways. The first was to recognise education as another life domain and examine the role of reading out loud within this domain. In this way, we have seen that teachers use forms of oral reading to teach reading and languages, to organise, illustrate, focus and instruct, both reading aloud themselves and asking learners to read aloud alone or in different groupings. If we want to fully grasp the role of oral reading in adult life, we need to take account of the fact that reading aloud is part of how adults teach and learn a great number of things, from Gaelic to knowledge about the respiratory system, and that this works more and less well depending on the learner and the circumstances.

We then turned to how adults have been taught to read aloud, finding participants reporting training in specific contexts, such as for drama, broadcasting or religious roles, alongside an overall message of (to repeat the phrasing of Observer F43): 'I don't remember being taught how to read aloud, but I do remember it being expected.' This begged the question of how most people learn to read aloud, and recognising the distinct natures of different reading aloud practices, we reflected on ideas of informal learning and the 'dynamic' nature of social practices.

The third way to explore the relationship between reading aloud and education is where we will end this chapter and look towards the next. This is the question of what the RABiT project, and the thinking of this book, could mean for education and specifically literacy education. One answer, potentially suggested by the discussions above, is that our educational systems need to think a bit more about how we teach and develop reading (including how we encourage young people to think of themselves as readers) and whether this includes enough attention to diverse forms of oral reading. At the same time, much of this and the previous chapter suggest that reading aloud can be a useful tool for learning all sorts of things, whether in groups or alone, and so another answer could be that we should revisit what oral reading (and, crucially, listening) could bring to pedagogical practices more generally. These two 'answers' would both be useful areas for future attention but are not, I feel, the main educational implication of our explorations of contemporary adult reading aloud, which is, rather, around expanding what is understood by 'reading' in the first place. The concluding chapter will develop this idea.

References

Burton, M. (2007a). *Reading (Developing Adult Teaching and Learning: Practitioner Guides)*. NIACE.

Burton, M. (2007b). *Oral Reading Fluency in Adults*. NRDC.

Carpentieri, J. D., Fairfax-Cholmeley, K., Litster, J., & Vorhaus, J. (2011). *Family Literacy in Europe: Using Parental Support Initiatives to Enhance Early Literacy Development*. NRDC.

Clanchy, M. T. (2012). *From Memory to Written Record: England 1066–1307*. John Wiley & Sons.

Collins, F. M. (2005). "She's sort of dragging me into the story!" Student teachers' experiences of reading aloud in Key Stage 2 classes. *Literacy*, 39(1), 10–17.

Dreher, S. (2003). A novel idea: Reading aloud in a high school English classroom. *The English Journal*, 93(1), 50–53.

Duncan, S. (2015). Reading aloud in Lewisham: An exploration of adult reading-aloud practices. *Literacy*, 49(2), 84–90. https://doi.org/10.1111/lit.12046.

Duncan, S., & Paran, A. (2018). Negotiating the challenges of reading literature: Teachers reporting on their practice. In J. Bland (Ed.), *Using Literature in English Language Education: Challenging Reading for 8–18 Year Olds* (pp. 243–259). Bloomsbury.

Ellström, P. E., & Nilsen, P. (2014). Promoting practice-based innovation through learning at work. In S. Billett, C. Harteis, & H. Gruber (Eds.), *International Handbook of Research in Professional and Practice-Based Learning* (pp. 1161–1185). Springer Netherlands.

Evangelou, M., Taggart, B., Sylva, K., Melhuish, E., Sammons, P., & Siraj-Blatchford, I. (2008). *What makes a successful transition from primary to secondary school? Effective Pre-school, Primary and Secondary Education 3–14 (EPPSE) Project*. Department for Children, Schools and Families.

Gibson, S. (2008). Reading aloud: A useful learning tool? *ELT Journal*, 62(1), 29–36. https://doi.org/10.1093/elt/ccm075.

Gregory, E., & Williams, A. (2002). *City Literacies: Learning to Read across Generations and Cultures*. Routledge.

Hoffman, J. V., Roser, N. L., & Battle, J. (1993). Reading aloud in classrooms: From the modal toward a 'model'. *The Reading Teacher*, 46(6), 496–503.

Hughes, N., & Schwab, I. (2010). *Teaching Adult Literacy: A Teacher Education Handbook: Principles and Practice*. McGraw-Hill Education.

Lave, J. (1991). Situating learning in communities of practice. In L. B. Resnick, J. M. Levine, & S. D. Teasley (Eds.), *Perspectives on Socially Shared Cognition* (pp. 63–82). American Psychological Association. https://doi.org/10.1037/10096-003.

Lave, J., & Wenger, E. (2001). Legitimate peripheral participation in communities of practice. In J. Clarke, A. Hanson, R. Harrison, & F. Reeve (Eds.), *Supporting Life-long Learning Volume I: Perspectives on Learning*. Routledge. https://www.taylor francis.com/books/e/9780203996287/chapters/10.4324/9780203996287-11.

Mace, J. (1998). *Playing with Time: Mothers and the Meaning of Literacy*. UCL Press.

Manguel, A., Nafisi, A., & Pennac, D. (2008, April 12). *Alberto Manguel, Azar Nafisi & Daniel Pennac: The rights of the reader event. Free the word!*International PEN Festival of World Literature, Southbank Centre, London.

McEneaney, J. E. (1997). Teaching them to read Russian: Four hundred years of the Russian Bukvar. *The Reading Teacher*, 51(3), 210–226.

Moss, W. (2000). Talk into text: Reflections on the relationship between author and scribe in writing through language experience. *RaPAL Bulletin*.

Pergams, O. R., Jake-Matthews, C. E., & Mohanty, L. M. (2018). A combined read-aloud think-aloud strategy improves student learning experiences in college-level biology courses. *Journal of College Science Teaching*, 47(5), 10–15.

Rogers, A. (2014). The classroom and the everyday: The importance of informal learning for formal learning. *Investigar Em Educação*, 2(1).

Sanchez Tyson, L. (2020). Literacy and oracy across the U.S.-Mexico border: A look at the Plazas Comunitarias programme. *Changing English*, 27(1), 91–99. https://doi.org/10.1080/1358684X.2019.1687285.

Shove, E., Pantzar, M., & Watson, M. (2012). *The Dynamics of Social Practice: Everyday Life and How it Changes*. Sage.

Street, B. V. (2001). Literacy empowerment in developing societies. In L. Verhoeven, & C. E. Snow (Eds.), *Literacy and Motivation: Reading Engagement in Individuals and Groups* (pp. 71–94). Routledge.

Van Steensel, R. (2006). Relations between socio-cultural factors, the home literacy environment and children's literacy development in the first years of primary education. *Journal of Research in Reading*, 29(4), 367–382. https://doi.org/10.1111/j.1467-9817.2006.00301.x.

Warner, L., & Crolla, C. (2015). The practice of reading aloud in the high school: A preliminary investigation. *English Teaching: Practice & Critique*, 14(3), 419–426. https://doi.org/10.1108/ETPC-06-2015-0045.

Warner, L., Crolla, C., Goodwyn, A., Hyder, E., & Richards, B. (2016). Reading aloud in high schools: Students and teachers across the curriculum. *Educational Review*, 68(2), 222–238. https://doi.org/10.1080/00131911.2015.1067881.

Westbrook, J., Sutherland, J., Oakhill, J., & Sullivan, S. (2018). 'Just reading': The impact of a faster pace of reading narratives on the comprehension of poorer adolescent readers in English classrooms. *Literacy*, 0(0). https://doi.org/10.1111/lit.12141.

Wu, X., Li, W., & Anderson, R. C. (1999). Reading instruction in China. *Journal of Curriculum Studies*, 31(5), 571–586.

Xerri, D. (2012). Pennac on the tube: Revaluing reading to children. *English, Drama, Media: The Professional Journal of the National Association for the Teaching of English*, October(24).

12

CONCLUSION

What does all this mean for literacy teaching and learning?

The last chapter ended with reflections on the educational implications of the RABiT study and the thinking of this book. The aim of this project was not to directly influence practice, within or outside of education, but rather to better understand the diversity of adult reading practices and therefore deepen our knowledge of reading itself. This deeper knowledge could then, in turn, influence literacy teaching and research. I argued that the main contribution this study makes is in supporting expanded conceptualisations of reading, illustrating that reading is not only a silent process, not only something done alone, and not only something we do to find out what has been written down on a particular piece of paper or screen. Rather, reading can be communal as well as individual; aloud as well as silent; whispered, shouted, chanted, sung; and to meditate, enjoy sounds, think, feel, pray, entertain, memorise, understand or express love as well as to impart information. There is room for the conceptualisations of reading which underpin literacy (including adult literacy) policy, curricula and forms of assessment to better reflect this breadth and diversity. In other words, this study can help us see that 'reading' is something bigger and more diverse than is sometimes presented, and those of us teaching, as well as those creating policy, curricula and assessments, need to work from understandings of reading which take this range into account.

There is also a second educational implication worth emphasising, particularly for literacy teachers. This study reinforces the message that we cannot assume that we have a firm grasp of our learners' life-wide literacy practices or that these practices are similar to our own. This is a point that Kalman (2005) and her co-researchers (and no doubt others) have made too. Participants in this study talked about forms of reading that I have never taken part in and would never have imagined. Very simply, we cannot guess at others' practices; we need to ask, to open up meaningful conversations and keep these conversations open. This is important, particularly for adult literacy teaching, because our teaching needs to be so firmly based on an understanding of learners' existing practices and existing ideas of reading and writing, as well as what learners want to do in the future and why. This is not a new point, but it is one that I feel is worth making again and again. Kalman expresses it well, highlighting the relevance of her literacy research in Mixquic, Mexico to educational policy in three guidelines:

1   educational actions must consider the context in which learners live and carry out their daily activities;
2   the starting point for educational interventions should be learners' existing knowledge and know-how; and
3   educational projects must recognise and respond to learners' heterogeneity
(Kalman, 2005, p. 139)

Adult literacy teaching starts with how learners understand, value and live literacy (whatever other factors, such as accreditation requirements, also need to be juggled); this is the basis of a social practice approach to literacy teaching. As noted in Chapter 1, Brian Street's life work reminds us that to understand literacy practices better we need to ask questions and challenge assumptions (Robinson-Pant, 2018). This doesn't mean that literacy teachers necessarily work on *only* what learners feel they want and need to do – literacy teachers bring their own expertise and can use this to develop learners' awareness of additional practices – but it does mean that literacy teaching needs to *start* from what learners bring. Burnett et al. (2014) end their edited collection *New Literacies around the Globe* with a 'charter for literacy education.' The first point of this charter captures this crucial dynamic:

An empowering literacy education involves a recognition of the linguistic, social and cultural resources learners bring to the classroom whilst encouraging them to diversify the range of communicative practices in which they participate.
(Burnett et al., 2014, pp. 161–162)

In order to recognise the 'linguistic, social and cultural resources learners bring to the classroom' literacy teachers need to have conversations with learners, find out more about what they do, what they value, what they find more enjoyable or more challenging and why. A wider point made throughout this book is that some literacy practices are less visible or less talked about and yet still extremely meaningful to those who take part in them. As much as anything, this project has reinforced the messages of the powerful 'Adult Learners' Lives' project (Barton et al., 2007; Ivanič et al., 2004): how little we may know of other people's practices, including what is meaningful to them and why, and how much can be gained from asking and talking.

What else does it mean?

The aims of this project and book as a whole were not, however, primarily educational, despite the rationale for the project coming very much from

180

experience of adult literacy education. The overall aim of the RABiT project was to create a record and analysis of contemporary adult reading aloud practices. One job for this conclusion is therefore to try to sum up by constructing an account of how this aim has been met. We can certainly say that some adults do indeed read out loud and listen to others reading, and we can say that this involves different sorts of texts, including books (both fiction and non-fiction), poems, play-scripts, meeting-minutes, documents, newspaper and magazine articles (on- and offline), religious texts, posters, textbooks, product packets, health and safety information, instructions, recipes, graffiti, political slogans, menus, tombstones, court statements, letters, birthday cards, postcards and emails. Adults read aloud alone and with others, reading and listening in pairs, smaller and larger groups, one voice at a time and in unison, and for purposes including to better understand, study, memorise, focus, compose, revise or redraft text, pray, worship, meditate, entertain, share time and texts with others, share information, teach, enjoy sounds, help others, count stock, relieve pain, celebrate lives and more.

We have seen that oral reading plays a significant role in the lives of at least some adults, and as part of family, home, work, religious, romantic and literary life, as part of community-building, friendship, partnership and marriage. It is part of our identities as members of cultural, religious and linguistic groups, how we engage with and produce literature, how we link ourselves to other people, past and present, close and distant, and how we grow and use our *Wordhords*. It is part of how we experience voices, how we are alone and with others, reading aloud as company, intimacy, mediation, fellowship, care and a sharing of time and love. Reading, for at least some adults, and at least sometimes, is more than a silent process: something voiced and heard quietly, loudly, sung, chanted, remembered, recited, performed, proclaimed, conjured, *cast*.

Over the course of the project, I have also tried out a few different forms of classification or typology. In the pilot study, I tried organising practices into four *domains* (spiritual life, family life, work and learning) and four *purposes* (to memorise, to understand, to write and for fellowship) (Duncan, 2015). Examining the RABiT questionnaire data, I reflected on what makes a literacy practice *common* or 'everyday,' whether this means frequent occurrence within an individual life, something that most people experience at some point in a life, or a more general cultural prevalence, and how each of these relate to the wider *visibility* of a practice. Sitting amongst the 160 pieces of Mass Observation writing, I started to see the Observers as the '*atypical typical*' (that is, a fairly idiosyncratic collection of people who nevertheless can present a range of potentially 'typical' reactions to a topic), as *researchers* themselves, creating their own classifications and analyses, and as *storytellers*, telling stories of the roles of reading aloud in their lives, overwhelmingly stories of loss and pain, youth and encounter.

Rereading and relistening to the interviews and recordings, I played with a further classification of three 'types' or categories of oral reading: those *serving others* (whether to entertain, soothe, provide information for, or help in some other way), those meeting a particular *cognitive or creative goal* (such as to revise, understand or memorise written text) and those *for their own sake*, reading aloud for the aesthetic, meditative or spiritual experience. Once again, this is an imperfect classification: what about an adult reading to a child, is this a service or an experience in itself? And couldn't reading aloud to be with others be a fourth category? Yet I argued that these 'types' are worth keeping in mind as a reminder of the extent of the differences between forms of oral reading and to illustrate just how different 'being good at reading aloud' would be in each case. Part 2 of this book moved through different aspects, or domains, of adult life, with attention to reading aloud with family, friends and partners; for work; as part of religion; in literary life; alone; and education. The crossovers between these, as with all the classifications above, raise questions that may help us think more carefully, or differently, about forms of reading and its roles in adult lives. We could also try picturing these various systems of classification as differently coloured shopping bags, swinging and bulging with examples of oral reading, the carrier straining under their weight, calling out 'Look what we found! Look at all this!'

Themes or threads

I have also introduced some themes or threads along the way and return to these briefly here.

Power, visibility and longevity

Chapter 3 linked observations from the questionnaire with ideas from literacy studies on power and visibility, arguing that what makes certain literacies powerful or valued has a relationship with what is noticed, talked about or 'visible,' and this visibility can be contextual. Literacy practices which are highly visible in one context may be invisible (and less powerful) in another, where other literacies dominate (Elster, 2003); for example, many of the religious reading practices discussed in this book are associated with extremely powerful institutions and are highly visible in their worship contexts but may be invisible in other contexts where reading is discussed. Chapter 6 played with the idea of 'mediation,' using this term to describe the idea that the person reading aloud (for example, someone reading from online news to his partner at lunch) is not only sharing news, and facilitating access to literacy, but also controlling what and how news from the outside is heard by the listener 'on the inside' – an exercise of power. Chapter 7 continued this thinking with examples from the workplace and prisons, where the reading aloud of documents to others can also be an exercise of power, leaving the listener vulnerable to the intensions (good or bad) of the reader.

These ideas of visibility, power and context underpin the thinking about oracy and literacy throughout this book, and we could extend this thinking to reflect on how relationships between oracy and literacy have shifted over time. When Lyons (2010) writes of the 'significant constitutional milestone' that was the Magna Carta of 1215, he notes,

> but for it to have any meaning for contemporaries it had to be orally proclaimed throughout the kingdom, in both English and French (the original was written in Latin). Important documents could always be forged or lost in transit; the voice of a messenger seemed more reliable and authentic [...] Documentary evidence might accompany all such agreements, but it did not carry the force of law.
>
> (p. 23)

We might reflect on how different things are now, where in many parts of the world it is the written word rather than the spoken that has 'the power'. And yet, as we have seen in Chapter 7, in Britain today (and many other countries) courts of law require the reading aloud of written statements, and weddings only become 'legal' with the speaking aloud of certain words: the vocalisation of written text.

Power and visibility may also relate to longevity. Observers' memories (good and bad) of being read to have often outlasted the physical books they once read from, suggesting the potential superior longevity of the oral/aural and reminding me of a conversation between two RABiT interviewees. They discussed community writing, community publishing initiatives and reading aloud events, and one noted that 'all that stuff that we published and wrote in the 1970s and 1980s and 1990s, there's hardly any of it left [...] half of the stuff got thrown away in the paper recycling and so on.' However, they both remembered well the oral reading events and the work that was read out, remarking how funny it is that the oral has outlived the written (NP & PN, British Library, C1765/63).

Role-taking, spaces and places

Chapter 8 explored how for some forms of religious oral reading we need to think about not only who the reader is reading to but who she is reading *as*; the reader may be reading as the writer of the religious text, she may be reading as an individual, or she may be reading as a unified congregation. In other words, as we read aloud, we may be taking on a role, lending our voice to someone or something. Exploring literary reading and writing, in Chapter 9 we borrowed Heathcote (1970) and Barrs' (1987) term 'role-taking' to think about reading as an act of becoming someone else (the writer, the narrator, a character) intensified with the physicality of oral reading, as we 'lend the text not only our consciousness, but, actually, our breath' (Barrs, 1987, p. 209). We used this idea of oral reading as role-taking to think about reading aloud supporting writing in two ways: (firstly) taking on the roles of listener, audience or judge to hear and edit writing, and (secondly) the way that the reading and hearing of others' writing builds up within the listener a bank of phrasing and rhythms until that listener is able to take on the role of writer, as Atwood also reminds us: 'From listening to the stories of others, we learn to tell our own' (2005, p. 79). Thinking about both religious and literary reading, we returned to Barrs (2000) to think about reading as a 'meeting place' of reader and writer, extending this idea to explore oral reading as a meeting place between reader, writer, text and all those other readers who have read that text in the past, are reading it right now or will read it in the future, across the world: a powerful compression of time and place.

Another sort of place came up in conversations about oral reading creating a 'space' between reader(s) and listener(s). Interviewee (and poet) CS describes:

> Sometimes it [oral reading] brings a different energy – it's a shared experience and, and you get to hear things that are incredible, and it is a different, a very different experience from reading it directly from a book or on a page, yeah so I think it becomes a shared [...] I am writing a lot in my PhD about the idea of correspondence, so this kind of, this making of meaning or things that happen between one thing and another [...] that live element of it brings a sort of tension, a dynamic to it that is different.
>
> (C1765/10)

Interviewee (and priest) NS describes something very similar:

> When I was at school, I came across an essay by a poet called Archibald McLeish and it talked about, as I recall, where the meaning lay in poetry. And he said, it was a completely new thought to me, that the meaning didn't lie in the head of the person who had written the poem, or was reciting the poem, or was hearing the poem, the meaning was something shared in between, and that thought has stayed with me in all sorts of contexts [...] if you say where is the meaning, is the meaning in the utterer or is the meaning in the hearer? – it's something between the two, and there's always a mystery about the meaning because nobody can quite nail it down but something very distinct and wonderful is happening when there is communication, and I just really love the German word for that, Zwischenraum – that there's a, there's a space in between in which meaning emerges.
>
> (C1765/38)

This 'space in between in which meaning emerges' is, according to both poet and priest, shared, creative, dynamic.

The final 'place' we explored is the *Wordhord* (taking interviewee BL's usage): the 'text of memory' (interviewee VH, C1765/33), that bank of texts, phrases, lines, language, rhythms inside each of us, accumulated throughout our lives and from which we can, if we are lucky, pull something up to recite whenever we choose (and at other times things may be belched up, unbidden?).

The fixed and the fluid

Over each of the chapters of the book we have played with ideas of 'the fixed and the fluid' on multiple levels, explicitly and implicitly. The first may be simply that a text read aloud is a fluid (or varied) version of the (fixed) written text, fluid because of the difference that different readers, voices and contexts make. In Chapter 8, we looked at Rosowsky's (2012) use of the term 'religious classical' to describe the fixed nature of religious language (and texts) in contrast to the fluid (and ever-changing) nature of most language use. We used this idea to think about the fixed nature of many religious texts that are read aloud or recited and the fact that their 'fixedness' is part of their power as 'meeting places' between all those reading them aloud, past and present. We also reflected on the situation where a relatively 'fixed' religious text (the Christian Bible, for example) can exist in different languages, language varieties and even editions in the same language, and so those reading it aloud may experience the co-presence of several versions at once – reading one and remembering another. RABiT participants describe this as both a 'curse' (getting muddled up) and a 'blessing,' enforcing new attentiveness or perspective on a familiar text (a form of defamiliarisation). A final variation of the 'fixed and the fluid' comes from interviewees CO and ST, who reflect on how reading aloud the same text again 'is always different' because we as readers are always that bit different.

Skills or competences, meanings, materials and social practice

In Chapter 2, I noted the usefulness of using Shove et al.'s (2012) model of the 'dynamics' of social practice to think through how individuals use and develop different literacy practices across different aspects of their lives. I argued that though there are many ways to write about the diverse skills and meanings within literacy practices, and their relationships to technologies, materials or objects (see for example, Bloome & Kim, 2016; Gregory & Williams, 2002; Herbert & Robinson, 2001; Papen, 2005), Shove et al.'s conceptualisation of social practice being made up of three interacting elements (meanings, materials and competences) is a particularly helpful tool for not only emphasising the importance of all three elements but as a way of reflecting on how the 'dynamics' between these three interactive elements drive practice development and change on both a social and an individual level. Throughout this book, participants describe their varied uses of oral reading and their awareness of the distinct meanings, competences and materials at play, and at times I have been explicit in my application of Shove et al.'s terminology (for example, in Chapters 7 and 11). This has reinforced my own feeling of its usefulness for thinking through how individuals develop (or learn) literacy practices informally, through activity in different domains and with diverse groups of people.

It has also led me to reflect on how useful this paradigm could be within more formalised adult literacy provision, as a way of talking with learners about relationships between the competences, meanings and materials within range of literacy practices. It could be a tool for reflection with learners on how being 'good' or 'effective' at reading or writing can be different for different reading or writing practices and as a way out of the otherwise dead-end of either seeing all literacy practices as the same thing (the same reading, the same writing, just in a different context) or as completely different, and therefore the idea of transferability of skills as an illusion (both false). It could allow learners and teachers to look carefully together at which skills/competences may be in common across distinct practices and which may be different, and why, and explore how we could gain the new expertise required to add another practice to our repertoires.

Identity, love and voice

These last three interwoven, intermingled threads are both too huge to sum up adequately and too fundamental to leave out. That oral reading often links to ways that adults enact elements of our identities is a key message of this book. People read aloud to be together as members of families (as part of being a father, a grandmother, a husband, a daughter) and as members of religious (reading aloud to worship, alone and with others) and linguistic communities (reading aloud to practise, use, voice or hear languages, alone or with others). These are often (though, importantly, not always) also ways of expressing or experiencing love – reading or listening with those we love, recording or sharing our voices, gifting time, warmth, voice and attention, reading aloud to soothe, heal, care or console, to honour or remember, in the presence or absence of those we love. One of the biggest questions of this project is around what difference the voice makes, what the voice *does* or adds, as well as how it relates to both identity and love. Each chapter of this book offers different answers, or perhaps elements of the same answer: the voice as metaphor for, representative of, and enactment of both individual and group identity; the voice as mode of multimodal communication; the voice as sometimes needing to be exercised and to be heard; the voice as exposing and protecting; as physical and ethereal; as intensely personal and abstractly human; as a tool, an interpretation, a temptation, a reaching-out.

All this positivity... a bit of balance

The aim of this study was to understand better the role of oral reading in adult life, taking the approach of asking people if and when they might read aloud and why. This has produced a detailed and, I hope, thought-provoking account.

It has also produced an overwhelmingly positive one, as those who engage in, and often value, forms of oral reading were keen to explain their practices. This book, then, runs the risk of providing an overly positive or unbalanced account. It risks suggesting that everyone does all these things (not so), or that for those who do read aloud oral reading makes up the majority of their reading (rarely the case; most people who enjoy reading aloud still do far more silent than oral reading). It risks suggesting that most people like reading aloud, or that those who like it like or do every form of it (not so).

Many people do not enjoy reading aloud themselves or listening to other people read. Many have bad memories of being forced to read aloud and feeling humiliated, or having had to listen to boring or unappealing voices or texts. We have heard from many different people who enjoy reading out loud and/or listening to others, but this will never mean that everyone does. We have also heard from those who find reading aloud helps them to understand difficult text or complex instructions, particularly when reading alone, and we have tried to explore reasons for this. This doesn't mean, though, that oral reading in this way will help everyone, and we should not forget voices from the RABiT regional community events (for example, Duncan, 2019a), which stressed that if reading something aloud, especially for the first time, and especially to an unfamiliar audience, it can be harder to understand something as 'you are concentrating on saying it right rather than taking it in.' Similarly, at another community event (Duncan, 2019b), participants had a discussion around how some find it much easier to understand something if others are reading it to them (or even recording themselves reading and listening back), while others find it easier to understand something if they read it themselves, whether aloud or silently. This is not to say that we should not take seriously the ideas in this book about what some people enjoy or find useful and why. These are all things that are worth thinking about, trying out and basing further thought and research on. But we do need to remember that what 'works' for one person may not work for someone else. This applies as much to people who classify themselves as neurodiverse or dyslexic as to those who do not.

What I am arguing and what I am not arguing

For the sake of clarity, and by way of a further summing up, here is what I am and am not arguing:

1 *I am arguing* that we cannot assume that we all understand the same things by words like 'reading.' Whenever we use the word 'reading' there is a chance that we, as speakers, are thinking of something a little different from what our listeners may be thinking. We need to be aware of this and have conversations to avoid misunderstandings (and to avoid, in literacy teaching situations, learners only mentioning forms of reading that they feel 'count' as reading for their teachers).

187

2 *I am arguing* that we pay more attention to different forms of reading (including, but not exclusively, reading aloud), thinking about when, why and how people do read, in and out of educational contexts.

3 *I am not arguing* that everyone participates in, enjoys or benefits from reading aloud or listening to others reading, and *I am not arguing* that we forget about the reasons why some people do not like to read aloud.

4 *I am not arguing* that everyone *should* do more reading aloud or that teachers (or parents or anyone else) should use more reading aloud.

5 *I am arguing* that we look, listen and think more about the reading aloud that some people already do and consider why and how they do it.

6 *I am arguing* that we cannot make assumptions about the practices of others; we cannot guess what others do or assume that others' practices are like our own. As literacy teachers, we need to talk to learners.

7 *I am arguing* that we use what we find out about real-life reading practices (such as this book's exploration of oral reading) to expand our conceptualisations, definitions and understandings of reading. Literacy policy, curricula and assessments should then be adjusted where appropriate, if only slightly, to acknowledge these expanded conceptualisations.

8 *I am arguing*, just as Street (1984, 2016), Kalman (2005) and Heath (1983), that literacy education (particularly adult literacy education) needs to be based on an evolving awareness of what people do and want to do with literacy, and this requires careful research or questioning.

9 *I am arguing* that, as a literacy research and teaching community, we make more use of Shove et al.'s (2012) model for the dynamics of social practices, where social practices are seen as made up of interrelationships between competences, meanings and materials, and that we do more work to examine how this could help us understand forms of literacy learning.

10 *I am arguing* that we keep re-evaluating the different possible relationships between literacy and oracy, between the written and the voiced, including in terms of how we understand power relationships and in the teaching and learning of literacy and language.

11 *I'm not arguing* that forms of silent reading are not important, fascinating or meaningful, or that we should ignore silent reading and aim for the dominance of oral reading; *neither am I arguing* that we should ignore equivalent forms of reading, or enactment of written text, related to uses of signed languages.

12 *I am arguing* that reading aloud should not be ignored or forgotten.

What next

More than the above arguments, though, I have tried to capture voices and accounts of contemporary oral reading from a range of participants so that we can all listen, read and think for ourselves about what they tell us. The Mass Observation pieces of writing are available to read through the Mass

Observation Project Archive in Sussex http://www.massobs.org.uk/the-ma ss-observation-project-1981-ongoing, and the interviews and recordings of practices in the British Library Sound Archive can be listened to at the British Library via the Sound and Moving Image catalogue http://sami.bl.uk. In early 2020, I worked on a Special Issue of the journal *Changing English* devoted to studies exploring forms of everyday reading and relationships between literacy and oracy. The editorial (Duncan, 2020) called for those interested in this area (whether working in applied linguistics, school English teaching, adult literacy, teacher education, prison reading groups or other contexts) to work together, exchange ideas and see what we come up with. I would also like to work with those developing literacy policy, curricula and assessments on how to take on board some of the ideas in this book. I hope to be part of more discussions between adult literacy teachers and researchers in different contexts, exploring possible implications for our work and developing further studies of oral reading in different parts of the world. Probably most of all I would like to read studies written by other people about reading aloud in distant contexts.

'Just listen to this!'

This chapter, like most conclusions, has tried to bring things together, but writing it has also reminded me that the conversations, recollections, reflections, events and recordings, electronic files, cardboard folders, notebooks and sticky notes still retain something un-capture-able, un-bundle-up-able.[1] Something a little unconquerable or unfathomable even? It may be apt to end, then, with these few words from a Mass Observation Reading Aloud Diary:

> Saturday: Read some bit of information out to my sister at the side of the river Thames on the North Greenwich Thames path. Read her a quote from John Masefield, "We must go down to the sea again, to the lonely sea and the sky...." This was written on the wall of the café in the Maritime Museum. [...]
> Sunday: I read a chapter of her book to my sister in the morning. And I read aloud the whole of the *I Must Go Down to the Sea* poem.
> In a cemetery with my sister reading tomb stones aloud, both of us, and I read the blurb about the cemetery.
> There were probably other things I or she or both of us read aloud to each other but this is written 48 hours later and I can't remember.
> (F65)

Note

1 Section heading, 'Just listen to this!', was a questionnaire participant response to the question of why read aloud.

References

Atwood, M. (2005). Introduction: Reading blind The Best American Short Stories 1989. In *Writing with Intent: Essays, Reviews, Personal Prose 1983–2005* (pp. 68–79). Caroll & Graf.

Barrs, M. (1987). Voice and role in reading and writing. *Language Arts*, 64(2), 207–218.

Barrs, M. (2000). The reader in the writer. *Reading*, 34(2), 54–60.

Barton, D., Ivanič, R., Appleby, Y., Hodge, R., & Tusting, K. (2007). *Literacy, Lives and Learning* (1st edition). Routledge.

Bloome, D., & Kim, M. (2016). Storytelling: Learning to read as social and cultural processes. *PROSPECTS*, 46(3), 391–405. https://doi.org/10.1007/s11125-017-9414-9.

Burnett, C., Davies, J., Merchant, G., & Rowsell, J. (2014). New meaning-making practices: A charter for literacy education. In C. Burnett, J. Davies, G. Merchant, & Rowsell, J. (Eds.), *New Literacies Around the Globe: Policy and Pedagogy* (pp. 154–166). Routledge.

Duncan, S. (2015). Reading aloud in Lewisham: An exploration of adult reading-aloud practices. *Literacy*, 49(2), 84–90. https://doi.org/10.1111/lit.12046.

Duncan, S. (2019a). *RABiT Discussion, Reflection and Next Steps for Adult Learners and Adult Education Teachers*. UCL Institute of Education. https://discovery.ucl.ac.uk/id/eprint/10080087/1/RABiT%20discussion%20reflection%20and%20next%20steps%20for%20Adult%20Learners%20and%20Adult%20Educators.pdf.

Duncan, S. (2019b). *RABiT Discussion, Reflection and Next Steps for Women, Library Users, Everyone and Anyone…*UCL Institute of Education. https://discovery.ucl.ac.uk/id/eprint/10080089/1/RABiT%20discussion%20reflection%20and%20next%20steps%20for%20Women%20Library%20Users%20Everyone%20and%20Anyone.pdf.

Duncan, S. (2020). Editorial. *Changing English*, 27(1), 1–4. https://doi.org/10.1080/1358684X.2020.1718333.

Elster, C. A. (2003). Authority, performance, and interpretation in religious reading: Critical issues of intercultural communication and multiple literacies. *Journal of Literacy Research*, 35(1), 663–692. https://doi.org/10.1207/s15548430jlr3501_5.

Gregory, E., & Williams, A. (2002). *City Literacies: Learning to Read Across Generations and Cultures*. Routledge.

Heath, S. B. (1983). *Ways with Words: Language, Life and Work in Communities and Classrooms*. Cambridge University Press.

Heathcote, D. (1970). How does drama serve thinking, talking and writing? *Elementary English*, 47(8), 1077–1081.

Herbert, P., & Robinson, C. (2001). Another language, another literacy. In B. V. Street (Ed.), *Literacy and Development: Ethnographic Perspectives* (pp.121–136). Routledge.

Ivanič, R., Appleby, Y., Tusting, K., & Barton, D. (2004). *Adult Learners' Lives Project: Setting the Scene: Progress Report*. NRDC.

Kalman, J. (2005). *Discovering Literacy: Access Routes to Written Culture for a Group of Women in Mexico*. UNESCO.

Lukkala, T. (2019). The soundscape of Orthodox Christian worship and participants' experiences – at the start of fieldwork. *Music and the Sacred*, 41(2). http://musiikinsuunta.fi/2019/02/.

Lyons, M. (2010). *A History of Reading and Writing in the Western World*. Palgrave MacMillan.

Papen, U. (2005). *Adult Literacy as Social Practice: More Than Skills*. Routledge.

Robinson-Pant, A. (2018, September 10). *Exploring Brian Street's understandings of literacy*. Literacy as Social Practice CTLR and BALID, University of Sussex.

Rosowsky, A. (2012). Performance and flow: The religious classical in translocal and transnational linguistic repertoires. *Journal of Sociolinguistics*, 16(5), 613–637. https://doi.org/10.1111/j.1467-9841.2012.00542.x.

Shove, E., Pantzar, M., & Watson, M. (2012). *The Dynamics of Social Practice: Everyday Life and How it Changes*. Sage.

Street, B. V. (1984). *Literacy in Theory and Practice*. Cambridge University Press.

Street, B. V. (2016). Learning to read from a social practice view: Ethnography, schooling and adult learning. *PROSPECTS*, 46(3), 335–344. https://doi.org/10.1007/s11125-017-9411-z.

INDEX